HEARTY FAMILY FAVORITES

150 Great Comfort-Food Recipes

TIME-LIFE BOOKS, ALEXANDRIA, VIRGINIA

TIME-LIFE BOOKS IS A DIVISION OF TIME LIFE INC.

HEARTY FAMILY FAVORITES

Project Manager	Donia Steele
Vice President of Sales and Marketing	Neil Levin
Director of Special Sales	Liz Ziehl
Production Manager	Carolyn Clark
Quality Assurance Manager	Miriam P. Newton

PRODUCED BY REBUS, INC.
NEW YORK, NEW YORK

Photographers: Christopher Lawrence, Steven Mays, Steven Mark Needham, Alan Richardson, Ellen Silverman, John Uher

HEARTY FAMILY FAVORITES is an adaptation of Creative Everyday Cooking.

First printing.
Printed in U.S.A.

TIME-LIFE is a trademark of Time Warner Inc. U.S.A.

Library of Congress Cataloging–in–Publication Data

Hearty family favorites : 150 great comfort-food recipes.
    p. cm.
Includes index.
ISBN 0-7835-4947-4
1. Cookery, American.   I. Time-Life Books.
TX715.H3977 1997
641.5973--dc21   97-10628
                                                    CIP

Books produced by Time-Life Custom Publishing are available at special bulk discount for promotional and premium use. Custom adaptations can also be created to meet your specific marketing goals. Call 1-800-323-5255.

CONTENTS

Linguine with Broiled Steak Strips and Tomato Salsa (page 27)

CHAPTER 1
PASTA

Chunky Rich
Spaghetti Sauce

▼

*A big batch of spaghetti sauce in the freezer is like money in the bank,
and it's well worth devoting a weekend afternoon to preparing it and packing
it away in family-size or single-serving portions. A hearty "ragù," this
sauce includes spicy sausage, ground beef, chunks of onion and carrot, and fresh
and dried mushrooms to deepen its meaty flavor.*

Working time: 40 minutes
Total time: 4 hours 15 minutes

Chunky Rich
Spaghetti Sauce

12 Servings

6 cloves garlic
3 medium onions
3 medium carrots
3 ribs celery
⅓ cup (packed) parsley sprigs
⅓ cup (packed) fresh basil leaves or
   1 tablespoon dried
1 ounce dried mushrooms
1 pound sweet Italian sausage

½ pound lean ground beef
1 tablespoon olive oil
2 cups dry red wine
1 can (35 ounces) whole tomatoes,
   with their juice
3 tablespoons tomato paste
1 pound fresh mushrooms
2 cups beef broth
1 tablespoon lemon juice

Step 3

1 In a food processor, mince the garlic. Add the onions and coarsely chop; set aside. In the same processor work bowl, coarsely chop the carrots. Add the celery and pulse to coarsely chop; set aside. Add the parsley and fresh basil (if using), and finely chop.

2 Place the dried mushrooms in a small bowl, cover with 1 cup hot tap water and set aside to soak.

3 Remove the sausage from its casings. Crumble the sausage meat and ground beef into a flameproof casserole or Dutch oven and cook over medium-high heat until no longer pink, about 5 minutes.

4 Add the oil, garlic, onions, carrots and celery, and cook, stirring occasionally, until the vegetables are softened, about 10 minutes.

5 Add the wine and cook, stirring frequently, until most of the wine has evaporated, about 15 minutes.

Step 5

6 Add the tomatoes and their juice and the tomato paste, and bring the mixture to a boil. Reduce the heat to low and simmer, uncovered, for 15 minutes.

7 Meanwhile, if the fresh mushrooms are small, leave them whole; otherwise, halve or quarter them. Strain the reconstituted dried mushrooms over a measuring cup; reserve the soaking liquid.

8 Bring the sauce back to a boil over medium-high heat and add the fresh mushrooms, dried mushrooms, beef broth, lemon juice, parsley and basil. Carefully pour the mushroom soaking liquid into the casserole, leaving any grit in the bottom of the measuring cup.

9 Return the mixture to a boil. Reduce the heat to low, partially cover and simmer for 3 hours, stirring occasionally.

Values are approximate per serving: Calories: 262 Protein: 12 gm Fat: 19 gm
Carbohydrates: 13 gm Cholesterol: 45 mg Sodium: 615 mg

Step 8

Pasta Twists with Chicken and Garlic-Pepper Cream

▼

This pasta dish calls for cooked chicken, which can be picked up at a deli counter or prepared in less than five minutes in the microwave (see the "microwave tip" that follows the recipe). Serve the pasta with French or Italian bread and a colorful salad, such as the one shown here made with radicchio, Bibb lettuce, sliced cucumber and strips of yellow bell pepper.

Working time: 30 minutes
Total time: 40 minutes

Pasta Twists with Chicken and Garlic-Pepper Cream

4 Servings

3 medium carrots
½ cup chicken broth
3 cloves garlic, peeled
1 package (8 ounces) cream cheese
2 tablespoons grated Parmesan cheese
½ teaspoon pepper

½ teaspoon salt
2 tablespoons milk
2 cups pasta twists, such as fusilli, rotini or rotelle (about ½ pound)
1½ cups cubed cooked chicken (about ½ pound)
1 bunch scallions (6 to 8)

Step 2

1 Bring a large pot of water to a boil.

2 Meanwhile, cut the carrots into matchsticks about 2 inches long.

3 In a medium saucepan, bring the chicken broth to a boil over medium-high heat. Add the carrots and garlic. Reduce the heat to medium-low, cover and simmer for 5 minutes. Reserving the broth, drain the carrots and garlic.

4 Place the garlic in a food processor and process to mince. Add the cream cheese, Parmesan, pepper, salt and reserved chicken broth. Process until smooth, 5 to 10 seconds. With the machine running, add the milk and process until smooth.

5 Add the pasta to the boiling water and cook until al dente, 10 to 12 minutes or according to package directions.

6 Meanwhile, cut the chicken into ½-inch cubes and coarsely chop the scallions.

7 Drain the pasta and, while it is still hot, toss it with the cream cheese mixture, the carrots, chicken and scallions. Serve hot.

Step 3

TIME-SAVERS

■ *Microwave tip:* *If you do not have already cooked chicken, you can cook chicken breast quickly in the microwave. Place about ¾ pound of skinless, boneless chicken breast in a shallow microwave-safe dish. Cover loosely and cook at 100% for about 4½ minutes, or until the chicken is cooked all the way through.*

■ *Do-ahead:* *The carrots can be prepared (Steps 2 and 3) and the garlic-pepper cream made (Steps 3 and 4) ahead. The chicken and scallions can also be cut up ahead of time.*

Values are approximate per serving: Calories: 594 Protein: 34 gm Fat: 27 gm
Carbohydrates: 53 gm Cholesterol: 128 mg Sodium: 699 mg

Step 7

Zesty Garden Pasta

In this autumnal variation on "pasta primavera"—pasta topped with spring vegetables—linguine is combined with broccoli and cauliflower, both of which appear at the end of the growing season. The vegetables are cooked until just crisp-tender, and the sauce is very light. Sliced black olives and grated Parmesan are tossed with the linguine, vegetables and sauce just before serving.

Working time: 25 minutes
Total time: 30 minutes

4 Servings

4 tablespoons butter
3 tablespoons flour
1 ½ cups chicken broth
1 ½ teaspoons oregano
½ teaspoon black pepper
Pinch of cayenne pepper
1 medium onion
Half a head of cauliflower
2 medium stalks broccoli
1 large fresh tomato or 2 whole
  canned tomatoes, well drained

½ pound linguine
1 tablespoon olive oil
3 cloves garlic, minced or crushed
  through a press
1 package (10 ounces) frozen peas,
  thawed
½ teaspoon salt
½ cup sliced pitted black olives
  (optional)
½ cup grated Parmesan
¼ cup chopped parsley (optional)

Step 3

1 Bring a large pot of water to a boil.

2 Meanwhile, in a small saucepan, melt 3 tablespoons of the butter over medium-high heat. Stir in the flour until it is no longer visible, about 30 seconds. Stir in 1 cup of the chicken broth, ½ teaspoon of the oregano, the black and cayenne peppers. Bring the mixture to a boil, then reduce the heat to low, cover and simmer, stirring occasionally, while you prepare the remaining ingredients.

3 Halve the onion lengthwise, then cut crosswise into thin slices. Cut the cauliflower and broccoli into florets. Coarsely chop the tomato.

4 Add the pasta to the boiling water and cook until al dente, 10 to 12 minutes, or according to package directions.

5 Meanwhile, in a large skillet, warm the remaining 1 tablespoon butter in the oil over medium-high heat until the butter is melted. Add the onion and garlic and cook until they begin to brown, about 5 minutes.

Step 6

6 Add the cauliflower, broccoli, peas, remaining 1 teaspoon oregano and the salt to the skillet. Cook, stirring, until the vegetables begin to soften, 3 to 5 minutes. Cover and cook 1 to 2 minutes.

7 Stir the tomato and the remaining ½ cup broth into the vegetable mixture.

8 Drain the pasta and place in a serving bowl. Toss the pasta with the vegetable mixture, olives (if using), Parmesan and 2 tablespoons of the parsley (if using), and toss to combine. Garnish the pasta with the remaining parsley.

Values are approximate per serving: Calories: 522   Protein: 21 gm   Fat: 20 gm
Carbohydrates: 68 gm   Cholesterol: 39 mg   Sodium: 934 mg

Step 7

Stuffed Manicotti with Sweet-and-Sour Tomato Sauce

▼

Agrodolce—an Italian sweet-and-sour sauce that may contain tomatoes, vinegar, currants and orange zest—was the inspiration for the sauce in this unusual baked pasta. The tomato sauce is sweetened with raisins, brown sugar and fennel seeds; the sweetness is balanced with a hint of cider vinegar. Shredded apple (along with onion, cabbage and carrot) is folded into ricotta cheese for the filling.

Working time: 40 minutes
Total time: 1 hour 5 minutes

Stuffed Manicotti with Sweet-and-Sour Tomato Sauce

6 Servings

5 cloves garlic
2 medium onions
½ pound cabbage
1 medium carrot
1 tart green apple, unpeeled
2 tablespoons butter
2 tablespoons olive or other vegetable oil
1½ teaspoons oregano
1 cup ricotta cheese
1 egg

1 cup grated Swiss cheese
¾ teaspoon salt
¼ teaspoon pepper
½ pound manicotti (12 to 14)
1 pound plum tomatoes or 12 canned tomatoes, well drained
2 tablespoons tomato paste
2 tablespoons cider vinegar
2 teaspoons brown sugar
¾ teaspoon fennel seeds
¼ cup raisins

Step 2

1 In a food processor, mince 3 of the garlic cloves. Add 1 of the onions and finely chop; remove and set aside. In the same work bowl, one at a time, shred the cabbage, carrot and apple.

2 Bring a large pot of water to a boil. Meanwhile, in a large skillet, warm 1 tablespoon of the butter in 1 tablespoon of the oil over medium-high heat until the butter is melted. Add the garlic-onion mixture, the cabbage, carrot, apple and oregano, and cook, stirring, until the vegetables are slightly softened, about 4 minutes.

3 In a bowl, combine the ricotta, egg, ½ cup of the Swiss cheese, ½ teaspoon of the salt and the pepper. Stir in the cooked vegetables.

4 Add the manicotti to the boiling water and cook until al dente, 8 to 10 minutes, or according to package directions.

Step 7

5 Preheat the oven to 425°. Lightly grease a 13 x 9 inch baking dish. Coarsely chop the remaining onion. Coarsely chop the tomatoes. Mince the remaining 2 cloves garlic, or put them through a press.

6 In a medium skillet, warm the remaining 1 tablespoon butter in the remaining 1 tablespoon oil over medium-high heat until the butter is melted. Add the garlic and onion, and stir-fry until the mixture is golden, 3 to 4 minutes. Add the tomatoes, tomato paste, vinegar, brown sugar, fennel seeds, remaining ¼ teaspoon salt and the raisins. Cover and simmer while you stuff the manicotti.

7 Drain the manicotti. Fill each pasta tube with about ⅓ cup of the cheese-vegetable filling. Place the filled pasta in the baking dish.

8 Spoon the sauce over the pasta and sprinkle with the remaining ½ cup Swiss cheese. Bake for 20 minutes, or until heated through.

Values are approximate per serving: Calories: 437 Protein: 18 gm Fat: 19 gm
Carbohydrates: 52 gm Cholesterol: 75 mg Sodium: 486 mg

Step 8

Green and White Fettuccine with Spicy Shrimp

In Italy, a pasta dish made of plain and spinach pasta is called "paglia e fieno," which means hay and straw. The "hay and straw" here is topped with shrimp cooked in a highly seasoned tomato sauce. When you buy the pasta, check the cooking times on the packages; some pastas cook more quickly than others. If this is the case, add the one that requires longer cooking first, then several minutes later, add the other pasta.

Working time: 40 minutes
Total time: 40 minutes

Green and White Fettuccine
with Spicy Shrimp

6 Servings

¾ **pound medium shrimp**
2 **medium onions**
3 **plum tomatoes or 5 canned whole tomatoes, well drained**
1 **large green bell pepper**
1 **tablespoon olive oil**
3 **cloves garlic, minced or crushed through a press**
2 **tablespoons curry powder**
¾ **pound fettuccine, half white and half green**

1 **cup tomato purée**
2 **tablespoons lime juice**
2 **teaspoons grated lime zest (optional)**
½ **teaspoon sugar**
¼ **teaspoon red pepper flakes**
½ **teaspoon salt**
½ **teaspoon black pepper**
1 **tablespoon butter**

Step 3

1 Shell and devein the shrimp.

2 Bring a large pot of water to a boil.

3 Meanwhile, thinly slice the onions. Coarsely chop the tomatoes. Dice the bell pepper.

4 In a large skillet, warm the oil over medium-high heat until hot but not smoking. Add the onions and garlic, and stir-fry until the onions begin to brown, about 3 minutes. Add the curry powder and stir-fry until the onions are well coated and the curry powder is fragrant, about 1 minute.

5 Add the pasta to the boiling water and cook until al dente, 7 to 9 minutes, or according to package directions.

Step 4

6 Meanwhile, add the tomatoes, bell pepper and tomato purée to the skillet, and bring to a boil over medium-high heat. Add the shrimp, lime juice, lime zest (if using), sugar, red pepper flakes, salt and black pepper, and let the mixture return to a boil. Reduce the heat to low, cover and simmer until the shrimp are cooked through, about 4 minutes.

7 Swirl the butter into the shrimp mixture. Drain the pasta and serve topped with the shrimp and sauce.

TIME-SAVERS

■ *Do-ahead:* *The shrimp can be shelled and deveined and the vegetables cut up ahead. The sauce can be made ahead through Step 6, but do not add the shrimp. When ready to serve, bring the sauce back to a simmer, add the shrimp and proceed with the recipe.*

Values are approximate per serving: Calories: 527 Protein: 29 gm Fat: 12 gm
Carbohydrates: 77 gm Cholesterol: 195 mg Sodium: 702 mg

Step 6

Baked Mushroom Manicotti with Three Cheeses

▼

Manicotti (the Italian word for "muffs") are large pasta tubes designed to be stuffed and baked. For this dish, they are filled with a ricotta-mushroom mixture and baked in a tomato sauce. If necessary, you can substitute cottage cheese for ricotta: Buy a one-pound carton of a fairly dry, small-curd cottage cheese and use it here just as you would the ricotta (or, for a smoother texture, purée it in a blender or food processor).

Working time: 20 minutes
Total time: 50 minutes

Baked Mushroom Manicotti
with Three Cheeses

4 Servings

2 cloves garlic
1 medium onion
½ pound mushrooms
1 tablespoon olive or other
  vegetable oil
8 large pasta tubes, such as
  manicotti
1½ cups tomato puree
2 tablespoons tomato paste

1½ teaspoons oregano
1 bay leaf
1 container (15 ounces) ricotta
  cheese
½ cup grated Parmesan cheese
½ teaspoon salt
¼ teaspoon pepper
⅔ cup grated mozzarella cheese

Step 6

1 Bring a large pot of water to a boil. Meanwhile, in a food processor, finely chop the garlic. Add the onion and finely chop. Add the mushrooms and finely chop.

2 In a medium skillet, warm the oil over medium-high heat until hot but not smoking. Add the vegetables and stir-fry until the onion wilts and the mushrooms release some of their moisture, 2 to 3 minutes.

3 Add the pasta to the boiling water and cook until almost done (it cooks more in the oven), about 9 minutes.

4 Meanwhile, remove half of the onion-mushroom mixture to a mixing bowl. To the vegetables remaining in the skillet, add the tomato puree, tomato paste, ½ teaspoon of the oregano and the bay leaf. Bring the mixture to a boil over medium heat. Reduce the heat to medium-low and simmer, uncovered, while you stuff the pasta.

5 Preheat the oven to 375°.

6 To the onion-mushroom mixture in the bowl, add the ricotta, Parmesan, remaining 1 teaspoon oregano, the salt and pepper.

Step 7

7 Drain the pasta, rinse it under cold water to cool it off slightly and drain again. Stuff each pasta tube with about ¼ cup of the stuffing.

8 Remove the tomato sauce from the heat. Remove and discard the bay leaf. Spread about ½ cup of the sauce evenly over the bottom of an 11 x 7-inch baking dish. Arrange the pasta tubes on top. Cover the pasta with the remaining sauce and sprinkle the mozzarella on top.

9 Bake for 25 minutes, or until heated through.

Values are approximate per serving: Calories: 439 Protein: 27 gm Fat: 20 gm
Carbohydrates: 41 gm Cholesterol: 56 mg Sodium: 1107 mg

Step 8

Pasta with
Stir-Fried Sesame Beef

▼

For this pasta dinner, steak slices are stir-fried with sesame oil and then briefly braised with carrots and celery in a Szechuan-style sesame sauce. The peanut butter used in the sauce is a frequent stand-in for Chinese ground roasted sesame seeds, which are sold in Oriental groceries as "sesame paste." This is not to be confused with tahini, which is a Middle Eastern paste made from unroasted sesame seeds.

Working time: 30 minutes
Total time: 40 minutes

Pasta with
Stir-Fried Sesame Beef

6 Servings

1¼ pounds flank steak
3 tablespoons Oriental sesame oil
2 tablespoons reduced-sodium soy
   sauce
¼ teaspoon black pepper
2 ribs celery
3 medium carrots
4 scallions
3 cloves garlic, minced
¼ cup chicken broth

2 teaspoons cornstarch
1 teaspoon lemon juice
4 drops hot pepper sauce
3 tablespoons smooth peanut butter
2 teaspoons grated lemon zest
   (optional)
½ teaspoon sugar
¼ teaspoon red pepper flakes
¼ cup chopped cilantro (optional)
¾ pound spaghettini or capellini

Step 2

1 Halve the flank steak lengthwise, with the grain. Cut each piece across the grain into ¼-inch-wide slices.

2 In a medium bowl, combine 1 tablespoon of the sesame oil, 1 tablespoon of the soy sauce and the black pepper. Stir to combine. Add the steak slices and toss to coat evenly. Cover loosely and set aside while you prepare the remaining ingredients.

3 Thinly slice the celery and carrots on the diagonal. Cut the scallions into 1½-inch lengths.

Step 3

4 In a large skillet, preferably nonstick, warm 1 tablespoon of the sesame oil over medium-high heat until hot but not smoking. Add the scallions and garlic, and cook until fragrant, about 30 seconds. Add the steak and stir-fry until browned but still slightly rare, about 5 minutes. Remove the meat to a plate and cover loosely to keep warm.

5 In a small bowl or measuring cup, blend the chicken broth and cornstarch. Bring a large pot of water to a boil.

6 Meanwhile, add the remaining 1 tablespoon sesame oil to the skillet and warm until hot but not smoking. Add the carrots, celery, broth mixture, remaining 1 tablespoon soy sauce, the lemon juice, hot pepper sauce, peanut butter, lemon zest (if using), sugar and red pepper flakes. Bring the mixture to a boil, then reduce the heat to low, cover and simmer for 5 minutes.

7 Return the meat to the skillet. Add the cilantro and cook until the beef is cooked through and medium-rare, about 3 minutes.

8 Meanwhile, add the pasta to the boiling water and cook until al dente, 3 to 5 minutes, or according to package directions. Drain the pasta and serve topped with the beef and sauce.

Step 6

Values are approximate per serving: Calories: 521   Protein: 29 gm   Fat: 22 gm
Carbohydrates: 51 gm   Cholesterol: 49 mg   Sodium: 377 mg

Ziti with Chicken and Asparagus in Lemon-Cheese Sauce

This luxurious dish is made with asparagus and a creamy sauce—similar to an Alfredo sauce, but lightened with cottage cheese instead of heavy cream. Although you could make this recipe with frozen asparagus, it will taste even better with fresh. Look for bright green, plump stalks and firm, tightly closed tips. To trim asparagus, bend the bottoms of the stalks; they will snap off naturally just above the tough, woody ends.

Working time: 25 minutes
Total time: 35 minutes

6 Servings

1 medium onion
1½ cups cottage cheese
¼ cup sour cream
¼ cup grated Parmesan cheese
2 tablespoons lemon juice
1 teaspoon grated lemon zest
    (optional)
1½ teaspoons dill weed
¼ teaspoon pepper
1 medium-size yellow squash

10 asparagus spears (about ½
    pound)
4 skinless, boneless chicken breast
    halves (about 1¼ pounds total)
½ pound ziti or other medium
    tube-shaped pasta
3 tablespoons olive or other
    vegetable oil
⅓ cup chicken broth

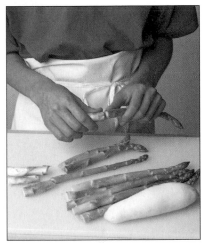

Step 4

1 In a food processor, coarsely chop the onion; set aside.

2 In the same work bowl, purée the cottage cheese. Beat in the sour cream, Parmesan, lemon juice, lemon zest (if using), dill and pepper. Set the lemon-cheese sauce aside.

3 Bring a large pot of water to a boil.

4 Meanwhile, cut the squash into thin slices. Snap off the tough ends of the asparagus stalks; cut the asparagus into 2-inch lengths. Cut the chicken across the grain into ¼-inch-wide strips.

5 In a large skillet, warm 2 tablespoons of the oil over medium-high heat until hot but not smoking. Add the onion and stir-fry until it begins to brown, about 5 minutes.

6 Add the pasta to the boiling water and cook until al dente, 9 to 11 minutes, or according to package directions.

Step 7

7 Meanwhile, add the chicken and the remaining 1 tablespoon oil to the skillet and cook the chicken for 5 minutes.

8 Add the squash, asparagus and chicken broth and bring the mixture to a boil. Reduce the heat to medium-low, cover and simmer until the vegetables are tender, about 5 minutes.

9 Drain the pasta and transfer to a large serving bowl. Toss the pasta with the lemon-cheese sauce and the chicken and vegetables.

TIME-SAVERS

■ *Do-ahead: The vegetables can be chopped and the lemon-cheese sauce (Step 2) made ahead.*

Values are approximate per serving: Calories: 419   Protein: 37 gm   Fat: 14 gm
Carbohydrates: 34 gm   Cholesterol: 70 mg   Sodium: 415 mg

Step 8

Pasta Risotto with Yellow Squash and Red Pepper

▼

In the classic Italian rice dish called risotto, rice is cooked slowly and stirred constantly to produce creamy, tender results. In this takeoff on the idea, orzo (a rice-shaped pasta) is cooked in broth—and pretty much left alone— to produce a similar dish. Along with the squash and bell pepper, the pasta is combined with peas, ham and Parmesan—all favorite risotto components.

Working time: 15 minutes
Total time: 35 minutes

Pasta Risotto with Yellow Squash and Red Pepper

4 Servings

1 small yellow squash	Pinch of red pepper flakes
1 medium red bell pepper	¾ pound orzo (about 2 cups)
3½ cups low-sodium chicken broth	1 cup frozen peas
2 tablespoons butter	¼ pound ham, preferably smoked, unsliced
2 cloves garlic, minced or crushed through a press	⅓ cup grated Parmesan cheese
1½ teaspoons oregano	¼ cup chopped parsley (optional)
½ teaspoon black pepper	

1 Dice the yellow squash and bell pepper.

2 In a medium saucepan, bring the chicken broth, butter, garlic, oregano, black pepper and red pepper flakes to a boil over high heat.

3 Add the orzo to the boiling broth, let the broth return to a boil, and cook, stirring frequently, over medium-high heat for 3 minutes.

4 Add the squash, bell pepper and peas, and let the mixture return to a boil. Reduce the heat to low, cover and simmer until the pasta and vegetables are cooked, about 7 minutes.

5 Meanwhile, cut the ham into 2-inch matchsticks.

6 When the pasta is done, stir in the ham, Parmesan and parsley (if using) and serve.

TIME-SAVERS

■ **Do-ahead:** *The vegetables and ham can be cut up ahead*

Step 3

Step 4

Step 5

Values are approximate per serving: Calories: 503 Protein: 24 gm Fat: 12 gm
Carbohydrates: 73 gm Cholesterol: 34 mg Sodium: 681 mg

Pasta Shells with Tuna, Peppers and Mushrooms

▼

Almost any kind of fish would work well with this simple pasta dish. Use canned salmon in place of the tuna. Or, if you have leftover cooked fish—firm types such as halibut, cod or swordfish are best—flake it into medium-size chunks and add it to the pasta at the end. If you have fresh fish on hand, cut it into chunks and cook it, covered, in the microwave; then add it at the end.

Working time: 15 minutes
Total time: 30 minutes

4 Servings

½ **pound small mushrooms**
1 **large red bell pepper**
1¼ **cups chicken broth**
2 **cloves garlic, minced or crushed through a press**
½ **pound small pasta shells (about 3 cups)**
4 **tablespoons butter**

⅓ **cup flour**
¾ **teaspoon oregano**
¼ **teaspoon black pepper**
1 **cup frozen peas**
½ **cup sour cream**
1 **can (6½ ounces) water-packed tuna, drained**

1 Bring a large pot of water to a boil.

2 Meanwhile, halve the mushrooms. Cut the bell pepper into strips.

3 In a medium saucepan, bring the chicken broth to a boil over medium-high heat. Add the mushrooms, bell pepper and garlic. Cover and return the liquid to a boil. Reduce the heat to medium-low and simmer, covered, for 5 minutes.

4 Add the pasta to the boiling water and cook until al dente, 10 to 12 minutes, or according to package directions.

5 Meanwhile, in another medium saucepan, melt the butter over medium heat. Stir in the flour and cook, stirring, until the flour is no longer visible, about 1 minute.

6 Stir in the oregano and black pepper. Add the broth, mushrooms and bell pepper and stir to blend well. Stir in the peas. Cook until heated through, 2 to 3 minutes.

7 Remove the pan of sauce from the heat and stir in the sour cream.

8 Drain the pasta and add it to the sauce, tossing to coat well. Fold in the tuna, taking care to leave it somewhat chunky.

TIME-SAVERS

■ **Do-ahead:** *The sauce can be made ahead and gently reheated.*

Values are approximate per serving: Calories: 525   Protein: 26 gm   Fat: 20 gm
Carbohydrates: 61 gm   Cholesterol: 61 mg   Sodium: 635 mg

Step 6

Step 7

Step 8

Linguine with Broiled Steak Strips and Tomato Salsa

▼

Instead of serving pasta tossed with a ground meat and tomato sauce, try this delicious combination of linguine topped with strips of steak broiled with a spicy tomato salsa. Chopped tomatoes, scallions, garlic, oil and vinegar form the basis of the salsa, which is used not only to baste the steak but also as a sauce for the pasta.

Working time: 15 minutes
Total time: 35 minutes

Linguine with Broiled Steak Strips and Tomato Salsa

4 Servings

2 medium fresh tomatoes, or 1 can (14 ounces) whole tomatoes, well drained
4 scallions
2 cloves garlic, minced or crushed through a press
¼ cup olive or other vegetable oil

2 tablespoons red wine vinegar
1 tablespoon Dijon mustard
¼ teaspoon pepper
1 small shell steak (¾ inch thick, about ¾ pound)
½ pound linguine or spaghetti

1 Preheat the broiler. Line a broiler pan with foil.

2 Bring a large pot of water to a boil.

3 Meanwhile, finely chop the tomatoes and scallions.

4 In a medium bowl, combine the tomatoes, scallions, garlic, olive oil, vinegar, mustard and pepper. Divide the tomato salsa in half and set aside one-half to toss with the cooked pasta.

6 Place the steak on the prepared broiler pan. Divide the other half of the tomato salsa in half again and spread it on the steak. Broil 4 inches from the heat for 7 minutes.

5 Add the pasta to the boiling water and cook until al dente, 10 to 12 minutes, or according to package directions.

7 Meanwhile, turn the steak over and cover with the remaining one-fourth of the salsa. Broil for another 7 minutes for rare; 9 minutes for medium-rare; 11 minutes for medium to well-done. Let stand for 5 minutes before slicing.

8 Drain the pasta and toss with the reserved tomato salsa.

9 Cut the steak on the diagonal into thin slices. Serve each portion of pasta topped with several slices of the steak.

TIME-SAVERS

■ *Do-ahead: The tomato salsa can be made well ahead. The steak can be broiled a short time ahead and served at room temperature over freshly cooked pasta.*

Values are approximate per serving: Calories: 543 Protein: 25 gm Fat: 27 gm
Carbohydrates: 49 gm Cholesterol: 50 mg Sodium: 165 mg

Step 4

Step 6

Step 8

Ziti with Eggplant-Garlic Sauce

People sometimes shy away from cooking eggplant because most recipes require a lot of oil—which this porous vegetable soaks up like a sponge. However, it can be broiled with just a light brushing of oil, as is done here. When buying eggplant, look for firm, glossy specimens; for this recipe, choose either a regular eggplant that weighs about one pound, or a few of the small, slender Italian variety.

Working time: 25 minutes
Total time: 50 minutes

Ziti with
Eggplant-Garlic Sauce

4 Servings

1 medium eggplant (about 1 pound)
3 tablespoons olive oil
12 cloves garlic
1 tablespoon butter
¼ cup fresh basil leaves or
   1 tablespoon dried
¼ cup sprigs of parsley (optional)
1 medium onion
2 large tomatoes

½ to ¾ cup chicken broth
1 tablespoon cornstarch
½ teaspoon oregano
¼ teaspoon sugar
¼ teaspoon red pepper flakes
¼ teaspoon black pepper
½ pound ziti
⅓ cup grated Parmesan cheese

Step 2

1 Preheat the broiler. Line a baking sheet with foil and lightly grease the foil.

2 Cut the eggplant lengthwise into quarters. Then cut each quarter crosswise into ¼-inch-thick slices.

3 Arrange the eggplant on the baking sheet. Brush the eggplant, on both sides, with 2 tablespoons of the oil. Broil 4 inches from the heat until lightly browned, about 4 minutes. Turn over and cook until browned on the second side, about 4 minutes. Set aside.

4 With the side of a large knife, smash the garlic and then peel. In a medium saucepan, warm the butter in the remaining 1 tablespoon oil over medium heat. Add the garlic and cook until golden.

Step 3

5 Meanwhile, bring a large pot of water to a boil. One at a time, in a food processor, coarsely chop the fresh basil, parsley (if using) and onion. By hand, coarsely chop the tomatoes.

6 Add the onion to the garlic in the saucepan and cook, stirring, until the onion begins to wilt, about 3 minutes.

7 In a small bowl, combine ½ cup of the broth, the cornstarch, basil, oregano, sugar, red pepper flakes and black pepper. Increase the heat under the saucepan to medium-high and add the broth mixture. Bring to a boil and cook until slightly thickened, 1 to 2 minutes. Add the tomatoes and parsley (if using). Reduce the heat to low, cover and simmer for 15 minutes, mashing the garlic with a fork and stirring to combine. If the mixture is too dry, add the remaining ¼ cup broth.

8 Meanwhile, add the pasta to the boiling water and cook until al dente, 10 to 12 minutes, or according to package directions. Drain the pasta, place it in a serving bowl, and top with the eggplant slices and the garlic sauce. Sprinkle with the Parmesan.

Values are approximate per serving: Calories: 444 Protein: 14 gm Fat: 17 gm
Carbohydrates: 62 gm Cholesterol: 13 mg Sodium: 328 mg

Step 4

Spaghetti Timbale

For an unusual pasta meal, try a timbale—a molded baked pasta dish. Cooked spaghetti is mixed with sausage, cheese, eggs and sour cream and is then placed in a springform pan so that after baking it can be turned out in a freestanding "cake." If you don't have a springform pan, you can bake the timbale in a 2-quart casserole dish; instead of unmolding it, cut it into wedges and serve it straight from the casserole.

Working time: 25 minutes
Total time: 1 hour

Spaghetti Timbale

6 Servings

1 cup shredded Monterey jack cheese (about ¼ pound)	½ cup sour cream
3 cloves garlic	2 eggs
1 medium onion	1½ teaspoons oregano
¾ pound sweet Italian sausage	¾ teaspoon nutmeg
¾ pound spaghetti	½ teaspoon salt
1 cup cottage cheese	½ teaspoon pepper
	¼ cup chopped parsley (optional)

Step 4

1 Preheat the oven to 375°. Grease and flour an 8½-inch springform pan.

2 Shred the cheese. In a food processor, mince the garlic. Add the onion and coarsely chop. Remove the sausage from its casings.

3 Bring a large pot of water to a boil.

4 Meanwhile, set a medium skillet over medium heat. Crumble the sausage into the skillet. Add the garlic-onion mixture and cook until the sausage is no longer pink, about 7 minutes. Remove the skillet from the heat and drain off the sausage fat.

5 Add the pasta to the boiling water and cook until al dente, 10 to 12 minutes, or according to package directions.

6 Meanwhile, in the same processor work bowl (no need to clean it out), purée the cottage cheese. Add the sour cream, eggs, oregano, nutmeg, salt and pepper, and pulse to combine.

Step 7

7 Drain the spaghetti and transfer it to a large mixing bowl. Add the sausage-onion mixture, the cottage cheese mixture, ½ cup of the shredded cheese and the parsley (if using). Toss to combine well.

8 Turn the mixture into the prepared springform pan and sprinkle with the remaining ½ cup shredded cheese. Cover with foil and bake for 20 minutes, or until heated through.

9 Preheat the broiler. Remove the foil from the timbale. Broil the timbale 4 inches from the heat until golden on top, 5 to 7 minutes.

10 Let the timbale sit for about 5 minutes before unmolding. To unmold, run a knife around the edges of the timbale and then release the sides of the springform. Cut the timbale into wedges to serve.

Values are approximate per serving: Calories: 527 Protein: 28 gm Fat: 25 gm
Carbohydrates: 47 gm Cholesterol: 133 mg Sodium: 844 mg

Step 10

Pasta with Chicken in Jalapeño Tomato Sauce

▼

Not so long ago, few Americans cooked with chilies. But now that Mexican and Tex-Mex cuisines are established favorites throughout the country, it's easier than ever to find fresh and bottled jalapeño peppers. When handling fresh chilies, remember to wear thin rubber gloves and to wash your hands thoroughly afterwards. The same components that make chilies feel hot on your tongue can burn your eyes and skin.

Working time: 25 minutes
Total time: 35 minutes

6 Servings

1 medium onion	1 tablespoon flour
2 skinless, boneless chicken breast halves (about ½ pound total)	1 can (28 ounces) crushed tomatoes, with their juice
2 small pickled jalapeño peppers	1 tablespoon tomato paste
2 tablespoons olive or other vegetable oil	1 package (10 ounces) frozen corn
3 cloves garlic, minced or crushed through a press	¼ teaspoon salt
1 tablespoon butter	¼ teaspoon black pepper
1 tablespoon cumin	¾ pound small pasta shells (about 3½ cups)
1½ teaspoons oregano	¼ cup (packed) cilantro sprigs (optional)

Step 1

1 Coarsely chop the onion. Cut the chicken into bite-size pieces. Seed the jalapeños and then mince them.

2 In a large skillet, warm 1 tablespoon of the oil over medium-high heat until hot but not smoking. Add the onion and garlic, and sauté until the onion begins to brown, about 5 minutes.

3 Bring a large pot of water to a boil. Meanwhile, add the remaining 1 tablespoon oil and the chicken to the skillet, and stir-fry until the chicken is browned, about 5 minutes. Transfer the chicken, onion and garlic to a bowl, cover loosely and set aside.

Step 3

4 Add the butter to the skillet and warm until melted. Add the cumin and oregano and stir-fry until fragrant, about 30 seconds. Stir in the flour and cook, stirring, until the flour is no longer visible, about 30 seconds. Add the tomatoes and their juice, the tomato paste, minced jalapeños, corn, salt and black pepper, and bring the mixture to a boil, stirring constantly. Reduce the heat to low, cover and simmer while you cook the pasta.

5 Add the pasta to the boiling water and cook until al dente, 10 to 12 minutes, or according to package directions.

6 Meanwhile, coarsely chop the cilantro (if using).

7 Return the onion and chicken to the sauce and stir to combine. Stir in the cilantro (if using). Drain the pasta and top with the sauce.

TIME-SAVERS

■ ***Do-ahead:*** *The jalapeño tomato sauce can be made ahead through Step 4.*

Values are approximate per serving: Calories: 397 Protein: 19 gm Fat: 9 gm
Carbohydrates: 62 gm Cholesterol: 27 mg Sodium: 438 mg

Step 7

Fettuccine with Spinach-Cheese Sauce

Italian pesto—a purée of fresh basil, pine nuts, Parmesan and olive oil—is the inspiration for this sauce. Here, spinach is puréed with walnuts, Parmesan, garlic and oil (olive or any light vegetable oil can be used). Dried basil or oregano, about 1/2 teaspoon of either, could be added for a subtle change in flavor. If you like, double the sauce recipe and freeze individual portions for busy-day meals.

Working time: 15 minutes
Total time: 35 minutes

Fettuccine with Spinach-Cheese Sauce

6 Servings

1 package (10 ounces) frozen
   spinach, thawed and well drained
3 cloves garlic
14 sprigs of parsley (optional)
¼ cup walnut pieces
½ cup grated Parmesan cheese

1 teaspoon salt
¼ teaspoon pepper
¾ cup olive or other vegetable oil
¾ pound fettuccine or other broad
   noodles

Step 3

1 Bring a large pot of water to a boil.

2 Meanwhile, squeeze the excess moisture out of the thawed spinach; set aside.

3 In a food processor, mince the garlic and parsley (if using). Add the walnuts, Parmesan, salt and pepper and pulse to blend.

4 Add the spinach and then the oil and pulse to form a purée.

5 Add the pasta to the boiling water and cook until al dente, 10 to 13 minutes or according to package directions.

6 Drain the pasta well and toss it in a serving bowl with the spinach-cheese sauce.

Step 4

TIME-SAVERS

■ *Microwave tip:* To thaw the spinach, remove it from the box, place it on a saucer or plate and cook at 100% for about 3 minutes.

■ *Do-ahead:* The spinach-cheese sauce (Steps 2 through 4) can be made ahead.

Step 6

Values are approximate per serving: Calories: 538 Protein: 13 gm Fat: 35 gm
Carbohydrates: 44 gm Cholesterol: 60 mg Sodium: 566 mg

Mock Lasagna

Lasagna is not a difficult dish to make, but sometimes handling the large pasta strips and layering all the ingredients can be a bit of a chore. Using small pasta shapes such as bow ties (whatever you have in the cupboard will do) and a one-pot sauce simplifies the process. The meat that gives the sauce its rich flavor is a coarse, spicy country sausage, not to be confused with country-style breakfast links.

Working time: 25 minutes
Total time: 50 minutes

Mock Lasagna

6 Servings

1 medium onion
½ pound country sausage
3 cloves garlic, minced or crushed
  through a press
½ pound bow tie pasta
1 can (15 ounces) tomato purée
2 tablespoons tomato paste

1 bay leaf
1½ teaspoons basil
½ teaspoon red pepper flakes
½ teaspoon salt
¼ teaspoon black pepper
2 cups grated part-skim mozzarella
  cheese

1 Bring a large pot of water to a boil. Meanwhile, coarsely chop the onion. Remove the sausage from its casings.

2 Crumble the sausage meat into a medium skillet over medium heat and cook, stirring, until the meat is no longer pink, about 5 minutes. Add the onion and garlic and cook, stirring, until the onion is translucent, 3 to 4 minutes.

3 Add the pasta to the boiling water and cook until al dente, 10 to 12 minutes, or according to package directions.

4 Meanwhile, add the tomato purée, tomato paste, bay leaf, basil, red pepper flakes, salt and black pepper to the skillet. Bring the mixture to a boil over medium-high heat. Reduce the heat to low, cover and simmer for 10 minutes.

5 Preheat the oven to 400°. Drain the pasta. Remove the bay leaf from the tomato sauce.

6 Cover the bottom of an 8-inch square baking pan with one-third of the sauce. Top with half the pasta and half the mozzarella. Top the cheese with half the remaining sauce and all of the remaining pasta. Top the pasta with the remaining sauce and mozzarella.

7 Bake for 15 minutes, or until heated through.

TIME-SAVERS

■ *Microwave tip: Cook the pasta as instructed. In a 2-quart microwave-safe dish, combine the onion, sausage and garlic. Cover and cook at 100% for 5 minutes, stirring once; drain off excess fat. Stir in the remaining sauce ingredients. Cover and cook at 100% for 4 minutes; then at 50% for 5 minutes. In an 8-inch square baking dish, assemble the lasagna as instructed. Top with the remaining sauce (but not the cheese). Cover loosely and cook at 50% for 8 minutes, or until heated through. Top with the remaining cheese and cook, uncovered, at 100% for 1 minute, to melt the cheese.*

Values are approximate per serving: Calories: 437   Protein: 20 gm   Fat: 22 gm
Carbohydrates: 40 gm   Cholesterol: 48 mg   Sodium: 940 mg

Step 1

Step 6

Step 6

Peppers Stuffed
with Pasta and Salmon

This multicolored meal of stuffed peppers is a delight to the eye as well as the palate. Be sure to choose peppers that are all the same size, so they will accommodate equal amounts of filling and cook evenly. This recipe calls for leftover pasta, but if you don't have any, cook a half-pound of pasta just until al dente; use a small, shaped pasta, such as elbow macaroni or pasta twists.

Working time: 25 minutes
Total time: 50 minutes

Peppers Stuffed with Pasta and Salmon

4 Servings

2 medium red bell peppers	¼ teaspoon black pepper
2 medium green bell peppers	4 cups cooked pasta (about ½
2 medium orange bell peppers	pound raw)
2 medium yellow bell peppers	¼ cup grated Parmesan cheese
2 tablespoons butter	¼ cup shredded mozzarella cheese
2 cloves garlic, minced or crushed	¼ cup sliced black olives
through a press	½ cup sour cream
1 teaspoon oregano	1 can (7 ounces) salmon, drained

1 Preheat the oven to 375°. Butter a baking dish large enough to hold the peppers snugly.

2 Cut the stem ends off the bell peppers and then seed and derib them. If necessary, slice a small piece off the bottoms of the peppers so they will stand upright. Place the peppers in the prepared baking dish.

Step 2

3 In a small skillet, warm the butter over medium-high heat until it is melted. Add the garlic and cook, stirring, until fragrant, 2 to 3 minutes. Remove the skillet from the heat and stir in the oregano and black pepper.

4 In a medium bowl, combine the pasta, Parmesan, half of the mozzarella, the olives, sour cream and garlic-oregano butter. Flake in the salmon and stir to combine well.

5 Dividing evenly, fill the peppers with the stuffing. Top with the remaining mozzarella. Bake for 25 to 30 minutes, or until the peppers are heated through and the cheese is melted.

Step 4

TIME-SAVERS

■ *Microwave tip: Prepare the bell peppers as described in Step 2. In a small microwave-safe bowl, combine the butter and garlic, and cook at 100% for 1 minute. Stir in the oregano and black pepper. Prepare the salmon stuffing as described in Step 4 and stuff the peppers, but do not top with the remaining mozzarella. Place the peppers in a microwave-safe baking dish and put 2 tablespoons of water in the dish. Cover loosely with plastic wrap and cook at 100% for 5 minutes. Cook at 50% for 18 minutes, rotating the dish once, until the peppers are crisp-tender and the stuffing is heated through. Top with the reserved mozzarella and serve.*

■ *Do-ahead: The stuffing mixture (Steps 3 and 4) can be made ahead. The stuffed peppers can be baked ahead and served warm or at room temperature.*

Values are approximate per serving: Calories: 461 Protein: 21 gm Fat: 20 gm
Carbohydrates: 50 gm Cholesterol: 54 mg Sodium: 474 mg

Step 5

Spaghettini with Spinach and Red Clam Sauce

▼

*Fresh spinach and ripe plum tomatoes add color and flavor to this clam sauce—
and once you prepare it, you may never go back to serving a canned version.
This is a great busy-day dish; it's on the table in only 30 minutes,
steaming hot and satisfying. Using bottled clam juice in this recipe emphasizes
the seafood flavor, but chicken broth can be substituted, if necessary.*

Working time: 20 minutes
Total time: 30 minutes

Spaghettini with Spinach and Red Clam Sauce

4 Servings

1 pound plum tomatoes (about 6) or 1 can (16 ounces) whole tomatoes, well drained
1 medium onion
2 tablespoons butter
2 tablespoons olive oil
3 cloves garlic, minced or crushed through a press
2 tablespoons flour
1 bottle (8 ounces) clam juice or 1 cup chicken broth
½ teaspoon salt
¼ teaspoon pepper
½ pound spaghettini or spaghetti
¼ pound fresh spinach (about 4 cups leaves) or 1 package (10 ounces) frozen chopped spinach
1 can (6½ ounces) canned clams, drained
⅔ cup grated Parmesan cheese

1 Bring a large pot of water to a boil.

2 Meanwhile, coarsely chop the tomatoes and onion.

3 In a large skillet, warm the butter in the oil over medium-high heat until the butter is melted. Add the onion and garlic and sauté until the onion just begins to brown, 2 to 3 minutes.

4 Stir in the flour and cook, stirring, until the flour is no longer visible, about 30 seconds.

Step 4

5 Stir in the tomatoes, clam juice, salt and pepper. Bring the liquid to a boil. Reduce the heat to medium-low, cover and simmer for 10 minutes.

6 Meanwhile, add the pasta to the boiling water and cook until al dente, 10 to 12 minutes, or according to package directions.

7 While the pasta and tomato sauce are cooking, stem and roughly chop the fresh spinach (or thaw the frozen chopped spinach in the microwave; then squeeze out the excess moisture).

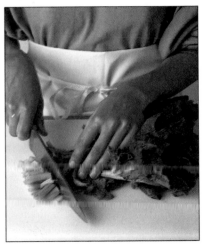

Step 7

8 Bring the tomato sauce to a boil over medium-high heat. Stir in the clams and spinach and cook until the fresh spinach just wilts (or the frozen spinach is heated through), about 1 minute.

9 Drain the pasta and toss it with the sauce and ⅓ cup of the Parmesan. Pass the remaining Parmesan on the side.

TIME-SAVERS

■ *Do-ahead: The sauce can be made ahead through Step 5.*

Values are approximate per serving: Calories: 471 Protein: 22 gm Fat: 18 gm
Carbohydrates: 55 gm Cholesterol: 42 mg Sodium: 774 mg

Step 8

Egg Noodles with Swiss Chicken Melt

▼

Concealed beneath a golden topping of Swiss and Parmesan cheeses is a toss of egg noodles, chicken and cabbage in a mustard cream sauce. It's easiest to make this dish from start to finish in a skillet, but if you don't have one that is broilerproof, transfer the noodle mixture to a baking dish before topping it with cheese and broiling. A simple salad or platter of crisp raw vegetable sticks is all you need to complete the meal.

Working time: 35 minutes
Total time: 40 minutes

42

Egg Noodles
with Swiss Chicken Melt

6 Servings

½ pound skinless, boneless chicken breasts
1 medium onion
2 cups shredded cabbage (about ¼ pound)
2 tablespoons olive or other vegetable oil
¾ pound egg noodles
3 tablespoons butter

3 tablespoons flour
1 cup chicken broth
1 cup sour cream
1 tablespoon Dijon mustard
1½ teaspoons tarragon
¼ teaspoon pepper
1½ cups grated Swiss cheese (about 6 ounces)
½ cup grated Parmesan cheese

Step 5

1 Bring a large pot of water to a boil.

2 Meanwhile, cut the chicken into bite-size pieces. Coarsely chop the onion. Shred the cabbage.

3 In a large broilerproof skillet, warm 1 tablespoon of the oil over medium-high heat until hot but not smoking. Add the onion and cook, stirring, until the onion begins to brown, 3 to 4 minutes.

4 Add the remaining 1 tablespoon oil. Add the chicken and stir-fry until the chicken is opaque and almost cooked through, 2 to 3 minutes.

5 Add the cabbage and cook, stirring frequently, until the cabbage is just wilted, about 1 minute. Remove the chicken and vegetables to a plate and cover loosely to keep warm.

6 Add the noodles to the boiling water and cook until al dente, 4 to 6 minutes, or according to package directions.

7 Preheat the broiler.

Step 8

8 Meanwhile, in the same skillet, melt the butter over medium-high heat. Stir in the flour and cook, stirring, until the flour is no longer visible, about 1 minute. Stir in the chicken broth, sour cream, mustard, tarragon and pepper. Bring to a boil, stirring constantly, until slightly thickened. Remove the skillet from the heat.

9 Drain the noodles. To the skillet, add the noodles, chicken-vegetable mixture, 1 cup of the Swiss cheese and ¼ cup of the Parmesan and stir to combine. Sprinkle the remaining ½ cup Swiss and ¼ cup Parmesan on top and broil 4 inches from the heat until the top is golden, 3 to 5 minutes.

Values are approximate per serving: Calories: 600 Protein: 30 gm Fat: 31 gm
Carbohydrates: 49 gm Cholesterol: 140 mg Sodium: 557 mg

Step 9

Rosemary Baked Chicken and Potatoes (page 59)

CHAPTER 2
POULTRY

Chicken Braised with Thyme and White Wine

Gentle braising produces this tender, juicy chicken; the golden onions that accompany it are stir-fried with garlic before they are simmered with the chicken. Thyme is the dominant herb in this dish, but it's not an overpowering one and blends beautifully with the garlic and tomato. Serve the chicken and onions with colorful broccoli and cauliflower florets, steamed and then tossed with a little melted butter.

Working time: 15 minutes
Total time: 50 minutes

Chicken Braised with Thyme and White Wine

4 Servings

2 medium onions
2 teaspoons olive or other
  vegetable oil
2½ pounds chicken parts
½ teaspoon salt
3 cloves garlic, minced or crushed
  through a press

1½ teaspoons thyme
3 bay leaves
2 tablespoons flour
1 cup dry white wine
½ cup chicken broth
2 tablespoons tomato paste
½ teaspoon pepper

Step 2

1 Thinly slice the onions.

2 In a large skillet, preferably nonstick, warm the oil over medium-high heat until hot but not smoking. Add the chicken and brown on all sides, about 12 minutes. Season with the salt. Remove the chicken to a plate and cover loosely to keep warm.

3 Pour off all but 1 tablespoon of fat from the skillet. Add the onions, garlic, thyme and bay leaves, and stir-fry until the onions begin to brown, about 3 minutes.

4 Stir in the flour and cook, stirring, until the flour is no longer visible, about 30 seconds. Add the wine, chicken broth, tomato paste and pepper, and bring to a boil, stirring constantly.

Step 4

5 Return the chicken (and any juices that have accumulated on the plate) to the skillet. Return the mixture to a boil, reduce the heat to low, cover and simmer until the chicken is cooked through, about 20 minutes. Halfway through, turn the chicken over.

6 Remove the bay leaves before serving.

TIME-SAVERS

■ *Microwave tip:* Follow the recipe through Step 4, but in Step 2, place the chicken in a shallow microwave-safe dish instead of on a plate. Add the sauce mixture (Steps 3 and 4) to the chicken, cover loosely with waxed paper and cook at 100% for 4 minutes. Cook at 50% until the chicken is tender and cooked through, about 8 minutes, rearranging the chicken parts halfway through.

■ *Do-ahead:* The whole dish can be made ahead and gently reheated.

Step 5

Values are approximate per serving: Calories: 395 Protein: 36 gm Fat: 23 gm
Carbohydrates: 10 gm Cholesterol: 113 mg Sodium: 569 mg

Turkey Stir-Fry with Apricot Glaze

▼

You can make a stir-fry with practically any vegetables you choose, but Asian vegetables add an authentic flavor and texture: This sweet-and-sour glazed stir-fry contains crunchy shreds of crunchy Napa cabbage. The pale green, oblong heads of Napa cabbage—also called Chinese or celery cabbage—have crisp ruffled leaves that are more delicate than regular green cabbage. Choose a small head of Napa for the best flavor.

Working time: 40 minutes
Total time: 45 minutes

Turkey Stir-Fry
with Apricot Glaze

4 Servings

4 quarter-size slices (¼ inch thick)
   fresh ginger, unpeeled
4 cloves garlic
1¼ pounds turkey scallops
3 tablespoons apricot jam
1 tablespoon brown sugar
3 tablespoons reduced-sodium soy
   sauce
2 tablespoons rice wine vinegar
2 tablespoons sherry (optional)
½ teaspoon black pepper

¼ teaspoon red pepper flakes
2 cups water
1 cup raw rice
4 medium scallions
¼ pound mushrooms
8 Napa cabbage leaves
1 large red bell pepper
3 tablespoons cornstarch
2 tablespoons vegetable oil
¼ cup chicken broth
2 tablespoons sesame seeds

Step 2

1 In a food processor, mince the ginger and garlic. By hand, cut the turkey into ¼-inch-wide strips.

2 In a large shallow bowl, combine the ginger-garlic mixture, apricot jam, sugar, soy sauce, vinegar, sherry (if using), black pepper and red pepper flakes. Add the turkey strips and toss to combine. Cover and set aside to marinate while you prepare the rest of the dish.

3 In a medium saucepan, bring the water to a boil. Add the rice, reduce the heat to medium-low, cover and simmer until the rice is tender and all the liquid is absorbed, about 20 minutes.

4 Meanwhile, in the same processor work bowl, coarsely chop the scallions. By hand, cut the mushrooms into ¼-inch slices. Shred the Napa cabbage. Cut the bell pepper into thin strips.

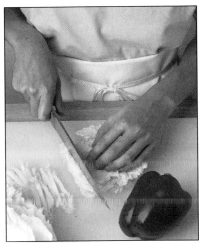

Step 4

5 Remove the turkey from the marinade, reserving the marinade. Dredge the turkey lightly in 2 tablespoons of the cornstarch. In a large skillet, warm 1 tablespoon of the oil over medium-high heat until hot but not smoking. Add the turkey and stir-fry until cooked through, about 5 minutes. Remove to a plate and cover loosely to keep warm.

6 In the skillet, heat the remaining 1 tablespoon oil. Add the scallions, mushrooms, Napa cabbage and bell pepper, and stir-fry until softened slightly, about 3 minutes. Add the reserved marinade and bring to a boil. Combine the remaining 1 tablespoon cornstarch and the chicken broth. Stir the broth mixture into the skillet, and cook, stirring, until the vegetables are crisp-tender.

7 Return the turkey (and any juices that have accumulated on the plate) to the skillet. Serve the turkey-vegetable mixture over the rice, sprinkled with sesame seeds.

Values are approximate per serving: Calories: 545   Protein: 41 gm   Fat: 12 gm
Carbohydrates: 68 gm   Cholesterol: 88 mg   Sodium: 627 mg

Step 6

Cheddar-Chicken Chowder

Although the term chowder is more commonly applied to a seafood stew, you'll immediately see the family resemblance in this thick, creamy chicken soup. Chunks of chicken replace the fish, and the broth is enriched with milk, butter and Cheddar cheese. For color contrast, make the soup with white Cheddar and garnish it with grated yellow Cheddar.

Working time: 30 minutes
Total time: 35 minutes

Cheddar-Chicken Chowder

4 Servings

4 scallions	¼ teaspoon pepper
4 tablespoons butter	2 medium carrots
1 small clove garlic, minced or crushed through a press	2 ribs celery
	1 pound skinless, boneless chicken breast
⅓ cup flour	
2 cups chicken broth	1 cup milk
1 cup water	1 cup grated white or yellow Cheddar cheese
1½ teaspoons thyme	

1 Coarsely chop the scallions.

2 In a large saucepan, warm the butter over medium-high heat until melted. Add the scallions and garlic and cook until the scallions have softened, about 3 minutes.

3 Stir in the flour and cook until it is no longer visible, about 30 seconds. Increase the heat to medium-high and stir in the chicken broth and water. Add the thyme and pepper and bring the mixture to a boil. Reduce the heat to low, cover and simmer while you prepare the remaining ingredients.

4 Roughly dice the carrots and celery. Cut the chicken into ½-inch chunks.

5 Uncover the broth and bring it to a boil over medium-high heat. Add the carrots, celery and chicken, and cook, stirring occasionally, until the chicken is cooked through, about 6 minutes.

6 Add the milk and cheese and cook until the cheese has melted, about 5 minutes.

TIME-SAVERS

■ **Do-ahead:** *The vegetables can be chopped or the whole soup made in advance.*

Values are approximate per serving: Calories: 491 Protein: 46 gm Fat: 26 gm
Carbohydrates: 17 gm Cholesterol: 152 mg Sodium: 834 mg

Step 3

Step 4

Step 6

Bacon-and-Onion Chicken with Rice

This hearty meal with a French country feel requires no fancy techniques—
cutting the onions into wedges is about all the preparation necessary. Do be sure,
though, to remove the fat from the pan juices before adding them to the rice.
A gravy separator—a specially designed measuring cup that allows you to pour off
the juices and leave the fat behind—is useful here.

Working time: 10 minutes
Total time: 55 minutes

Bacon-and-Onion Chicken
with Rice

4 Servings

3 medium onions	**½ teaspoon salt**
6 slices bacon	**½ teaspoon pepper**
2½ pounds chicken parts	**2 cups water**
3 cloves garlic, minced or crushed through a press	**1 cup raw rice**

Step 2

1 Cut the onions into ½-inch wedges.

2 Lay 3 strips of the bacon in the bottom of a large flameproof casserole or Dutch oven. Cover the bacon with half of the chicken, half of the onion wedges and all of the garlic. Sprinkle with ¼ teaspoon each of the salt and pepper. Top the chicken with the remaining 3 strips bacon. Then layer the remaining chicken, onion wedges, and ¼ teaspoon each salt and pepper.

3 Cover the casserole and cook over low to medium-low heat until the chicken is cooked through, about 40 minutes.

4 About 20 minutes before the chicken is done, bring the water to a boil in a medium saucepan. Add the rice, reduce the heat to medium-low, cover and simmer until the rice is tender and all the liquid is absorbed, about 20 minutes.

5 Preheat the broiler. Line a broiler pan with foil.

6 When the chicken is done, transfer the chicken, onions and bacon to the broiler pan. Broil 4 inches from the heat to brown the chicken and crisp the bacon, about 5 minutes.

Step 6

7 Meanwhile, degrease the pan juices and then stir into the rice. Serve the chicken, bacon and onions with the rice.

TIME-SAVERS

■ *Microwave tip: Prepare Steps 1 and 2 as directed above, using a 4- or 5-quart microwave-safe casserole. Cover and cook at 100% for 5 minutes. Cook at 50% for 20 minutes, or until the chicken is cooked through; rotate the dish twice and rearrange the chicken once. Cook the rice and broil the chicken and bacon in the conventional manner.*

■ *Do-ahead: The chicken and onions can be cooked ahead and then broiled just before serving. If cooking ahead, refrigerate the pan juices to make it easier to remove the fat, and then bring the juices back to a simmer while you broil the chicken.*

Values are approximate per serving: Calories: 695   Protein: 43 gm   Fat: 38 gm
Carbohydrates: 42 gm   Cholesterol: 158 mg   Sodium: 645 mg

Step 7

Southwestern Chicken Stew

Serve this spicy stew with corn bread and a tossed green salad. If you are making this for kids, consider spending the extra money for boneless chicken breasts (about 1⅓ pounds), which will make the stew easier to eat. For that variation, cut the chicken into 1-inch cubes, skip the browning step, and add the uncooked chicken along with the corn near the end. The small pieces will quickly cook through.

Working time: 25 minutes
Total time: 50 minutes

Southwestern Chicken Stew

6 Servings

2½ pounds chicken parts
1 tablespoon olive or other vegetable oil
2 medium onions
5 cloves garlic, crushed through a press or lightly bruised
2 tablespoons flour
3 tablespoons chili powder

1 can (28 ounces) whole tomatoes, with their juice
1 can (4 ounces) chopped mild green chilies, drained (optional)
¾ teaspoon salt
¼ teaspoon pepper
1 package (10 ounces) frozen corn

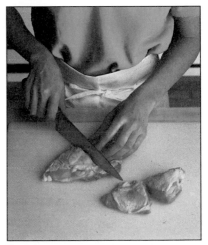
Step 1

1 If you are using chicken breasts, cut them in half.

2 In a large skillet or flameproof casserole, warm the oil over medium-high heat. Add the chicken and cook it until golden on all sides, 5 to 10 minutes. Remove the chicken from the pan and set aside.

3 Halve and slice the onions. Add the onions and garlic to the skillet and cook over medium-high heat, stirring frequently, until the onion is softened but not browned, about 5 minutes.

4 Stir in the flour and chili powder and cook for 1 minute.

5 Stir in the tomatoes and their juice, breaking up the tomatoes with a spoon, and the green chilies (if using). Add the chicken, the salt and pepper. When the mixture returns to a boil, cover the skillet, reduce the heat to medium-low and simmer the stew, stirring occasionally, until the chicken is fully cooked, about 20 minutes.

6 Stir in the corn and cook for 5 minutes. Serve hot.

Step 4

TIME-SAVERS

■ *Microwave tip: In a large microwave-safe casserole, combine the oil, chopped onions, garlic and chili powder. Cover with plastic wrap and cook at 100% for 5 to 6 minutes, stirring once. Add the chicken, re-cover and cook at 100% for 10 to 12 minutes, stirring once. Stir the flour into the tomato juice and add to the casserole along with the tomatoes, green chilies (if using), salt, pepper and corn. Re-cover and cook at 100%, stirring occasionally, until the mixture is heated through and the flavors are blended, 10 to 12 minutes.*

■ *Do-ahead: The whole dish can made ahead and even frozen. Reheat gently on the stovetop, in the oven or in the microwave.*

Values are approximate per serving: Calories: 399   Protein: 28 gm   Fat: 23 gm
Carbohydrates: 22 gm   Cholesterol: 96 mg   Sodium: 659 mg

Step 6

Wine-Roasted Cornish Game Hens

▼

This company dish is sophisticated looking, but requires no exotic ingredients. Have the supermarket butcher split the hens, or split them yourself (see the step-by-step photographs overleaf). Or, roast them whole, which will take a little extra cooking time, and cut them in half before serving. Since the recipe calls for only ¼ cup of wine, you may want to use a table-quality wine and serve the rest with dinner.

Working time: 15 minutes
Total time: 1 hour 15 minutes

Wine-Roasted Cornish Game Hens

4 Servings

2 Cornish game hens, about 1 pound each, split in half	**2 teaspoons Dijon mustard**
¼ cup dry red wine	**½ teaspoon crumbled rosemary**
3 tablespoons olive or other vegetable oil	**½ teaspoon sage**
2 cloves garlic, minced or crushed through a press	**½ teaspoon thyme**
	¼ teaspoon pepper

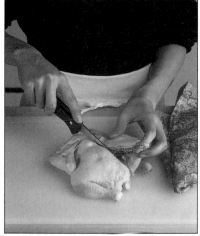

Step 2

1 Preheat the oven to 425°.

2 If the butcher has not split the hens for you, place them breast-side up on a work surface. With a sharp knife, cut all the way through the breasts, following the bone. Turn the hens over and cut through the backbones to halve them.

3 Place the halved hens in one layer, skin-side up, in a baking dish or roasting pan.

4 In a small bowl, stir together the wine, olive oil, garlic, mustard, rosemary, sage, thyme and pepper.

5 Pour the wine mixture over the hens. Place the hens in the oven and roast for 15 minutes.

6 Lower the oven temperature to 350° and roast until the juices run clear when the hens are pierced with a fork, about 15 minutes longer. Baste the hens every 15 minutes with the wine mixture.

Step 2

7 To serve, give each person half a hen with some of the pan juices spooned on top.

TIME-SAVERS

■ *Microwave tip: Prepare Steps 2, 3, 4 and 5 above, using a shallow microwave-safe baking dish. Sprinkle about ½ teaspoon of paprika evenly over the hens. Loosely cover with waxed paper and cook at 100% for about 12 minutes, or until the hens are cooked through. Rearrange the hens halfway through the cooking.*

■ *Do-ahead: The wine basting mixture (Step 4) can be made ahead. The hens can also be baked ahead of time and served at room temperature or reheated in the oven or microwave.*

Step 6

Values are approximate per serving: Calories: 336   Protein: 27 gm   Fat: 24 gm
Carbohydrates: 1 gm   Cholesterol: 88 mg   Sodium: 158 mg

Rosemary Baked Chicken and Potatoes

▼

*After ten minutes of preparation, this chicken dish goes in the oven;
an hour later, a dinner of crisp, Parmesan-crusted chicken and potatoes,
redolent with rosemary, is ready to put on the table. Some bread and
a tossed salad or a green vegetable round out the meal. Try this simple recipe
with other herbs, such as tarragon, basil or oregano.*

Working time: 10 minutes
Total time: 1 hour 10 minutes

Rosemary Baked Chicken and Potatoes

4 Servings

3 tablespoons olive or other vegetable oil
2 cloves garlic, minced or crushed through a press
¼ cup chopped fresh rosemary or 2½ teaspoons dried
¼ cup fine unseasoned breadcrumbs

¼ cup grated Parmesan cheese
½ teaspoon pepper
2½ pounds chicken parts
1 pound small red potatoes, unpeeled

1 Preheat the oven to 425°. Line a broiler pan with foil.

2 In a small bowl, combine the oil with the garlic and 2 tablespoons of the fresh rosemary (or 1 teaspoon of the dried).

3 In another small bowl, combine the breadcrumbs, Parmesan, pepper and remaining 2 tablespoons fresh rosemary (or 1½ teaspoons dried).

4 Place the chicken skin-side up on the broiler pan. Sprinkle the breadcrumb-Parmesan mixture over the chicken.

5 If the potatoes are small, leave them whole; otherwise, halve them. Place the potatoes around the chicken.

6 Drizzle the rosemary-garlic oil over the chicken and potatoes and bake for 20 minutes.

7 Reduce the oven temperature to 375° and continue baking for 30 to 40 minutes, or until the potatoes are tender and the chicken is golden and cooked through.

TIME-SAVERS

■ *Microwave tip: Prepare and arrange the ingredients as instructed in Steps 2 through 6 in a shallow microwave-safe baking dish. Cover loosely with waxed paper and cook at 100% for 15 minutes. Transfer the chicken and potatoes to a foil-lined broiler pan and broil until crisp and cooked through, 8 to 10 minutes.*

■ *Do-ahead: The rosemary-garlic oil (Step 2) and the breadcrumb-Parmesan mixture (Step 3) can be made ahead.*

Values are approximate per serving: Calories: 649 Protein: 41 gm Fat: 41 gm
Carbohydrates: 26 gm Cholesterol: 149 mg Sodium: 284 mg

Step 4

Step 5

Step 6

Lentil and Smoked Turkey Stew with Tomatoes

▼

Lentils, like split peas, need no presoaking before they are cooked—and they'll simmer to tenderness in a fraction of the time it takes to cook dried beans. The lentils here are cooked with smoked turkey, red wine and tomatoes. Smoked turkey—available in supermarket delis or meat cases—gives this stew something of the taste of sausage, but with much less fat.

Working time: 20 minutes
Total time: 1 hour

Lentil and Smoked Turkey Stew with Tomatoes

4 Servings

1 large onion
1 tablespoon vegetable oil
3 cloves garlic, minced or crushed through a press
1 cup lentils
2 cans (14½ ounces each) stewed tomatoes, with their juice
½ cup low-sodium chicken broth
½ cup dry red wine or low-sodium chicken broth
1½ teaspoons thyme
¼ teaspoon sugar
¼ teaspoon pepper
1 bay leaf
¾ pound smoked turkey, unsliced
¼ cup chopped parsley (optional)

1 Coarsely chop the onion.

2 In a large saucepan, warm the oil over medium-high heat until hot but not smoking. Add the onion and garlic, and stir-fry until the mixture begins to brown, 3 to 5 minutes.

3 Add the lentils, stewed tomatoes and their juice, the chicken broth, wine, thyme, sugar, pepper and bay leaf. Bring the mixture to a boil over medium-high heat. Reduce the heat to low, cover and simmer, stirring occasionally, until the lentils are tender, about 40 minutes.

4 Meanwhile, cut the turkey into ½-inch cubes.

5 When the lentils are done, remove and discard the bay leaf. Remove about 1 cup of the lentils and purée them in a food processor. Return the lentil purée to the saucepan and add the cubed turkey and parsley (if using). Cook over medium-high heat until the turkey is heated through, about 3 minutes.

TIME-SAVERS

■ **Do-ahead:** *The entire stew can be made well ahead and gently reheated.*

Step 3

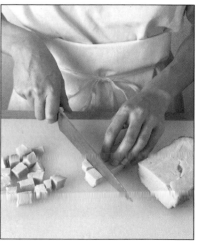

Step 4

Step 5

Values are approximate per serving: Calories: 370 Protein: 33 gm Fat: 8 gm
Carbohydrates: 46 gm Cholesterol: 37 mg Sodium: 1362 mg

Broiled Chicken with Garlic-Herb Sauce

▼

The sage-flavored sauce for this savory dish is thickened with kneaded butter, a technique borrowed from classic French cooking. To make kneaded butter (called beurre manié), you simply stir or rub together a small amount of butter and flour and then add it bit by bit to a hot broth or pan juices to make a rich, smooth sauce. If you don't care for the sage used here, substitute basil or thyme.

Working time: 15 minutes
Total time: 35 minutes

Broiled Chicken with Garlic-Herb Sauce

4 Servings

2 whole boneless chicken breasts, skin on (about 1½ pounds total)
3 tablespoons butter, at room temperature
3 cloves garlic, minced or crushed through a press
¼ cup chopped parsley (optional)
1½ teaspoons crumbled sage
¼ teaspoon pepper
2 tablespoons flour
½ cup chicken broth
¼ cup water

1 Preheat the broiler. Line a broiler pan with foil.

2 Meanwhile, cut each chicken breast in half.

3 In a small bowl, combine the butter, garlic, parsley (if using), sage and pepper.

4 Place the chicken on the broiler pan. Spread each breast half with ½ teaspoon of the garlic-herb butter. Broil 4 inches from the heat for 8 minutes, or until golden.

5 Turn the chicken over and spread each breast half with another ½ teaspoon garlic-herb butter. Broil for 10 minutes, or until the chicken is firm and the juices run clear when pierced with a knife.

6 Meanwhile, use your fingers to mix the flour into the remaining garlic-herb butter.

7 In a small skillet or saucepan, bring the chicken broth and water to a boil over medium-high heat. Stir the butter-flour mixture, bit by bit, into the hot broth. Reduce the heat to medium-low and simmer for 1 minute.

8 Remove the chicken from the broiler pan. Pour any juices from the pan into the garlic-herb sauce and stir to combine. Serve the chicken breasts topped with some sauce.

TIME-SAVERS

■ *Do-ahead: The garlic-herb butter (Step 3) can be made ahead; just be sure it's at room temperature before using.*

Values are approximate per serving: Calories: 279 Protein: 28 gm Fat: 16 gm
Carbohydrates: 4 gm Cholesterol: 101 mg Sodium: 277 mg

Step 4

Step 6

Step 7

Chicken and Rice in Green Vegetable Broth

In spite of its low calorie count, this light version of chicken-in-a-pot is both nourishing and satisfying. And in the tradition of homemade chicken soup, it's even more welcome when the weather turns cold and gray. If it's more convenient, you can use frozen spinach, and if your family prefers it, the soup can be made with chicken breasts instead of legs.

Working time: 20 minutes
Total time: 40 minutes

Chicken and Rice in Green Vegetable Broth

4 Servings

2 chicken legs (about 14 ounces total)

3 cups low-sodium or regular chicken broth

2 cups water

½ cup raw rice

1 teaspoon thyme

½ teaspoon pepper

2 cups shredded cabbage (about 6 ounces)

2 cups fresh spinach leaves, or half a 10-ounce package frozen chopped spinach, thawed

1 Remove and discard the skin from the chicken legs.

2 In a large saucepan, combine the chicken broth, water, rice, thyme and pepper. Add the chicken, cover and bring to a boil over high heat. Reduce the heat to low and simmer, covered, for 15 minutes.

3 Meanwhile, shred the cabbage and fresh spinach (or thaw the frozen spinach in the microwave).

4 Remove the chicken to a cutting board. Remove the meat from the bones and cut it into bite-size pieces.

5 Return the chicken pieces to the broth. Add the cabbage and spinach and bring to a boil over medium-high heat. Boil the broth just until the cabbage and chicken are wilted and heated through, about 1 minute.

TIME-SAVERS

■ *Do-ahead:* The chicken can be cooked in the broth and removed from the bone ahead of time. The whole soup can be made and reheated.

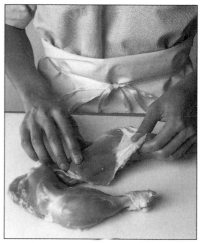

Step 1

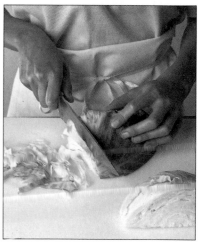

Step 3

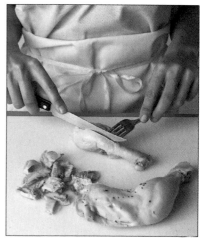

Step 4

Values are approximate per serving: Calories: 191 Protein: 16 gm Fat: 4 gm
Carbohydrates: 23 gm Cholesterol: 45 mg Sodium: 119 mg

Tomato-Tarragon Braised Chicken Breasts

▼

Braising—long, slow cooking in broth, wine or sauce—is commonly used to tenderize tough cuts of meat. But since chicken breasts are tender to begin with, a brief braising simply renders them mouth-watering and juicy and suffuses them with the savors of tomatoes, tarragon and garlic. Serve a simple vegetable side dish and offer lots of Italian or French bread to sop up the sauce.

Working time: 10 minutes
Total time: 35 minutes

Tomato-Tarragon Braised Chicken Breasts

4 Servings

3 tablespoons flour
¼ teaspoon pepper
4 chicken breast halves, bone-in (about 2½ pounds total)
1 tablespoon olive or other vegetable oil
1 cup canned crushed tomatoes
½ cup chicken broth

8 medium shallots, peeled but left whole, or 1 medium onion, cut into wedges
2 cloves garlic, minced or crushed through a press
3 tablespoons minced fresh tarragon or 1 teaspoon dried
1 teaspoon brown sugar

Step 3

1 In a plastic or paper bag, combine the flour and pepper, and shake to mix. Add the chicken and shake to coat lightly. Remove the chicken and reserve the excess seasoned flour.

2 In a large skillet, warm the oil over medium-high heat until hot but not smoking. Add the chicken, skin-side down, and cook until golden brown, about 6 minutes.

3 Turn the chicken over and cook for 3 minutes longer. Remove the chicken to a plate and cover loosely to keep warm.

4 Stir in the reserved seasoned flour. Add the tomatoes, chicken broth, shallots (or onion wedges), garlic, tarragon and sugar. Bring the mixture to a boil over medium-high heat. Return the chicken (and any juices that have accumulated on the plate) to the skillet. Reduce the heat to medium-low, cover and simmer for 5 minutes.

Step 4

5 Turn the chicken over, baste the sauce and simmer until the chicken is cooked through, 10 to 15 minutes longer.

TIME-SAVERS

■ *Do-ahead: The whole dish can be made ahead and gently reheated.*

Values are approximate per serving: Calories: 476 Protein: 49 gm Fat: 25 gm
Carbohydrates: 12 gm Cholesterol: 145 mg Sodium: 367 mg

Step 5

Chili-Rubbed Chicken with Corn-Avocado Salad

Rubbing chicken with a spice paste before broiling gives it an intense flavor and a crisp coating. Here, mayonnaise and lime juice form the base for a Southwestern-inspired paste that is flavored with chili powder, cumin and garlic. The corn-avocado side dish, a cross between a salad and a salsa, is tossed with the same mayonnaise mixture used on the chicken.

Working time: 20 minutes
Total time: 35 minutes

Chili-Rubbed Chicken with Corn-Avocado Salad

4 Servings

½ cup mayonaise
⅓ cup lime juice
1 tablespoon olive or other vegetable oil
¼ cup chopped parsley (optional)
2 cloves garlic, minced or crushed through a press
2 teaspoons grated lime zest (optional)
2 tablespoons chili powder
1 tablespoon cumin

½ teaspoon salt
¼ teaspoon pepper
4 whole chicken legs (drumstick and thigh, about 2¼ pounds total)
1 package (10 ounces) frozen corn, thawed
1 avocado
12 cherry tomatoes
2 tablespoons chopped cilantro (optional)

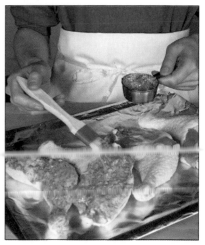

Step 2

1 Preheat the broiler. Line a broiler pan with foil and lightly grease the foil.

2 In a serving bowl, combine the mayonnaise, lime juice, oil, parsley (if using), garlic, lime zest (if using), chili powder, cumin, salt and pepper. Measure out ¼ cup of the chili mayonnaise to rub on the chicken.

3 Place the chicken legs skin-side down on the broiler pan. Coat them with half of the reserved ¼ cup of chili mayonnaise. Broil 4 inches from the heat for about 8 minutes, or until the chicken begins to brown.

4 Turn the chicken legs over and coat them with the remaining 2 tablespoons of chili mayonnaise. Broil for about 8 minutes, or until the chicken is browned and cooked through.

Step 3

5 Meanwhile, thaw the corn in the microwave or under warm running water; drain well and add to the chili mayonnaise in the serving bowl.

6 Dice the avocado and halve the cherry tomatoes, and add them to the serving bowl. Toss to combine and coat with the dressing. Stir in the cilantro (if using).

7 Serve the hot chicken legs with the corn-avocado salad on the side.

TIME-SAVERS

■ *Do-ahead: The chili mayonnaise (Step 2) and the corn-avocado salad (Steps 5 and 6) can be made ahead.*

Values are approximate per serving: Calories: 692 Protein: 37 gm Fat: 51 gm
Carbohydrates: 25 gm Cholesterol: 132 mg Sodium: 593 mg

Step 6

Oven-Braised Turkey Breast with Cider-Mayonnaise Sauce

▼

This oven-braised turkey breast is just right for a buffet or casual dinner party. Serve it sliced, accompanied with the creamy sauce, or provide sandwich fixings and use the sauce as a spread. The sauce is made by reducing the cider-based cooking broth to an intensely flavorful syrup and then combining it with mayonnaise. Although reducing the broth can take over an hour, it can be done in stages, at the cook's convenience.

Working time: 30 minutes
Total time: 2 hours 25 minutes

Oven-Braised Turkey Breast with Cider-Mayonnaise Sauce

6 Servings

1 quart apple cider or apple juice
2 medium onions
3 medium carrots
2 ribs celery
3 cloves garlic
½ teaspoon whole peppercorns
3 cloves
1 teaspoon thyme

1 bay leaf
1½ pounds skinless, boneless
  turkey breast
1 cup mayonnaise
3 tablespoons lemon juice
2 tablespoons Dijon mustard
2 teaspoons grated lemon zest
  (optional)

1 Preheat the oven to 375°.

2 In a large flameproof casserole or Dutch oven, bring the cider to a boil.

3 Meanwhile, halve the onions. Halve the carrots and celery crosswise. Add the onions, carrots, celery, garlic, peppercorns, cloves, thyme and bay leaf to the cider. Bring the mixture to a boil, then add the turkey. Cover the casserole and place it in the oven for 35 minutes.

4 Turn the turkey over and cook for 15 minutes longer, or until the turkey is cooked through.

5 Remove the turkey from the broth, loosely cover and set aside. Strain the broth into a medium saucepan and discard the solids. Over medium heat, reduce the broth to ½ cup; it should be the color and consistency of maple syrup. This will take about 1 hour and 15 minutes. Watch the mixture carefully for the last half hour of reducing. If the saucepan you are using is on the big side, transfer the broth to a smaller saucepan to avoid burning the broth. Let the reduced broth cool to room temperature and then refrigerate.

6 Meanwhile, in a small bowl, combine the mayonnaise, lemon juice, mustard and lemon zest (if using).

7 Stir the cooled reduced cider into the mayonnaise. Thinly slice the turkey and serve with the sauce.

TIME-SAVERS

■ *Microwave tip: To reduce the broth in the microwave, strain it and place it in a 1-quart glass measuring cup. Cook at 100% for 10 minutes. Check the amount of reduction and cook at 100% for another 10 minutes. Continue microwaving for 1 or 2 minutes at a time until it is reduced to ⅓ cup.*

Values are approximate per serving: Calories: 493   Protein: 28 gm   Fat: 31 gm
Carbohydrates: 25 gm   Cholesterol: 92 mg   Sodium: 454 mg

Step 3

Step 5

Step 7

Chicken and Mixed Vegetable Grill

▼

Chicken breasts and skewers of zucchini, eggplant and bell peppers are marinated in a tangy lemon-mustard vinaigrette for a delicious indoor or outdoor grilled meal. If your family does not like eggplant, use small, whole mushrooms instead. To save on last-minute preparation, place the chicken in the marinade in the morning, cover the dish and refrigerate it until you are ready to start dinner.

Working time: 25 minutes
Total time: 50 minutes

Chicken and Mixed Vegetable Grill

6 Servings

2 scallions
¼ cup olive or other vegetable oil
2 tablespoons lemon juice
2 tablespoons grainy mustard
5 cloves garlic, minced or crushed through a press
3 teaspoons grated lemon zest (optional)
1½ teaspoons basil
1½ teaspoons oregano
½ teaspoon salt

¼ teaspoon black pepper
Pinch of cayenne pepper
4 chicken breast halves, bone in, with skin (about 2½ pounds total)
1 medium zucchini
1 medium yellow or green bell pepper
Half a small eggplant (halved lengthwise), unpeeled

1 Preheat the broiler or start the charcoal. If broiling, line a broiler pan with foil.

2 Coarsely chop the scallions.

3 In a small bowl, combine the scallions, oil, lemon juice, mustard, garlic, lemon zest (if using), basil, oregano, salt, black pepper and cayenne.

4 Place the chicken breasts in a shallow nonmetallic dish and spoon the marinade over them; let marinate while you prepare the vegetables.

5 Cut the zucchini into ½-inch-thick rounds. Cut the bell pepper into 1-inch squares. Halve the eggplant lengthwise and then cut crosswise into ½-inch pieces. Thread the vegetables on skewers.

6 Remove the chicken from the marinade, reserving the marinade. If broiling, place the chicken skin-side down on the foil-lined broiler pan; if grilling, place the chicken skin-side up. Grill or broil 4 inches from the heat for 7 minutes.

7 Turn the chicken over (if broiling, brush with some of the pan juices). Brush the skewered vegetables with the reserved marinade. Grill or broil the chicken and vegetables for 12 minutes, or until the chicken is cooked through. If the vegetables are done before the chicken, remove them.

TIME-SAVERS

■ **Do-ahead:** *The chicken can be marinated for several hours or all day. The vegetables can be cut up and threaded on skewers ahead of time.*

Values are approximate per serving: Calories: 263 Protein: 31 gm Fat: 13 gm
Carbohydrates: 4 gm Cholesterol: 86 mg Sodium: 191 mg

Step 4

Step 5

Step 7

Coq au Vin

▼

Coq au vin—chicken in wine sauce—is a classic French bistro dish. In the traditional recipe, the onions and mushrooms are braised separately, and the dish is served with boiled potatoes; here, the chicken and all the vegetables cook in a single pot. One way to get the most out of this recipe is to double it: Serve it once for a company dinner and save the leftover portion for a family meal later in the week.

Working time: 15 minutes
Total time: 1 hour 10 minutes

Coq au Vin

4 Servings

¼ **pound bacon (4 to 6 slices)**
2½ **pounds chicken parts**
¼ **cup plus 3 tablespoons flour**
1 **pound small red potatoes, unpeeled**
½ **pound small mushrooms**
3 **medium carrots**
1½ **cups chicken broth**
1½ **cups dry red wine**
2 **cups frozen pearl onions or ½ pound small white boiling onions**

3 **cloves garlic, minced or crushed through a press**
1½ **teaspoons thyme**
½ **teaspoon salt**
¼ **teaspoon pepper**
1 **bay leaf**
3 **tablespoons butter, at room temperature**

Step 1

1 In a large flameproof casserole or Dutch oven, cook the bacon over medium heat until crisp, about 10 minutes. Drain the bacon, crumble and set aside.

2 Meanwhile, dredge the chicken in ¼ cup of the flour; discard any excess dredging mixture.

3 Add the chicken to the casserole and sauté over medium heat until golden, about 8 minutes per side.

4 Meanwhile, halve the potatoes. If the mushrooms are small, leave them whole; otherwise, halve or quarter them. Cut the carrots into 1½-inch lengths.

Step 4

5 Increase the heat under the casserole to medium-high and add the chicken broth, wine, potatoes, mushrooms, carrots, onions, garlic, thyme, salt, pepper and bay leaf, and bring to a boil. Reduce the heat to low, cover and simmer, stirring occasionally, until the potatoes and carrots are tender and the chicken is cooked through, about 30 minutes.

6 Blend the butter with the remaining 3 tablespoons flour. Bring the casserole back to a boil over medium-high heat. Add the butter-flour mixture about a half a tablespoon at a time and stir well after each addition. Cook, stirring occasionally, until the sauce has thickened slightly, 2 to 3 minutes.

7 Stir in the bacon and discard the bay leaf before serving.

Values are approximate per serving: Calories: 772 Protein: 46 gm Fat: 43 gm
Carbohydrates: 50 gm Cholesterol: 175 mg Sodium: 1037 mg

Step 6

Chunky Chicken-Potato Soup

▼

Making soup is one of the best ways to use leftovers, since exact quantities are not critical to the soup's success. This recipe calls for about half a pound of leftover chicken, but a little bit more or less won't do any harm. And if you don't have broccoli on hand, you can omit it or replace it with cauliflower (add it when you put in the potatoes) or sliced mushrooms (add them at the end with the chicken).

Working time: 20 minutes
Total time: 35 minutes

4 Servings

2 medium all-purpose potatoes (about 1 pound)	**¼ teaspoon pepper**
1 medium onion	**1½ cups cubed cooked chicken (about ½ pound)**
4 tablespoons butter	**1 cup broccoli florets**
¼ cup flour	**1½ cups milk**
4½ cups chicken broth	**1 can (16 ounces) corn, drained**

Step 1

1 Peel the potatoes and cut them into ½-inch cubes. Coarsely chop the onion.

2 In a large saucepan, melt the butter over medium heat until hot but not smoking. Add the onion and cook, stirring, until wilted, 1 to 2 minutes.

3 Stir in the flour and cook, stirring constantly, until the flour and butter are completely blended, about 1 minute.

4 Slowly pour in the chicken broth, stirring constantly. When the mixture returns to a boil, add the potatoes and pepper, reduce the heat to medium-low, cover the pan and simmer, stirring occasionally, until the potatoes are tender, about 15 minutes.

5 Meanwhile, cut the chicken into 1-inch cubes. Cut the broccoli into florets.

6 Increase the heat to medium and when the soup returns to a boil, stir in the chicken, milk, corn and broccoli. Cook until the broccoli is crisp-tender and the chicken is heated through, 2 to 3 minutes longer.

Step 5

TIME-SAVERS

■ *Microwave tip: If you would like to make this soup but don't have any leftover chicken, you can cook chicken quickly in the microwave. Place 1 pound of skinless, boneless chicken breast in a shallow microwave-safe baking dish. Loosely cover and cook at 100% for 5 minutes, rotating the dish once. Let stand for 5 minutes.*

■ *Do-ahead: The potatoes, onion and chicken can be cut up ahead of time. The whole dish can also be cooked ahead of time and then reheated on the stovetop or in the microwave.*

Step 6

Values are approximate per serving: Calories: 471   Protein: 28 gm   Fat: 22 gm
Carbohydrates: 44 gm   Cholesterol: 94 mg   Sodium: 1354 mg

Chicken Enchiladas
with Green Sauce

▼

The basic ingredient in a Mexican "salsa verde," or green sauce, is tomatillos, small fruits that resemble—but are botanically unrelated to—tomatoes. They grow within a papery husk, have a tart apple-like flavor and are never eaten raw. You'll find canned green tomatillos in the Mexican foods section of many supermarkets, or in Latin grocery stores. The cans may be labeled either "tomatillos" or "tomatitos verdes."

Working time: 35 minutes
Total time: 1 hour

Chicken Enchiladas with Green Sauce

1 Servings

1 cup chicken broth	¼ teaspoon black pepper
1 teaspoon oregano	1 can (11 ounces) tomatillos, with
1½ pounds skinless, boneless	their juice
chicken breast	1 cup sour cream
2 cloves garlic	4 scallions
1 medium onion	1 can (4 ounces) chopped mild
1 fresh or bottled jalapeño pepper,	green chilies, drained
seeded	8 flour tortillas
¼ cup (packed) cilantro sprigs	½ cup shredded Cheddar cheese

Step 3

1 In a medium saucepan, bring the chicken broth and oregano to a boil over medium-high heat. Add the chicken and let the liquid return to a boil. Reduce the heat to low, cover and simmer until the chicken is cooked through, about 10 minutes. With a slotted spoon, remove the chicken and set aside to cool. (Save the broth for another use.)

2 Meanwhile, in a food processor, mince the garlic. Add the onion, jalapeño and cilantro, and coarsely chop. Add the black pepper and the tomatillos and their juice, and purée. Add ½ cup of the sour cream and pulse to blend.

3 Coarsely chop the scallions. In a medium bowl, combine the scallions with the remaining ½ cup sour cream and the chilies. When the chicken is cool enough to handle, shred it and add to the bowl.

4 Preheat the oven to 425°. Grease an 11 x 7-inch baking dish

Step 5

5 Pour the tomatillo sauce into a shallow bowl. Dip a tortilla into the sauce to coat both sides. Place the tortilla on a plate and spoon about ⅓ cup of the chicken mixture onto the bottom third of the tortilla. Roll the tortilla up and place it crosswise in the prepared baking dish. Repeat with the remaining tortillas and chicken mixture. Spoon any remaining sauce over the enchiladas. Top with the Cheddar. Bake for 25 minutes, or until heated through.

TIME-SAVERS

■ *Microwave tip: In an 11 x 7-inch baking dish, combine ½ cup broth, the oregano and chicken. Cover loosely and cook at 100% for 10 minutes. Remove the chicken (discard the broth); wipe out the dish. Proceed with Steps 2 through 5, but use only ¼ cup of the tomatillo juice and don't sprinkle on the Cheddar. Cover with waxed paper and cook (on an inverted saucer) at 100% for 5 minutes; cook at 50% for 10 minutes, or until heated through. Top with the Cheddar and cook at 50% for 2 minutes to melt the cheese.*

Values are approximate per serving: Calories: 637 Protein: 53 gm Fat: 20 gm
Carbohydrates: 59 gm Cholesterol: 139 mg Sodium: 929 mg

Step 5

Chicken on a Bed
of Sautéed Spinach

Despite its impressive appearance, this party-worthy dish is cooked in a single skillet. You'll need a broilerproof skillet (with a flameproof handle) for this recipe. Do not, however, use a cast-iron skillet; the iron may react with the spinach, creating an unpleasant metallic flavor. You can also substitute other greens for the spinach, or add a small amount of a more pungent green, such as watercress.

Working time: 20 minutes
Total time: 40 minutes

Chicken on a Bed of Sautéed Spinach

4 Servings

¼ cup flour
¼ teaspoon pepper
4 skinless, boneless chicken breast halves (about 1¼ pounds total)
1 medium red onion
1 pound fresh spinach
2 tablespoons olive or other vegetable oil

1 clove garlic, minced or crushed through a press
3 tablespoons butter
¼ teaspoon nutmeg
⅔ cup chicken broth
⅓ cup milk
1 cup shredded Swiss cheese (about ¼ pound)

1 In a shallow bowl, combine the flour and pepper. Dredge the chicken lightly in the seasoned flour, reserving the excess. Thinly slice the onion. Stem the spinach.

2 In a large broilerproof skillet, warm 1 tablespoon of the oil over medium-high heat until hot but not smoking. Add the onion and garlic, and cook until the onion begins to brown, about 3 minutes.

3 Add the spinach and cook, stirring, just until it wilts, 2 to 3 minutes. Remove the spinach and onion to a plate and keep warm.

Step 3

4 Add the remaining 1 tablespoon oil to the skillet and warm over medium-high heat until hot but not smoking. Add the chicken breasts and cook until golden all over, about 5 minutes per side. Remove the chicken to a plate and cover loosely to keep warm.

5 Add the butter to the skillet and melt over medium heat. Stir in the reserved dredging mixture and the nutmeg and cook, stirring, until the flour absorbs all of the butter.

6 Gradually add the chicken broth and milk, stirring to keep the mixture smooth. Bring the mixture to a bare simmer and cook, stirring, until the sauce is slightly thickened, 1 to 2 minutes.

Step 7

7 Return the chicken to the skillet and spoon the sauce over the chicken. Bring the liquid to a boil. Reduce the heat to medium-low, cover and cook until the chicken is cooked through, 8 to 10 minutes. Meanwhile, preheat the broiler.

8 Stir ½ cup of the Swiss cheese into the sauce in the skillet. Sprinkle the remaining ½ cup Swiss cheese on top. Place the skillet under the broiler until the cheese is just golden, about 2 minutes.

9 Serve the chicken with some of the sauce on a bed of sautéed spinach and onion.

Values are approximate per serving: Calories: 471 Protein: 45 gm Fat: 26 gm
Carbohydrates: 13 gm Cholesterol: 134 mg Sodium: 494 mg

Step 8

Marinated Chicken
with Red Potato Salad

▼

This baked chicken and potato salad dish can be made over a period of one or two days. The marinade, basting mixture and potato salad can all be prepared ahead and refrigerated. And the chicken can be served either hot or at room temperature. Although ideally the chicken should marinate for 4 hours, it will taste fine if you marinate it for only an hour or so.

Working time: 25 minutes
Total time: 1 hour 10 minutes

Marinated Chicken
with Red Potato Salad

4 Servings

2 lemons	1 pound red potatoes, unpeeled
1 orange	¼ cup mayonnaise
¼ cup maple syrup	2 tablespoons red wine vinegar
3 tablespoons olive oil	2 tablespoons capers, drained
2½ teaspoons thyme	(optional)
¾ teaspoon black pepper	½ teaspoon salt
2½ pounds chicken parts	1 large yellow or red bell pepper

Step 1

1 Grate the zest from the lemons and orange. Squeeze the juice from the orange (about ½ cup) and the lemons (about ½ cup total); set the juices aside. In a small bowl, combine the grated lemon and orange zests and the maple syrup. Set aside until ready to cook the chicken.

2 In a shallow nonaluminum pan, thoroughly blend the reserved citrus juices, 1 tablespoon of the oil, 2 teaspoons of the thyme and ½ teaspoon of the black pepper. Add the chicken and turn to coat completely. Cover with plastic wrap and refrigerate. Marinate for at least 4 hours or overnight, turning the chicken every once in awhile to marinate evenly.

3 Halve the potatoes if they are large. Steam them in a vegetable steamer until they are tender, about 15 minutes.

4 Meanwhile, in a medium bowl, combine the mayonnaise, the remaining 2 tablespoons oil, the vinegar, capers, the remaining ½ teaspoon thyme and ¼ teaspoon black pepper, and the salt.

5 When the potatoes are done, add them, while they are still hot, to the dressing and toss to coat. Let cool to room temperature.

Step 5

6 Meanwhile, cut the bell pepper into bite-size pieces. Add it to the cooled potatoes, toss to combine, cover with plastic wrap and refrigerate until serving time.

7 About 45 minutes before serving time, preheat the oven to 425°. Line a baking sheet with foil. Remove the chicken from the marinade (discard the marinade) and place it skin-side up on the baking sheet. Bake for 25 minutes.

8 Drizzle the citrus zest-maple syrup mixture over the chicken and bake for about 15 minutes longer, or until the chicken is cooked through and browned.

Step 8

Values are approximate per serving: Calories: 614 Protein: 37 gm Fat: 37 gm
Carbohydrates: 34 gm Cholesterol: 118 mg Sodium: 575 mg

Baked Lime-Ginger Chicken with Garlic Rice

▼

The crisp-crusted chicken in this delicious entrée is marinated in spicy lime juice, rolled in breadcrumbs and drizzled with a buttery ginger-garlic baste before baking. The accompanying rice is flavored with the same ginger-garlic mixture. For a change, lemon or orange juice and zest could be used instead of the lime in the marinade. Serve the chicken and rice with a salad of greens, tomatoes and mushrooms.

Working time: 25 minutes
Total time: 1 hour 5 minutes

Baked Lime-Ginger Chicken
with Garlic Rice

6 Servings

3 tablespoons lime juice
3 teaspoons grated lime zest (optional)
¼ teaspoon red pepper flakes
½ teaspoon salt
½ teaspoon black pepper
2½ pounds chicken parts
5 quarter-size slices (¼ inch thick) fresh ginger, unpeeled
3 tablespoons butter

2 tablespoons olive or other vegetable oil
6 cloves garlic, minced or crushed through a press
1¼ cups fine unseasoned breadcrumbs
1 cup raw rice
2 cups chicken broth
2 teaspoons chopped parsley (optional)

Step 5

1 Preheat the oven to 375°. Line a broiler pan with foil.

2 In a large shallow dish, combine the lime juice, zest, red pepper flakes, salt and black pepper. Add the chicken and toss to coat well with the marinade.

3 Mince the ginger.

4 In a medium saucepan, warm the butter in the oil over medium-high heat until the butter is melted. Add the ginger and garlic, and cook over low heat, stirring occasionally, for 5 minutes to release the flavors. Remove from the heat and set aside.

5 Place the breadcrumbs in a large shallow dish. Roll the chicken parts in the breadcrumbs to coat them evenly and then place them on the prepared broiler pan.

6 Drizzle the chicken with 3 tablespoons of the ginger garlic mixture and bake until the chicken is cooked through, about 45 minutes.

Step 6

7 Meanwhile, return the saucepan with the ginger-garlic mixture to medium-high heat. Add the rice and sauté until the rice is lightly coated with the oil, 1 to 2 minutes. Add the chicken broth and bring to a boil. Reduce the heat to medium-low, cover and simmer until the rice is tender and all the liquid is absorbed, about 20 minutes.

8 When the chicken is done, pour any pan juices from the broiler pan into the cooked rice. Stir the parsley (if using) into the rice and serve.

Values are approximate per serving: Calories: 578 Protein: 30 gm Fat: 31 gm
Carbohydrates: 42 gm Cholesterol: 113 mg Sodium: 817 mg

Step 7

Chicken Marengo

Like many sauced-and-simmered poultry dishes, chicken Marengo actually tastes better the second day: the flavors of its diverse ingredients have time to mingle and mellow, and the sauce permeates the chicken more deeply. Refrigerating the dish overnight also allows you to skim any fat that congeals on top when the sauce is chilled. To cut calories further, skin the chicken parts before cooking.

Working time: 20 minutes
Total time: 1 hour 15 minutes

Chicken Marengo

8 Servings

1 tablespoon vegetable oil
2½ pounds chicken parts
6 small white onions (about ½ pound total)
3 cloves garlic, minced or crushed through a press
2 cans (16 ounces each) crushed tomatoes
1 bottle (12 ounces) dark beer

½ cup orange juice
2 tablespoons tomato paste
1 tablespoon grated orange zest (optional)
¾ teaspoon salt
½ teaspoon black pepper
¾ pound small whole mushrooms
3 large carrots
2 large green bell peppers

Step 1

1 In a Dutch oven or flameproof casserole, warm the oil over medium-high heat until hot but not smoking. Add the chicken and brown on all sides, about 20 minutes.

2 Meanwhile, peel the onions, but leave them whole.

3 Remove the chicken from the casserole and set aside. Add the onions and garlic to the pan and sauté over medium-high heat until the onions begin to brown, about 5 minutes.

Step 3

4 Add the tomatoes, beer, orange juice, tomato paste, orange zest (if using), salt and black pepper. Bring the mixture to a boil. Add the whole mushrooms and the chicken and return to a boil. Reduce the heat to medium-low, cover and simmer for 30 minutes, turning the chicken occasionally.

5 Meanwhile, cut the carrots into 1½-inch chunks. Cut the bell peppers into strips.

6 Add the carrots and bell peppers to the casserole and cook, stirring occasionally, until the carrots are crisp-tender, about 15 minutes longer.

TIME-SAVERS

■ *Microwave tip: In a 5-quart microwave-safe casserole, arrange the chicken with the thicker portions toward the outside of the dish. Halve the onions and cut the carrots into 1-inch chunks and add them to the casserole. Omit the oil. Cover and cook at 100% for 10 minutes, turning the chicken pieces over once. Stir in the remaining ingredients, but decrease the tomatoes to 1 can (16 ounces) and the beer to 6 ounces. Cover the casserole and cook at 100% for 10 minutes, then at 50% for 20 minutes, or until the vegetables are tender and the chicken is cooked through.*

Step 6

Values are approximate per serving: Calories: 309 Protein: 21 gm Fat: 17 gm
Carbohydrates: 19 gm Cholesterol: 72 mg Sodium: 512 mg

Rum-Maple Roast Turkey with Wild Rice Stuffing

One of the best things about the method used to roast this turkey—in addition to its magnificent flavor and color—is that it requires virtually no basting. Two cups of rum are poured into the roasting pan and the turkey is roasted tightly covered for half the cooking time. The turkey is then roasted uncovered and basted once or twice with the rum-laced pan juices to brown it.

Working time: 55 minutes
Total time: 4 hours 15 minutes

Rum-Maple Roast Turkey
with Wild Rice Stuffing

12 Servings

2⅔ cups chicken broth
1 cup raw brown rice
⅓ cup raw wild rice
1 large onion
½ pound mushrooms
1 tablespoon olive oil
3 cloves garlic, minced
½ pound country sausage
1 teaspoon sage

1 teaspoon thyme
1¼ teaspoons pepper
½ cup maple syrup
1 tablespoon reduced-sodium soy sauce
12-pound turkey
2 teaspoons salt
2 cups rum
2 tablespoons flour

Step 3

1 In a medium saucepan, bring the chicken broth, brown rice and wild rice to a boil over medium-high heat. Reduce the heat to low, cover and simmer until the rices are tender and all the liquid is absorbed, about 45 minutes. Uncover and set aside.

2 Meanwhile, in a food processor, chop the onion and mushrooms.

3 In a large skillet, warm the oil over medium-high heat until hot but not smoking. Add the onion and garlic, and stir-fry until the onion begins to brown, about 5 minutes. Remove the sausage casings; add the meat to the skillet and cook until no longer pink, about 6 minutes.

4 Add the mushrooms, sage, thyme and ¼ teaspoon of the pepper, and cook until the mushrooms are just softened, 3 to 5 minutes. Stir in the cooked rice and set aside to cool slightly.

5 Preheat the oven to 350°. In a small bowl, combine the maple syrup and soy sauce.

Step 6

6 When ready to roast the turkey, stuff it with about 4 cups of the stuffing and truss. (Bake the remaining stuffing in a covered baking dish for 40 minutes.) Rub the turkey with the salt and remaining 1 teaspoon pepper. Place the turkey breast-side up in a roasting pan with a cover. Drizzle the maple-soy sauce mixture over the turkey. Pour the rum into the roasting pan, cover and roast for 1½ hours without taking the lid off.

7 Baste the turkey with the pan juices, then roast it, uncovered, basting once or twice, until done, about 1 hour and 10 minutes.

8 Skim the fat from the pan juices, reserving 1 tablespoon of fat. In a small saucepan, combine ¼ cup of the pan juices with the 1 tablespoon fat and the flour. Stir over medium heat until smooth. Blend in the rest of the pan juices and stir until the gravy is smooth and thickened.

Values are approximate per serving: Calories: 602   Protein: 71 gm   Fat: 21 gm
Carbohydrates: 28 gm   Cholesterol: 186 mg   Sodium: 932 mg

Step 6

Pepper-Pecan Chicken

Crunchy pecans make an irresistible crust on this oven-baked chicken. To tenderize the chicken before baking, it is marinated briefly in buttermilk (or, if you have time, for several hours or overnight in the refrigerator). If you don't have buttermilk, use soured milk: Stir 1½ teaspoons of vinegar or lemon juice into ½ cup of milk; let stand for a few minutes, until the milk looks curdled.

Working time: 15 minutes
Total time: 55 minutes

Pepper-Pecan Chicken

4 Servings

2½ pounds chicken parts
½ cup buttermilk or plain yogurt
2 cloves garlic
½ cup pecans
⅔ cup fine unseasoned breadcrumbs

3 tablespoons cold butter, cut into pieces
½ teaspoon salt
½ teaspoon black pepper
Pinch of cayenne pepper
2 tablespoons honey

1 Preheat the oven to 425°. Line a broiler pan with foil.

2 In a large bowl, toss the chicken with the buttermilk (or yogurt) to coat evenly and set aside.

Step 2

3 In a food processor, mince the garlic. Add the pecans and coarsely chop. Add the breadcrumbs, butter, salt, black and cayenne peppers. Pulse on and off just to incorporate the butter. Transfer the pecan-breadcrumb mixture to a shallow bowl.

4 Drain the chicken pieces and dredge them in the pecan-breadcrumb mixture. Place the chicken, skin-side up, on the prepared pan.

5 Drizzle the honey over the chicken.

6 Bake the chicken for 15 minutes, then reduce the oven temperature to 375°. Bake for another 25 minutes, or until the chicken is cooked through.

Step 4

TIME-SAVERS

■ *Do-ahead: The chicken can be marinated in the buttermilk and the pecan-breadcrumb mixture can be made ahead. The chicken can be baked ahead and served at room temperature.*

Values are approximate per serving: Calories: 636 Protein: 39 gm Fat: 42 gm
Carbohydrates: 26 gm Cholesterol: 153 mg Sodium: 636 mg

Step 5

Chicken Breasts Stuffed with Broccoli, Bacon and Cheddar

Instead of stuffing and roasting an entire chicken, you can make an elegant—
but remarkably easy—chicken dish by stuffing whole breasts. And
you'll cut the cooking time by three-fourths in the bargain. Be sure the skin on the
chicken breasts is not torn, or it will be difficult to stuff them properly. To round
out the meal, serve steamed rice and lightly buttered carrots.

Working time: 40 minutes
Total time: 40 minutes

Chicken Breasts Stuffed with Broccoli, Bacon and Cheddar

4 Servings

4 slices bacon
1 cup chopped cooked broccoli, fresh or frozen, thawed
½ cup grated sharp Cheddar cheese
¼ cup whole-milk ricotta or small curd cottage cheese

2 tablespoons chopped pimiento (optional)
¼ teaspoon pepper
2 whole boneless chicken breasts, with full skin on (about 1½ pounds total)
About 1 tablespoon olive oil

1 In a medium skillet, cook the bacon over medium heat until crisp, about 10 minutes. Reserving the fat in the pan, drain the bacon on paper towels; crumble and set aside.

2 Make the stuffing: In a large bowl, blend the broccoli, Cheddar, ricotta, pimiento (if using), pepper and the reserved bacon.

3 Using your fingers, make a pocket for stuffing by gently separating the skin from the flesh, but keeping the skin attached at the edges.

Step 3

4 With the chicken breasts skin-side down on the work surface, stuff the pockets with the filling.

5 Pull the skin up and over the filling to cover it completely. Use toothpicks to hold the skin in place on the flesh side of the breasts.

6 Pour off all but 1 tablespoon of bacon fat from the skillet. Add 1 tablespoon of olive oil and warm over medium-high heat. Add the chicken breasts, skin-side up, and sear over medium-high heat for 2 minutes. Turn the breasts over and sear the other side, adding more oil if necessary to prevent sticking.

Step 4

7 Reduce the heat to medium and cook the breasts, skin-side up, for 10 minutes. Turn over and cook for 5 minutes longer.

8 To serve, remove the toothpicks and halve each breast crosswise.

TIME-SAVERS

■ *Microwave tip: Cook the bacon on paper towels at 100% for 3 to 4 minutes. Increase the amount of olive oil used in Step 6 to at least 2 tablespoons. If you are using fresh broccoli, cut up about 1 stalk and place it in a shallow microwave-safe dish with 3 tablespoons of water. Cover and cook at 100% for 3 minutes, or until crisp-tender.*

■ *Do-ahead: The stuffing can be made ahead, but do not mix in the crumbled bacon until you are ready to stuff the chicken.*

Values are approximate per serving: Calories: 478 Protein: 44 gm Fat: 32 gm
Carbohydrates: 3 gm Cholesterol: 139 mg Sodium: 330 mg

Step 8

New Orleans-Style Chicken Stew

▼

The flavors in this spicy stew are reminiscent of a Cajun gumbo, a dish that starts with a roux, a cooked blend of flour and fat. To achieve the proper rich brown color of the dark roux used in a gumbo, it can take up to half an hour of stirring over low heat. Here, the seasoned flour in which the chicken is dredged serves to thicken and mellow the sauce, but without the time and attention required by a traditional roux.

Working time: 25 minutes
Total time: 55 minutes

4 Servings

1 bunch scallions (6 to 8)
2 ribs celery
1 large red bell pepper
4 skinless, boneless chicken breast
   halves (about 1¼ pounds total)
¼ cup flour
1 teaspoon thyme
⅛ teaspoon cayenne pepper
2 tablespoons butter
1 tablespoon vegetable oil

3 cloves garlic, minced or crushed
   through a press
1 can (14 ounces) stewed tomatoes,
   with their juice
¼ cup chicken broth
3 drops hot pepper sauce
1 bay leaf
¼ pound kielbasa or other
   precooked garlic sausage

Step 3

1 Coarsely chop the scallions. Dice the celery and bell pepper. Cut the chicken into bite-size pieces.

2 In a plastic or paper bag, combine the flour, thyme and cayenne, and shake to mix. Add the chicken and shake to coat lightly. Remove the chicken and reserve the excess seasoned flour.

3 In a large skillet, warm 1 tablespoon of the butter in the oil over medium-high heat until the butter is melted. Add the chicken and cook until it is browned all over, about 7 minutes. Remove the chicken to a plate and cover loosely to keep warm.

4 Add the remaining 1 tablespoon butter to the skillet and heat until melted. Add the garlic and the reserved dredging mixture. Cook, stirring, until the flour is no longer visible, about 1 minute.

Step 6

5 Add the tomatoes and their juice, the chicken broth, scallions, celery, bell pepper, hot pepper sauce and bay leaf, and bring to a boil over medium-high heat. Reduce the heat to low, cover and simmer, stirring occasionally, until the vegetables are tender, about 15 minutes.

6 Meanwhile, dice the sausage.

7 Return the stew to a boil over medium-high heat. Return the chicken (and any juices that have accumulated on the plate) to the skillet along with the sausage, and heat until the chicken is cooked through, about 3 minutes. Remove the bay leaf before serving.

TIME-SAVERS

■ ***Do-ahead:*** *The vegetables, chicken and sausage can be cut up ahead. The whole stew can be made ahead and gently reheated.*

Values are approximate per serving: Calories: 402 Protein: 39 gm Fat: 19 gm
Carbohydrates: 18 gm Cholesterol: 117 mg Sodium: 792 mg

Step 7

Chicken with 40 Cloves of Garlic

This earthy Provençal dish is, as the title claims, made with 40 cloves of garlic—but they are rendered sweet and mild by an hour's baking in the oven. The garlic is cooked without peeling, which saves preparation time and lets each diner choose how to eat it: mashed into the pan juices and spooned over the chicken, spread onto slices of toasted French bread—or simply set aside by anyone who's not a garlic fan.

Working time: 15 minutes
Total time: 1 hour 30 minutes

Chicken with 40 Cloves of Garlic

6 Servings

1 tablespoon butter
1 tablespoon olive or other
    vegetable oil
4 pounds chicken parts
½ cup chicken broth
½ cup dry white wine
40 cloves garlic (about 3 large
    heads), unpeeled

1 teaspoon oregano
1 teaspoon thyme
¾ teaspoon marjoram
¾ teaspoon savory (optional)
½ teaspoon pepper

1 Preheat the oven to 375°.

2 In a large nonstick skillet, warm the butter in the oil over medium-high heat until the butter is melted. Add half the chicken and brown all over, about 10 minutes. Repeat with the remaining chicken. Transfer the chicken to a large casserole, Dutch oven or deep baking dish.

Step 2

3 Pour off all but 1 tablespoon of fat from the skillet. Add the chicken broth, wine, garlic, oregano, thyme, marjoram, savory (if using) and pepper to the skillet. Bring to a boil, scraping up any browned bits from the bottom of the pan.

4 Pour the contents of the skillet over the chicken. Tightly cover the casserole with aluminum foil and/or a lid. Bake until the garlic is completely softened and the chicken is cooked through, 45 minutes to 1 hour.

Step 3

TIME-SAVERS

■ *Microwave tip: Place the garlic cloves, broth, wine and seasonings in a large, shallow microwave-safe baking dish. Arrange the garlic around the outer edges of the casserole, cover and cook at 100% for 5 minutes. Meanwhile, brown the chicken as directed in Step 2. Add the chicken to the baking dish, arranging the meatier portions of the chicken toward the rim of the dish. Cover and cook at 100% for 20 minutes, or until the chicken is cooked through; rearrange the chicken once. If the garlic is not completely softened by the time the chicken is done, remove the chicken to a plate (cover loosely to keep warm) and continue cooking the garlic until it is soft enough to spread.*

■ *Do-ahead: The whole dish can be made ahead and served warm or gently reheated.*

Step 4

Values are approximate per serving: Calories: 410   Protein: 38 gm   Fat: 25 gm
Carbohydrates: 7 gm   Cholesterol: 124 mg   Sodium: 216 mg

Bloody Mary Grilled Chicken

All the makings of a Bloody Mary—except for the vodka—are combined in this vivid barbecue sauce. Tomato paste and chopped tomato reinforce the flavor and thicken the sauce; lemon juice, horseradish, Worcestershire and hot pepper sauce give it characteristic zing. Serve the chicken with celery stalks still bearing their leafy tops—just what you'd use to garnish a Bloody Mary in a glass.

Working time: 10 minutes
Total time: 45 minutes

Bloody Mary Grilled Chicken

4 Servings

1 cup tomato juice
¼ cup tomato paste
¼ cup lemon juice
1 tablespoon Worcestershire sauce
3 drops of hot pepper sauce
1 teaspoon horseradish
2 cloves garlic, minced or crushed
   through a press

1 teaspoon sugar
½ teaspoon salt
¼ teaspoon black pepper
2 scallions
1 fresh plum tomato or 1 whole
   canned tomato, well drained
2½ pounds chicken parts

1 Preheat the broiler or start the charcoal. If broiling, line a broiler pan with foil.

2 In a medium saucepan, combine the tomato juice, tomato paste, lemon juice, Worcestershire sauce, hot pepper sauce, horseradish, garlic, sugar, salt and black pepper. Bring to a boil over medium-high heat. Reduce the heat to medium and simmer, uncovered, for 10 minutes, stirring occasionally.

3 Meanwhile, coarsely chop the scallions and tomato.

4 If broiling, place the chicken on the broiler pan. Spoon half the sauce over the chicken and grill or broil 4 inches from the heat for 12 minutes, or until the chicken begins to brown.

5 Stir the scallions and tomato into the remaining sauce. Turn the chicken over and spoon the remaining sauce on the chicken. Cook 4 inches from the heat until the chicken is cooked through, about 12 minutes.

TIME-SAVERS

■ *Microwave tip: Prepare the sauce in the conventional manner as directed above. While the sauce is simmering, arrange the chicken in a shallow microwave-safe baking dish. Cover with waxed paper and cook at 100% for 15 minutes, rearranging the chicken pieces once about halfway through. To finish the cooking and to crisp the skin, grill or broil the chicken (following the basting instructions in Steps 4 and 5) for about 3 minutes on the first side and 8 to 10 minutes on the second side.*

■ *Do-ahead: The barbecue sauce (Step 2) can be made in advance.*

Values are approximate per serving: Calories: 331 Protein: 35 gm Fat: 17 gm
Carbohydrates: 8 gm Cholesterol: 110 mg Sodium: 609 mg

Step 2

Step 3

Step 4

Layered Turkey Enchilada Casserole

This Mexican-inspired casserole uses the same principle as lasagna, in which layers of pasta, sauce, cheese and meat are baked together. Here the tomato sauce is flavored with cumin and chili powder, and corn tortillas take the place of lasagna noodles. Serve the enchilada casserole with condiments such as crushed red pepper, chopped scallions and sour cream. And if you have leftover cooked chicken, use it in place of the turkey.

Working time: 20 minutes
Total time: 45 minutes

Layered Turkey Enchilada Casserole

6 Servings

1 can (16 ounces) tomato sauce
1 can (4 ounces) chopped mild
   green chilies, drained
1 clove garlic, minced or crushed
   through a press
1 tablespoon chili powder
2 teaspoons cumin
1 teaspoon oregano

¼ teaspoon black pepper
½ pound cooked turkey, unsliced
1 bunch scallions (6 to 8)
9 corn tortillas
1 package (10 ounces) frozen corn,
   thawed
2½ cups grated Cheddar cheese
   (about ¾ pound)

Step 3

1 Preheat the oven to 375°. Lightly grease a shallow 1-quart baking dish.

2 In a medium bowl, combine the tomato sauce, green chilies, garlic, chili powder, cumin, oregano and black pepper.

3 Cut the turkey with the grain into 2-inch-wide pieces and then cut the pieces across the grain into ¼-inch-thick strips. Coarsely chop the scallions.

4 Line the bottom of the baking dish with 3 tortillas, overlapping them. Spread one-third of the sauce over the tortillas.

5 Cover the tortillas with half the turkey, scallions and corn, and 1 cup of the Cheddar. Top with 3 more tortillas, half the remaining sauce, all of the remaining turkey, corn and scallions, and 1 cup of the Cheddar.

Step 5

6 Top with another 3 tortillas, the remaining sauce and the remaining ½ cup Cheddar.

7 Bake the casserole, uncovered, for 25 minutes.

TIME-SAVERS

■ *Microwave tip: Prepare Steps 2 through 5 as described above, layering the ingredients in a shallow 1-quart microwave-safe baking dish. Top the casserole with the remaining 3 tortillas and remaining sauce (but not the ½ cup Cheddar). Cover loosely with waxed paper and cook at 100% for 5 minutes; then cook at 50% for 10 minutes, or until heated through. Top with the remaining Cheddar and cook, uncovered, at 100% for 1 minute to melt the cheese.*

■ *Do-ahead: The sauce (Step 2) can be made ahead. The whole casserole can be made ahead and reheated.*

Values are approximate per serving: Calories: 474 Protein: 32 gm Fat: 23 gm
Carbohydrates: 39 gm Cholesterol: 89 mg Sodium: 1048 mg

Step 6

Chicken Thighs Creole with Almond-Onion Pilaf

▼

Meaty chicken thighs, one of the least expensive chicken parts, are delicious braised in a piquant Louisiana-style tomato sauce and served with a savory rice pilaf. The almond-onion rice will finish cooking about 15 minutes before the chicken is done; just take the rice pan off the heat and let it stand, covered, until serving time.

Working time: 30 minutes
Total time: 45 minutes

Chicken Thighs Creole with Almond-Onion Pilaf

4 Servings

2 medium onions
4 cloves garlic
2 stalks celery
1 medium green bell pepper
¼ cup flour
2 teaspoons paprika
½ teaspoon salt
¼ teaspoon black pepper
Pinch of cayenne pepper
8 chicken thighs (about 2½ pounds total)

2 tablespoons vegetable oil
1½ cups chicken broth
1 cup canned crushed tomatoes or 1 can (8 ounces) tomato sauce
1 teaspoon thyme
1 cup raw rice
1 cup water
½ cup sliced almonds

Step 4

1 In a food processor, chop the onions and garlic. Remove and set aside. In the same work bowl, chop the celery and bell pepper.

2 In a plastic or paper bag, combine the flour, paprika, salt, black pepper and cayenne. Add the chicken and shake to coat lightly. Remove the chicken and reserve the excess seasoned flour.

3 In a large skillet, warm 1 tablespoon of the oil over medium-high heat until hot but not smoking. Add the chicken and cook until golden all over, about 4 minutes per side. Remove the chicken to a plate and cover loosely to keep warm.

4 Add half of the onion-garlic mixture to the skillet and stir-fry over medium-high heat for 1 minute. Add the chopped celery and bell pepper. Stir in 1 tablespoon of the reserved dredging mixture and cook, stirring, until the flour is no longer visible.

Step 5

5 Stir in ½ cup of the chicken broth, the crushed tomatoes and thyme. Bring the mixture to a boil over medium-high heat.

6 Return the chicken (and any accumulated juices) to the skillet and return the mixture to a boil. Reduce the heat to medium-low, cover and simmer until the thighs are cooked through, about 15 minutes.

7 Meanwhile, in a medium saucepan, warm the remaining 1 tablespoon oil over medium-high heat until hot but not smoking. Add the remaining onion-garlic mixture and cook, stirring, for 5 minutes.

8 Add the rice and cook, stirring, for 1 minute. Add the remaining 1 cup broth and the water and bring to a boil. Reduce the heat to medium-low, cover and simmer until the rice is done, 15 to 20 minutes. Stir in the almonds. Serve the pilaf topped with chicken and sauce.

Values are approximate per serving: Calories: 854 Protein: 48 gm Fat: 49 gm Carbohydrates: 55 gm Cholesterol: 189 mg Sodium: 936 mg

Step 6

Lemon-Stuffed Roasted Chicken

▼

*Lemon, garlic and basil—irresistible Mediterranean flavors— suffuse the
meat of this simple but delicious roast chicken. Lemon halves placed
inside the bird flavor it from within, while lemon slices and a coating of herb
butter keep the outside tender and flavorful. If you make this dish often,
vary the herbs, using rosemary, thyme or oregano, for instance, instead of basil.*

Working time: 15 minutes
Total time: 1 hour 25 minutes

4 Servings

4 tablespoons butter
4 scallions
3 cloves garlic, minced or crushed
  through a press
3 teaspoons basil

½ teaspoon pepper
3 lemons
3-pound roasting chicken
½ teaspoon salt

Step 3

1 Preheat the oven to 425°. Line a roasting pan with foil.

2 In a small saucepan or in the microwave, melt the butter.

3 Chop the scallions. In a small bowl, combine the melted butter, scallions, garlic, 2 teaspoons of the basil and ¼ teaspoon of the pepper.

4 Prick 2 of the lemons all over with a fork and then halve them. Cut the third lemon into thin slices.

5 Place the chicken in the roasting pan. Sprinkle the remaining 1 teaspoon basil, ¼ teaspoon pepper and the salt in the cavity of the chicken, then stuff the lemon halves into the cavity.

6 Arrange the lemon slices over the chicken and spoon on some of the scallion-basil butter. Roast the chicken for 15 minutes.

7 Lower the oven temperature to 350° and roast the chicken for 45 minutes longer, basting every 15 minutes with the butter mixture. The chicken is done when the juices run clear and the internal temperature registers 170° on a meat thermometer.

Step 5

8 Let the chicken rest for 5 to 10 minutes before carving. Serve the chicken with some of the pan juices spooned on top.

TIME-SAVERS

■ **Microwave tip:** *Combine the butter, chopped scallions, garlic, 2 teaspoons of the basil and ¼ teaspoon of the pepper into a small microwave-safe bowl. Cook at 100% for 1½ minutes, or until the butter is melted. Prepare the lemons and chicken as directed in Steps 4 through 6. Place the chicken in a microwave-safe pie plate or baking dish and loosely cover with waxed paper. Cook at 100% for 20 minutes, rotating the dish and basting the chicken occasionally. To brown the chicken, place it under a preheated broiler, 4 inches from the heat, for 2 or 3 minutes.*

■ **Do-ahead:** *The scallion-basil butter (Step 3) can be made ahead and melted again before using.*

Values are approximate per serving: Calories: 510 Protein: 43 gm Fat: 35 gm
Carbohydrates: 5 gm Cholesterol: 165 mg Sodium: 521 mg

Step 6

Jamaican Jerk Chicken

▼

If you sampled this dish in the Caribbean, where it originated, the chicken would be fiery hot and spicy. When you make it at home, you can fine-tune the heat to your family's taste. To lessen the impact of the jalapeño, remove the seeds and ribs. For a still milder dish, use a pickled jalapeño instead of a fresh one, and use only half of it.

Working time: 15 minutes
Total time: 55 minutes

Jamaican Jerk Chicken

4 Servings

1 fresh or pickled jalapeño pepper
4 cloves garlic
4 quarter-size slices (¼ inch thick) fresh ginger, unpeeled
¼ cup (packed) parsley sprigs (optional)
2 teaspoons basil
1 teaspoon cinnamon
½ teaspoon allspice

1 teaspoon salt
½ teaspoon black pepper
3 tablespoons yellow mustard
2 tablespoons lime juice
2 tablespoons red wine vinegar or cider vinegar
1 tablespoon vegetable oil
1 teaspoon brown sugar
2½ pounds chicken parts

1 Preheat the oven to 375°. Line a broiler pan with foil.

2 If desired, remove the seeds and ribs from the jalapeño. In a food processor, combine the jalapeño, garlic, ginger, parsley (if using), basil, cinnamon, allspice, salt and black pepper, and finely chop.

Step 2

3 Add the mustard, lime juice, vinegar, oil and brown sugar, and process to a purée.

4 Place the chicken in a large bowl, add the spice mixture and toss to coat the chicken well.

5 Place the chicken skin-side up on the prepared broiler pan and bake for 35 minutes.

6 Remove the chicken from the oven and preheat the broiler. Broil the chicken 4 inches from the heat until cooked through and well browned on top, 2 to 5 minutes.

Step 3

TIME-SAVERS

■ *Do-ahead: The spice mixture can be made well ahead, or the chicken can be coated with the spice mixture and set aside to marinate a day ahead.*

Values are approximate per serving: Calories: 356   Protein: 35 gm   Fat: 21 gm
Carbohydrates: 5 gm   Cholesterol: 110 mg   Sodium: 803 mg

Step 4

Tarragon Chicken Pot Pie

Chicken pot pie is an old-fashioned country supper dish, but this version has two modern make-ahead options. The filling can be prepared in advance and the thawed pastry shell filled and baked shortly before serving. Or, you can assemble the whole pie, freeze it and then bake it later (15 minutes at 425° and then 1 hour and 15 minutes at 375°) without thawing.

Working time: 25 minutes
Total time: 1 hour

6 Servings

½ **pound small red potatoes, unpeeled**
1 **cup chicken broth**
¾ **pound skinless, boneless chicken breast**
1 **large green bell pepper**
2 **stalks celery**
2 **carrots**
½ **pound small mushrooms**
1 **cup frozen peas**
1 **teaspoon tarragon**

¼ **teaspoon black pepper**
3 **tablespoons flour**
3 **tablespoons butter, softened**
½ **cup fine unseasoned breadcrumbs**
Two 9-inch **frozen pie shells, thawed**
1 **egg yolk**
1 **tablespoon milk**
2 **tablespoons grated Parmesan cheese**

Step 6

1 Preheat the oven to 425°. Line a baking sheet with foil. Cut the potatoes into ¼-inch dice.

2 In a large skillet, bring the broth to a boil over medium-high heat. Add the potatoes. When the broth returns to a boil, cover the skillet, reduce the heat to low, and simmer for 9 minutes.

3 Meanwhile, cut the chicken into bite-size pieces. Dice the bell pepper. Thinly slice the celery and carrots.

4 Return the broth to a boil over medium-high heat. Add the chicken, bell pepper, celery, carrots, mushrooms, peas, tarragon and black pepper. Cover the skillet again and return the liquid to a boil.

5 Meanwhile, mix the flour and butter together until completely blended. Bit by bit, stir the flour-butter mixture into the chicken mixture and cook, stirring, until the liquid thickens, about 2 minutes.

Step 7

6 Cook until the chicken is done, 1 to 2 minutes longer. Stir in the breadcrumbs. Let the filling cool slightly.

7 Spoon the filling into one of the pie crusts. Top with the second crust and crimp to seal. Cut slits in the top crust.

8 In a small bowl, stir together the egg yolk and milk. Brush the top crust of the pie with the egg-yolk glaze and sprinkle it with the Parmesan.

9 Place the pie on the prepared baking sheet and bake for 15 minutes. Reduce the oven temperature to 325° and bake for 10 minutes longer, or until the crust is golden.

Values are approximate per serving: Calories: 580 Protein: 22 gm Fat: 29 gm Carbohydrates: 57 gm Cholesterol: 86 mg Sodium: 820 mg

Step 8

Quick Turkey Fricassee with Egg Noodles

A fricassee is a type of stew, usually made with chicken or veal. Turkey breast is the basis for this recipe, complemented by mild-tasting vegetables including summer squash and mushrooms. To preserve the delicate flavors (and to save time) the ingredients are not browned first; the addition of egg yolks and milk produces a pale, creamily sauced dish that's splendid over noodles.

Working time: 20 minutes
Total time: 35 minutes

Quick Turkey Fricassee with Egg Noodles

6 Servings

1 pound skinless, boneless turkey breast
2 medium zucchini
2 medium yellow squash
½ pound small mushrooms
1¾ cups chicken broth
2 cloves garlic, minced or crushed through a press
¾ teaspoon thyme
½ teaspoon salt
½ teaspoon pepper
1 cup frozen pearl onions or 3 coarsely chopped scallions (white part only)
½ pound egg noodles
2 tablespoons cornstarch
2 egg yolks
¼ cup milk
1 tablespoon chopped parsley (optional)

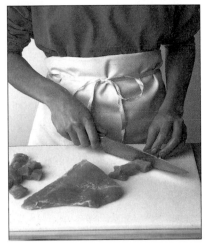

Step 1

1 Cut the turkey into bite-size pieces. Cut the zucchini and yellow squash into ¼-inch slices. If the mushrooms are small, leave them whole; otherwise, halve them. Bring a large pot of water to a boil.

2 Meanwhile, in a medium skillet, bring 1½ cups of the chicken broth, the garlic, thyme, salt and pepper to a boil over medium-high heat. Add the turkey, mushrooms and pearl onions to the boiling broth. Return the mixture to a boil, reduce the heat to low, cover and simmer until the turkey is barely done, 8 to 10 minutes.

3 Add the noodles to the boiling water and cook until al dente, 10 to 12 minutes, or according to package directions.

4 Meanwhile, in a small bowl, combine the remaining ¼ cup broth with the cornstarch. Increase the heat under the turkey mixture to medium-high and bring it to a boil. Stir in the cornstarch mixture and then add the zucchini and yellow squash. Stir constantly until the liquid has thickened slightly. Reduce the heat to medium, cover and simmer until the vegetables are just tender, about 4 minutes.

Step 2

5 In a small bowl, beat the egg yolks and milk together. Ladle out about ¼ cup of hot broth from the skillet and slowly beat it into the egg-milk mixture to warm it. Then add the warmed mixture to the turkey fricassee in the skillet. Cook at a bare simmer, stirring frequently, until thickened, about 5 minutes.

6 Drain the noodles and top them with the fricassee and parsley.

TIME-SAVERS

■ **Do-ahead:** *The vegetables and turkey can be cut up ahead. The fricassee can be prepared through Step 4 and then reheated and thickened with the egg-milk mixture (Step 5) just before serving.*

Values are approximate per serving: Calories: 316 Protein: 27 gm Fat: 6 gm
Carbohydrates: 39 gm Cholesterol: 155 mg Sodium: 544 mg

Step 5

Chicken Breasts Moroccan Style

North African cooking often mingles sweet, spicy and savory ingredients; typically, fruits and nuts are cooked with meat and rice, and seasoned with citrus and cinnamon. In this elegant rendition, an almond-raisin pilaf is stuffed under the skin of whole chicken breasts, which are then basted with oregano butter and roasted. The stuffing technique is simple; just be careful not to tear the skin as you loosen it.

Working time: 20 minutes
Total time: 1 hour 10 minutes

Chicken Breasts
Moroccan Style

4 Servings

2 cups chicken broth
½ cup raisins
2 cloves garlic, minced or crushed
   through a press
1½ teaspoons oregano
½ teaspoon pepper
1 cup raw rice
¼ cup chopped parsley (optional)

4 scallions
1 tablespoon grated orange zest
   (optional)
½ cup sliced almonds
2 whole boneless chicken breasts,
   with full skin on (about
   1½ pounds total)
2 tablespoons butter

1 In a medium saucepan, bring the chicken broth, raisins, garlic, ½ teaspoon of the oregano and ¼ teaspoon of the pepper to a boil. Add the rice, reduce the heat to medium-low, cover and simmer until the rice is tender and all the liquid is absorbed, about 20 minutes.

2 Meanwhile, coarsely chop the parsley (if using) and the scallions. Grate the orange zest (if using).

3 When the rice is done, remove it from the heat and stir in the parsley, scallions, orange zest and almonds. Set the rice aside to cool to room temperature, uncovered.

4 Preheat the oven to 425°. Line a roasting pan with foil.

5 Using your fingers, make a pocket for stuffing by gently separating the skin from the flesh of the chicken breasts, but keeping the skin attached at the edges.

6 With the chicken breasts skin-side up on the work surface, fill the pockets with the stuffing, using about ¾ cup of stuffing per breast. Pull the skin up and over the stuffing to cover it completely and use toothpicks to hold the skin in place.

7 Place the chicken breasts skin-side up in the roasting pan. Place the remaining stuffing in a small baking dish and cover it with foil.

8 Melt the butter on the stovetop or in the microwave. Stir in the remaining ¼ teaspoon pepper and 1 teaspoon oregano.

9 Brush the chicken breasts with the herbed butter. Place the chicken and extra stuffing in the oven and bake until the chicken is cooked through, 15 to 20 minutes.

10 To serve, remove the toothpicks and halve each breast crosswise.

Values are approximate per serving: Calories: 688 Protein: 45 gm Fat: 31 gm
Carbohydrates: 57 gm Cholesterol: 124 mg Sodium: 666 mg

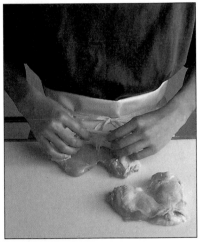

Step 5

Step 6

Step 6

Chicken Cacciatore

The Italian word "cacciatore" means hunter, and is applied to a number of hearty meat or poultry dishes made with tomato sauce and mushrooms. This version is made with chicken parts: you can use either a cut-up whole chicken, or all chicken breasts, legs or thighs, as your family prefers. For a lower-calorie meal, remove the skin from the chicken before cooking, and skim the fat from the pan juices before serving.

Working time: 20 minutes
Total time: 55 minutes

Chicken Cacciatore

6 Servings

¼ cup flour
¼ teaspoon pepper
2½ pounds chicken parts
About 2 tablespoons olive or other
   vegetable oil
1 medium onion
3 cloves garlic, minced or crushed
   through a press

1 can (16 ounces) crushed tomatoes
1½ cups chicken broth
4 tablespoons tomato paste
1½ teaspoons oregano
1 bay leaf
¼ pound small mushrooms
1 large zucchini
¼ cup chopped parsley (optional)

1 In a plastic bag or small paper bag, combine the flour and pepper. Add the chicken pieces and shake to coat lightly. Reserve the excess seasoned flour.

Step 1

2 In a casserole or Dutch oven, warm 2 tablespoons of the oil over medium-high heat until hot but not smoking. Add the chicken in one layer and fry until golden brown on all sides, 6 to 8 minutes.

3 Meanwhile, coarsely chop the onion.

4 Remove the chicken from the casserole and set aside. Add the onion and garlic and cook over medium-high heat until the onion begins to brown, about 5 minutes, adding more oil if necessary. Stir in the reserved seasoned flour and cook, stirring, until the flour is incorporated.

5 Stir in the crushed tomatoes, chicken broth, tomato paste, oregano and bay leaf. Bring the mixture to a boil. Add the chicken and mushrooms. Reduce the heat to medium-low, cover and simmer for 30 minutes, turning the chicken occasionally.

Step 5

6 Meanwhile, cut the zucchini into ¼-inch-thick slices.

7 Add the zucchini to the casserole and cook until just tender, about 5 minutes. Before serving, remove the bay leaf and stir in the parsley (if using).

TIME-SAVERS

■ *Do-ahead: The chicken can be partially cooked (through Step 2) ahead of time. The whole stew can also be made ahead and reheated.*

Step 7

Values are approximate per serving: Calories: 385 Protein: 27 gm Fat: 25 gm
Carbohydrates: 13 gm Cholesterol: 96 mg Sodium: 549 mg

Turkey Porcupines

Using turkey instead of beef, and adding ginger and scallions to the ground meat mixture, gives a new twist to this traditional meatball entrée. The "porcupines" can be served on their own—with some bread to help you finish the ginger-spiked tomato sauce—or over pasta for a meal that's healthfully high in carbohydrates.

Working time: 20 minutes
Total time: 40 minutes

4 Servings

3 cloves garlic
3 quarter-size slices (¼ inch thick)
   fresh ginger, unpeeled
4 scallions
¼ cup cilantro sprigs (optional)
1 pound ground turkey
¼ cup raw rice
1 egg

½ teaspoon salt
¼ teaspoon pepper
1 tablespoon olive or other
   vegetable oil
1 cup chicken broth
½ cup canned crushed tomatoes
1 tablespoon cornstarch

Step 2

1 In a food processor, finely chop the garlic, ginger, scallions and cilantro (if using).

2 In a medium bowl, stir together the turkey, rice, egg, salt, pepper and half of the ginger-scallion mixture. Form the mixture into balls (using about 2 tablespoons each).

3 In a large skillet, warm the oil over medium-high heat until hot but not smoking. Add the remaining ginger-scallion mixture and cook, stirring frequently, until the mixture begins to brown, about 3 minutes.

4 Add ¾ cup of the chicken broth and the crushed tomatoes and bring the mixture to a boil. Add the turkey balls and return to a boil. Reduce the heat to low, cover and simmer, stirring occasionally, until the rice is cooked, about 20 minutes.

5 In a small bowl, combine the remaining ¼ cup chicken broth with the cornstarch.

6 Uncover the skillet and return the mixture to a boil over high heat. Add the broth-cornstarch mixture and cook, stirring, until the sauce has thickened, about 1 minute.

Step 2

TIME-SAVERS

■ *Do-ahead: The ginger-scallion mixture (Step 1) and the turkey meatballs (Step 2) can be made ahead; keep the meatballs refrigerated until ready to use. The whole dish can be made ahead and gently reheated.*

Step 3

Values are approximate per serving: Calories: 281   Protein: 24 gm   Fat: 14 gm
Carbohydrates: 15 gm   Cholesterol: 136 mg   Sodium: 693 mg

Baked Chicken with Sweet-and-Sour Fruit

Cider vinegar, brown sugar, apples and plums create the basic flavor interplay in this sweet-and-sour chicken dish. You can use any kind of plum in the recipe: blue-black Friars, ruby-skinned Larodas, jade-green Kelseys or frosty-purple Italian prune plums, which are freestone and thus easier to pit. Combine two different varieties for an even more colorful presentation.

Working time: 25 minutes
Total time: 45 minutes

Baked Chicken with Sweet-and-Sour Fruit

4 Servings

1 tablespoon olive or other vegetable oil	2 tablespoons butter
2 teaspoons tarragon	2 tablespoons flour
½ teaspoon salt	1⅓ cups chicken broth
½ teaspoon pepper	2 tablespoons cider vinegar
2½ pounds chicken parts	2 teaspoons brown sugar
1 small onion	1 large apple, unpeeled
	2 plums

1 Preheat the oven to 425°.

2 In a small bowl, combine the oil, 1 teaspoon of the tarragon, the salt and pepper.

3 Place the chicken in a roasting pan. Brush the chicken with the seasoned oil, and bake for 15 minutes. Reduce the heat to 375° and bake until the chicken is cooked through, about 25 minutes longer.

Step 3

4 Meanwhile, coarsely chop the onion.

5 In a medium skillet, warm the butter over medium heat until melted. Add the onion and cook until slightly softened, about 4 minutes.

6 Stir in the flour and cook, stirring, until the flour is no longer visible, about 30 seconds. Stir in the chicken broth, vinegar, brown sugar and remaining 1 teaspoon tarragon. Bring the mixture to a boil, then reduce the heat to low, cover and simmer while the chicken cooks.

Step 7

7 About 10 minutes before the chicken is done, cut the apple and plums into ¼-inch-thick wedges. Return the sauce to a boil over medium-high heat. Reduce the heat to medium, add the apple and plums, and cook until the fruit is just tender, about 7 minutes.

8 Pour the sauce over the chicken in the roasting pan and toss to coat well.

Step 7

Values are approximate per serving: Calories: 577 Protein: 38 gm Fat: 39 gm
Carbohydrates: 18 gm Cholesterol: 160 mg Sodium: 795 mg

Szechuan Chicken Wings

For this simple Szechuan-style dish, chicken wings are marinated in a tart, hot sauce made with tangerine juice, ginger, soy sauce, red pepper flakes, garlic and honey, then broiled until browned and crispy. For a sit-down supper, serve the chicken with colorful steamed vegetables; for a picnic, accompany this ideal finger food with potato salad dressed with a sesame-soy vinaigrette and, for dessert, chunks of honeydew melon.

Working time: 15 minutes
Total time: 1 hour

Szechuan Chicken Wings

4 Servings

3 quarter-size slices (¼ inch thick) fresh ginger, unpeeled
3 cloves garlic
2 scallions
2 tangerines or 1 orange
⅓ cup reduced-sodium soy sauce
2 tablespoons Oriental sesame oil
1 tablespoon honey
¾ teaspoon red pepper flakes
12 chicken wings
2 teaspoons cornstarch

Step 2

1 In a food processor, mince the ginger and garlic. Trim and discard the dark green tops from the scallions; add the white and tender green parts to the processor and finely chop.

2 Grate the zest from the tangerines (or orange) and measure out 1½ teaspoons. Juice the tangerines (or orange) and measure out ⅓ cup.

3 In a large shallow dish, combine the ginger-garlic-scallion mixture with the tangerine (or orange) juice and zest, the soy sauce, sesame oil, honey and red pepper flakes. Add the chicken wings and toss to coat well with the marinade. Cover with the plastic wrap and set aside to marinate, stirring occasionally, for at least 30 minutes (or overnight).

4 Preheat the broiler. Line a broiler pan with foil.

5 Remove the chicken wings from the marinade and reserve the marinade. Place the chicken wings on the broiler pan and broil 4 inches from the heat for 7 to 10 minutes. Turn the chicken wings over and broil for 7 to 10 minutes longer, or until crisp and well browned. If the wing tips begin to char, wrap them with a bit of aluminum foil.

Step 3

6 Meanwhile, pour the reserved marinade into a saucepan. Blend in the cornstarch and bring to a boil over medium heat, stirring constantly. Reduce the heat to low and simmer while the chicken cooks.

7 Serve the chicken wings with the sauce on the side.

TIME-SAVERS

■ *Microwave tip: To make the sauce (Step 6), place the reserved marinade in a small microwave-safe bowl and blend in the cornstarch. Cook at 100% for 3 minutes, or until the mixture comes to a boil.*

■ *Do-ahead: The chicken wings can be marinated well ahead. The whole dish can be prepared ahead, the chicken served at room temperature and the sauce reheated; add a bit of water or chicken broth to the sauce if it has thickened too much.*

Values are approximate per serving: Calories: 438   Protein: 32 gm   Fat: 29 gm
Carbohydrates: 11 gm   Cholesterol: 95 mg   Sodium: 886 mg

Step 6

Spicy White Bean Turkey Stew

Even if you are counting calories, you can still sit down to a hearty bowl of stew brimming with turkey, beans and vegetables. Beans—virtually fat-free storehouses of complex carbohydrate and protein—are the key to the satisfying nature of this one-dish meal. To enhance the stew's sense of richness and to thicken it, some of the beans are coarsely puréed and then stirred back into the stew.

Working time: 20 minutes
Total time: 40 minutes

Spicy White Bean Turkey Stew

4 Servings

3 cloves garlic
1 bunch scallions (6 to 8)
1 large green bell pepper
1 large red bell pepper
½ pound turkey cutlets
1 tablespoon olive or other
   vegetable oil
1 teaspoon cumin
½ teaspoon ground ginger

¼ teaspoon black pepper
¼ teaspoon red pepper flakes
Pinch of cayenne pepper
1 can (14½ ounces) whole
   tomatoes, with their juice
½ cup low-sodium chicken broth
1 can (20 ounces) cannellini or
   white kidney beans

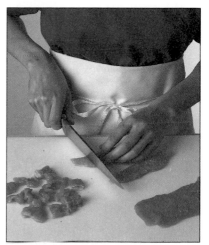

1 In a food processor, mince the garlic. Add the scallions and coarsely chop; remove and set aside. In the same processor work bowl, add the bell peppers and pulse on and off to cut them into bite-size pieces.

2 Cut the turkey into bite-size pieces.

Step 2

3 In a large nonstick skillet or medium saucepan, warm the oil over medium-high heat until hot but not smoking. Add the garlic-scallion mixture and cook until it begins to brown, 2 to 3 minutes.

4 Add the turkey and cook until the turkey is no longer pink, 4 to 5 minutes.

5 Add the cumin, ginger, black pepper, red pepper flakes and cayenne and stir-fry until the spices are fragrant, about 30 seconds. Add the tomatoes and their juice, the chicken broth and chopped bell peppers. Bring the mixture to a boil over medium-high heat, breaking up the tomatoes with a spoon. Reduce the heat to low, cover and simmer for 15 minutes.

Step 5

6 Meanwhile, drain the beans, rinse them under cold running water and drain well. Remove 1 cup of the beans to a small bowl and mash them, with a fork or potato masher, to a coarse purée.

7 Increase the heat to medium-high and add the whole beans and the bean purée. Cook uncovered, stirring frequently, until heated through, about 5 minutes.

TIME-SAVERS

■ *Do-ahead: All of the ingredients can be prepared ahead or the whole soup can be made ahead and reheated.*

Values are approximate per serving: Calories: 244   Protein: 23 gm   Fat: 6 gm
Carbohydrates: 26 gm   Cholesterol: 35 mg   Sodium: 386 mg

Step 6

Crispy Oven-Fried Chicken

▼

Oven-fried chicken is much lower in fat than pan-fried—and it needs no tending by the cook. Because the chicken tastes as delicious at room temperature as it does hot, it makes ideal outdoor or picnic food. Serve it with a tossed salad, iced tea and baking powder biscuits. For an added twist, mix some shredded Cheddar cheese into the biscuit dough before you roll it out.

Working time: 20 minutes
Total time: 1 hour 15 minutes

Crispy Oven-Fried Chicken

4 Servings

2 cloves garlic, peeled
4 slices white bread, torn into
  pieces
¼ cup grated Parmesan cheese
  (about 1 ounce)
½ teaspoon salt

¼ teaspoon pepper
1 teaspoon crumbled sage or thyme
2 tablespoons butter
¼ cup milk
2½ pounds chicken parts

Step 3

1 Preheat the oven to 375°. Line a baking sheet with foil.

2 Make the breading: Place the peeled garlic cloves in a food processor or blender. Process until finely chopped. Add the bread, Parmesan, salt and pepper and process, pulsing the machine on and off, until the bread is finely crumbed.

3 Add the sage to the mixture and process to distribute evenly.

4 Cut the butter into small pieces and add it to the breadcrumbs. Process the mixture until the butter is completely incorporated, then transfer the breading to a plastic or paper bag.

5 Place the milk in a shallow bowl. Dip the chicken pieces in the milk, then place them, a few at a time, in the bag of breading, and shake the bag until the chicken is well coated.

Step 5

6 Place the chicken pieces on the foil-lined baking sheet, leaving space between them. Bake the chicken until the coating is crisp and the juices run clear when the chicken is pierced with a knife, 45 to 55 minutes.

TIME-SAVERS

■ *Do-ahead: The whole dish can be made ahead and served at room temperature. The breading can also be made well ahead. You might even want to double or triple the quantities for the breading and keep it on hand. Because of the butter in it, the breading mixture should be stored in the refrigerator (or freezer).*

Step 6

Values are approximate per serving: Calories: 449   Protein: 39 gm   Fat: 26 gm
Carbohydrates: 14 gm   Cholesterol: 132 mg   Sodium: 657 mg

Quick Chicken Ratatouille

Yellow squash, zucchini, eggplant and tomatoes form the basis of ratatouille, a French country vegetable dish that showcases summer produce. Here, chicken is added for a satisfying main dish. If you'd like to use fresh tomatoes instead of canned, substitute one pound of meaty, ripe tomatoes, cut into large chunks. If your family doesn't care for eggplant, simply substitute more yellow squash or zucchini.

Working time: 35 minutes
Total time: 45 minutes

Quick Chicken Ratatouille

6 Servings

2 medium white or yellow onions
4 skinless, boneless chicken breast
halves (about 1¼ pounds total)
3 tablespoons flour
¼ teaspoon black pepper
3 tablespoons olive oil
4 cloves garlic, minced or crushed
through a press
1 can (14½ ounces) stewed
tomatoes, with their juice

Pinch of sugar
½ small eggplant (about ½ pound)
1 small red bell pepper
1 small zucchini
1 small yellow squash
¼ cup chopped fresh basil or 1½
teaspoons dried
1 teaspoon oregano

Step 1

1 Cut the onions into quarters and set aside. Cut the chicken into bite-size pieces. In a plastic or paper bag, combine the flour and black pepper, and shake to mix. Add the chicken and shake to coat lightly. Remove the chicken and reserve the excess seasoned flour.

2 In a large saucepan, warm 2 tablespoons of the oil over medium-high heat until hot but not smoking. Add the chicken and cook until golden, about 5 minutes. Remove the chicken to a plate and cover loosely to keep warm.

3 Add the remaining 1 tablespoon oil, the onions and garlic to the saucepan and sauté until the mixture begins to brown, 3 to 5 minutes.

4 Add the reserved dredging mixture and stir until the flour is no longer visible. Add the tomatoes and their juice and the sugar, and bring to a boil. Reduce the heat to low, cover and simmer while you prepare the vegetables.

Step 4

5 Quarter the eggplant lengthwise, then cut crosswise into ¼-inch slices. Cut the bell pepper lengthwise into slivers. Halve the zucchini and yellow squash lengthwise, then cut crosswise into ¼-inch half-rounds. Coarsely chop the fresh basil (if using).

6 Return the tomato sauce to a boil over medium-high heat. Add the eggplant, bell pepper, yellow squash, basil (fresh or dried) and oregano to the saucepan and let return to a boil. Reduce the heat to medium-low, cover and simmer until the vegetables are tender, 8 to 10 minutes.

7 Uncover and return the mixture to a boil over medium-high heat. Return the chicken (and any juices that have accumulated on the plate) to the saucepan and stir in the zucchini. Cook until the zucchini is just tender and the chicken is cooked through, about 2 minutes.

Values are approximate per serving: Calories: 228 Protein: 24 gm Fat: 8 gm
Carbohydrates: 15 gm Cholesterol: 55 mg Sodium: 239 mg

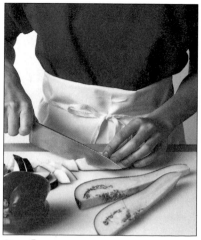

Step 5

Grilled Steaks with Red Wine-Mushroom Sauce (page 155)

CHAPTER 3
MEAT

London Broil Teriyaki

▼

The subtle basting sauce for this grilled steak is made with reduced-sodium soy sauce flavored with garlic and a touch of sweetness. You can substitute marmalade or honey for the apricot jam in the sauce; or, if you have none of these on hand, add 2 to 3 tablespoons of brown sugar. To give the sauce another flavor dimension, replace about 1 tablespoon of the oil with Oriental sesame oil.

Working time: 15 minutes
Total time: 35 minutes

London Broil Teriyaki

6 Servings

1 cup reduced-sodium soy sauce	**3 cloves garlic, peeled**
¼ cup vegetable oil	**2 pounds top round (1¼ inches thick)**
¼ cup apricot jam	
4 teaspoons cornstarch	**12 mushrooms**
¼ teaspoon pepper	**24 cherry tomatoes**

1 Preheat the broiler or start the charcoal. If broiling, line a jelly roll pan with foil.

2 Make the teriyaki sauce: In a small saucepan, combine the soy sauce, oil, apricot jam, cornstarch, pepper and whole garlic cloves. Stir to blend, then bring to a boil over medium heat, stirring constantly. Remove from the heat.

Step 3

3 Brush the steak with the teriyaki sauce. If broiling, place the steak on the jelly roll pan before brushing it with the sauce.

4 Broil or grill the steak 4 inches from the heat, turning once and brushing the second side with teriyaki sauce: 5 to 7 minutes per side for rare, 8 to 10 minutes per side for medium-rare, 11 to 13 minutes per side for well done.

5 Meanwhile, dividing the mushrooms and tomatoes evenly, thread them onto skewers.

6 About 4 minutes before the steak is done, brush the skewered vegetables with some teriyaki sauce and place them on the grill or under the broiler for 2 minutes. Turn them over, brush with more teriyaki sauce and cook for 2 minutes longer.

Step 5

7 Cut the steak across the grain and on the diagonal into thin slices. Serve with the skewered vegetables. Remove and discard the garlic from the remaining teriyaki sauce, and bring it to a boil before serving it alongside the steak.

TIME-SAVERS

■ *Do-ahead: The teriyaki sauce can be made ahead of time.*

Values are approximate per serving: Calories: 401   Protein: 38 gm   Fat: 19 gm
Carbohydrates: 18 gm   Cholesterol: 95 mg   Sodium: 1672 mg

Step 6

Sweet and Savory Spareribs

Pork ribs make luscious barbecue fare, but they can be fatty. Boiling them for about 10 minutes ahead of time eliminates much of the fat, and also partially cooks them so that they take less time on the grill. The mouthwatering barbecue sauce is made from pantry-shelf ingredients; another time, try it on steaks or burgers. Macaroni salad or Texas toast (thick slabs of buttered, grilled bread) are great partners for the ribs.

Working time: 10 minutes
Total time: 45 minutes

Sweet and Savory
Spareribs

4 Servings

1 cup ketchup	2 teaspoons dry mustard
¼ cup tomato paste	3 cloves garlic, minced or crushed
3 tablespoons cider vinegar	through a press
2 tablespoons Dijon mustard	12 spareribs, in two racks (about
⅓ cup brown sugar	6 ribs per rack; 3 pounds total)

Step 4

1 Preheat the broiler or start the charcoal. If broiling, line a broiler pan with foil.

2 Bring a large skillet of water to a boil.

3 Meanwhile, make the barbecue sauce: In a small saucepan, combine the ketchup, tomato paste, vinegar, Dijon mustard, sugar, dry mustard and garlic. Bring to a boil over medium heat. Reduce the heat to low, cover and simmer while you prepare the spareribs.

4 Add the spareribs to the boiling water in the skillet. Return the water to a boil over medium-high heat. Reduce the heat to medium-low, cover and simmer for 10 minutes. Remove the spareribs with tongs. Place them, bone-side up, on the grill or the prepared broiler pan.

5 Thickly spread about half the barbecue sauce over the ribs. Grill or broil 4 inches from the heat until dark mahogany with some charred patches, about 9 minutes.

6 Turn the ribs over, paint them with the remaining barbecue sauce and grill or broil about 9 minutes longer.

7 Cut the racks into individual ribs and serve.

Step 5

TIME-SAVERS

■ *Microwave tip: To precook the ribs in the microwave: Cut the racks into individual ribs and arrange them in a large, shallow microwave-safe baking dish, with the meatier portions toward the outside of the dish. Loosely cover with waxed paper and cook at 100% for 5 minutes. Drain off any accumulated fat and rearrange the ribs. Re-cover and cook at 50% for 10 minutes, rearranging the ribs once. Barbecue the ribs as described above.*

■ *Do-ahead: The barbecue sauce (Step 3) can be made ahead. The ribs can also be parboiled ahead, or even completely grilled ahead and then served at room temperature.*

Values are approximate per serving: Calories: 698   Protein: 40 gm   Fat: 41 gm
Carbohydrates: 39 gm   Cholesterol: 161 mg   Sodium: 1203 mg

Step 7

Lamb Chops
with Mushroom Sauce

▼

*Treat the family (or favored friends) to this savory dinner of
thick lamb chops, simply broiled and then topped with a tarragon-scented
mushroom-wine sauce. In the spring, fresh asparagus and steamed
new red potatoes would be fitting accompaniments. In the fall or winter,
serve the chops with glazed carrots and buttery whipped potatoes.*

Working time: 30 minutes
Total time: 40 minutes

Lamb Chops
with Mushroom Sauce

4 Servings

5 to 6 shallots or 1 small onion
2 cloves garlic
½ pound mushrooms
4 tablespoons butter
8 small lamb chops, well trimmed
  (1 inch thick, about ¼ pound
  each)
1 tablespoon flour

¼ cup dry white wine
1 tablespoon chopped fresh
  tarragon or ½ teaspoon dried
½ teaspoon salt
¼ teaspoon pepper
⅓ cup heavy cream
3 tablespoons fine unseasoned
  breadcrumbs

1 Preheat the broiler. Line a broiler pan with foil.

2 In a food processor, finely chop the shallots (or onion) and garlic. Remove and set aside.

3 In the same processor work bowl, coarsely chop the mushrooms.

4 In a large skillet, warm 2 tablespoons of the butter over medium-high heat until melted. Add the shallot-garlic mixture and stir-fry until the shallots are translucent, about 3 minutes.

5 Add the remaining 2 tablespoons butter and the mushrooms and stir-fry until the mushrooms begin to wilt, about 3 minutes.

6 Place the lamb chops on the broiler pan and broil 4 inches from the heat for 8 minutes.

7 Meanwhile, add the flour to the mushrooms and stir to thoroughly combine. Stir in the wine, tarragon, salt and pepper. Bring to a boil over medium-high heat and cook for 2 minutes. Stir in the cream, reduce the heat to medium and simmer, uncovered, until the sauce has thickened slightly, about 2 minutes.

8 Turn the lamb chops over. Spoon about 2 tablespoons of the mushroom sauce over each chop. Sprinkle the chops with the breadcrumbs and broil 4 inches from the heat until they are medium-rare, about 8 minutes; cook 2 minutes longer for medium; 3 minutes longer for well-done.

TIME-SAVERS

■ ***Do-ahead:*** *The mushroom sauce can be made ahead through Step 7, but do not add the cream until just before serving; bring the mixture to a simmer, add the cream, then proceed with the recipe.*

Values are approximate per serving: Calories: 397 Protein: 29 gm Fat: 27 gm
Carbohydrates: 11 gm Cholesterol: 139 mg Sodium: 521 mg

Step 5

Step 7

Step 8

Hearty Beef Goulash Soup

▼

To turn the traditional Hungarian meat stew called goulash into a soup, the amount of liquid used—in this case, tomato juice and beef broth—has been increased. And where goulash in its stew form would most likely be served with noodles, this soup has diced potatoes cooked in it instead. If you do not have tomato juice on hand, use half tomato sauce (or purée) and half water in its place.

Working time: 30 minutes
Total time: 50 minutes

4 Servings

6 small red potatoes, unpeeled (about ¾ pound)
1 medium onion
2 tablespoons olive or other vegetable oil
2 cloves garlic, minced or crushed through a press

½ pound ground round
3 cups tomato juice
1¾ cups beef broth
2 teaspoons paprika
½ teaspoon black pepper
1 small green bell pepper
1 small red bell pepper

1 Cut the potatoes into ¼-inch dice. Coarsely chop the onion.

2 In a large saucepan or flameproof casserole, warm the oil over medium-high heat until hot but not smoking. Add the onion and garlic and sauté until the onion is just translucent, 1 to 2 minutes.

3 Crumble the ground beef into the pan and cook, breaking the meat up with a spoon, until the meat just begins to brown, 5 to 10 minutes.

4 Add the tomato juice, beef broth, paprika, black pepper and potatoes. Bring the mixture to a boil, reduce the heat to medium-low, cover and simmer, stirring occasionally, for 10 minutes.

5 Meanwhile, cut the bell peppers into ¼-inch dice.

6 Stir the bell peppers into the soup and cook until the potatoes are tender, about 10 minutes longer. Serve hot.

TIME-SAVERS

■ *Microwave tip:* *In a 3-quart microwave-safe casserole, combine the potatoes, onion, garlic, bell peppers and 1 tablespoon of oil (omit the other tablespoon of oil). Cover and cook at 100% for 4 minutes. Crumble in the beef, re-cover and cook at 100% for 8 minutes, stirring once to break up the beef. Drain off any excess fat. Stir in the remaining ingredients, re-cover and cook at 100% for 10 minutes or until the mixture comes to a boil. Cook at 50% for 8 minutes or until the potatoes are tender.*

■ *Do-ahead:* *All of the vegetables can be diced or chopped ahead of time. And the entire soup can be made ahead and reheated.*

Values are approximate per serving: Calories: 322 Protein: 15 gm Fat: 17 gm
Carbohydrates: 28 gm Cholesterol: 39 mg Sodium: 1068 mg

Step 1

Step 3

Step 6

Pan-Broiled
Garlic-Mustard Pork Chops

It takes about five minutes to do the preparatory work required for this satisfying dish of herb-crusted pork chops. Simply place the chops in the marinade in the morning or the night before, and at mealtime it's only 15 minutes or so of hands-on cooking until you're ready to serve. And, except for the chops, you probably won't need to add a thing to your shopping list, as all of the other ingredients are likely to be in your pantry.

Working time: 20 minutes
Total time: 6 hours 20 minutes

Pan-Broiled
Garlic-Mustard Pork Chops

4 Servings

- **3 tablespoons olive or other vegetable oil**
- **2 tablespoons Dijon mustard**
- **5 cloves garlic, minced or crushed through a press**
- **3 tablespoons chopped parsley (optional)**

- **2 teaspoons thyme**
- **½ teaspoon pepper**
- **4 center-cut pork chops (about ¾ inch thick , 1¾ pounds total)**

Step 1

1 In a shallow dish large enough to hold the pork chops snugly in one layer, combine the oil, mustard, garlic, parsley (if using), thyme and pepper.

2 Add the pork chops and turn to coat thoroughly. Cover and refrigerate for at least 6 hours or overnight, turning the pork chops occasionally if convenient.

3 When ready to cook, let the chops return to room temperature.

4 Heat an ungreased cast-iron skillet over medium-high heat until very hot, about 3 minutes. Carefully add the chops and cook, without turning them, until browned and crusty on the bottom, 4 to 5 minutes.

5 Turn the chops over and cook on the second side until they are cooked through, 4 to 5 minutes.

Step 2

Values are approximate per serving: Calories: 465   Protein: 31 gm   Fat: 36 gm
Carbohydrates: 3 gm   Cholesterol: 110 mg   Sodium: 305 mg

Step 5

Cajun Meat Loaf

Chili powder, garlic and cayenne pepper add a spicy twist to this delicious beef-and-pork meat loaf. Serve the meat loaf hot, with buttered carrots and cornbread, or cold in a sandwich. If you intend to serve the meat loaf cold, pour off any excess fat from the loaf pan before refrigerating it. If you do not have any tomato juice on hand, you can use tomato sauce or purée diluted with a bit of water.

Working time: 25 minutes
Total time: 1 hour 20 minutes

Cajun Meat Loaf

6 to 8 Servings

1 medium onion
1 tablespoon vegetable oil
4 cloves garlic, crushed through a
  press
3 tablespoons chili powder
1 teaspoon salt
1 teaspoon paprika
Pinch cayenne pepper
1 cup tomato juice

1 pound ground beef
1 pound ground pork
2 slices whole wheat or white
  bread, torn into small pieces
  (about 1 cup)
2 eggs, lightly beaten
2 tablespoons Worcestershire sauce
½ teaspoon sugar
¼ teaspoon hot pepper sauce

Step 3

1 Preheat the oven to 350°.

2 Coarsely chop the onion. In a large skillet, warm the oil over high heat. Add the onion, garlic, chili powder, salt, paprika and cayenne. Cover, reduce the heat to low and cook, stirring occasionally, until the onions are softened but not browned, about 10 minutes.

3 Remove the skillet from the heat, stir in the tomato juice and set the mixture aside to cool slightly.

4 In a large bowl, combine the beef and pork.

5 Add the bread, eggs, Worcestershire sauce, sugar, hot pepper sauce and onion mixture and mix lightly but thoroughly.

Step 4

6 Place the mixture in a 9 x 5-inch loaf pan. Or, place the mixture on a foil-lined baking sheet and form it into a 9 x 5 inch loaf.

7 Bake the meat loaf for 55 minutes, or until a meat thermometer registers 160° at the center of the loaf. Allow to stand for 5 to 10 minutes before slicing.

TIME-SAVERS

■ *Microwave tip: In a microwave-safe bowl, combine the oil, onion, garlic, chili powder, paprika and cayenne. Omit the salt. Loosely cover with plastic wrap and cook at 100% for 4 to 5 minutes, stirring once. Add the tomato juice. Proceed with Steps 5 and 6 as above. Shape the mixture into a loaf in a shallow microwave-safe baking dish. Loosely cover with waxed paper and cook at 100% for 5 minutes. Then cook at 50% for 20 minutes, rotating the dish halfway through. Let stand 5 minutes.*

Step 5

Values are approximate per serving: Calories: 346 Protein: 21 gm Fat: 25 gm
Carbohydrates: 8 gm Cholesterol: 145 mg Sodium: 564 mg

Chili-Braised Short Ribs

Long, slow braising with tomatoes, onions and chili spices produces meltingly tender beef short ribs—and a rich sauce that just begs to be pooled on some mashed potatoes, rice or noodles. If you're making this recipe ahead of time and want to freeze it, you might consider taking the meat off the bones before storing it so you can use a smaller, space-saving container.

Working time: 30 minutes
Total time: 2 hours 30 minutes

Chili-Braised Short Ribs

6 Servings

2 tablespoons vegetable oil
4 pounds lean beef short ribs
2 medium onions
3 ribs celery
1 can (14½ ounces) stewed
    tomatoes, with their juice
1 can (8 ounces) tomato sauce

2 cups beef broth
3 tablespoons chili powder
1 tablespoon cumin
½ teaspoon salt
½ teaspoon pepper
3 tablespoons flour

Step 1

1 In a large Dutch oven, warm the oil over medium-high heat until hot but not smoking. In batches, add the short ribs and brown them all over, about 9 minutes.

2 Meanwhile, coarsely chop the onions. Cut the celery into 1-inch lengths.

3 Remove the ribs to a plate and cover loosely to keep warm. Add the onions to the pan and cook over medium-high heat until slightly softened, about 1 minute.

4 Add the celery, stewed tomatoes and their juice, the tomato sauce, beef broth, chili powder, cumin, salt and pepper. Return the short ribs to the pan (with any juices that have accumulated on the plate). Bring the mixture to a boil over medium-high heat. Reduce the heat to low, cover and simmer, stirring occasionally, until the ribs are tender, about 2 hours.

Step 5

5 Skim off any visible fat from the surface of the sauce. Measure out 3 tablespoons of the fat and discard the remainder. Blend the 3 tablespoons of fat with the flour. Stir the flour mixture into the sauce and bring to a boil; cook, stirring, over medium heat until the sauce thickens slightly, about 4 minutes.

Values are approximate per serving: Calories: 658 Protein: 53 gm Fat: 42 gm
Carbohydrates: 16 gm Cholesterol: 158 mg Sodium: 1011 mg

Step 5

Sausage and New Potato Kebabs with Mustard Glaze

▼

In these hearty mustard-glazed kebabs, all the elements of the meal—meat, vegetable and potatoes—are cooked together on one skewer. Serve the kebabs with a selection of sharp and sweet mustards, pickles, coleslaw, rolls and butter and amber beer or ale. If you have kids who might not like kielbasa, substitute cut-up hot dogs, but watch the cooking time, which should be a bit shorter.

Working time: 35 minutes
Total time: 35 minutes

Sausage and New Potato
Kebabs with Mustard Glaze

4 Servings

8 small red potatoes (about 1 pound), unpeeled

2 medium or 1 large zucchini (about 1 pound)

1 pound kielbasa or other fully cooked garlic sausage

3 tablespoons olive or other vegetable oil

1 tablespoon Dijon mustard

¼ teaspoon pepper

Step 5

1 Preheat the broiler or start the charcoal. If broiling, line a baking sheet with foil.

2 In a medium saucepan, bring 4 cups of water to a boil.

3 Meanwhile, halve the potatoes.

4 Place the potato halves in the boiling water and cook until just barely tender when pierced with a knife, 10 to 12 minutes. Drain well.

5 Meanwhile, cut the zucchini and kielbasa into 1-inch rounds (you will need about 16 pieces of each). If using a large zucchini, halve it lengthwise first, then cut it into half-rounds.

6 Make the mustard glaze: In a small bowl, combine the oil, mustard and pepper.

7 Dividing the ingredients evenly, thread the potatoes, zucchini and kielbasa alternately on skewers.

8 Brush the kebabs lightly with the mustard glaze. If broiling, place the kebabs on the foil-lined baking sheet before brushing them with the glaze.

Step 7

9 Broil or grill the kebabs 4 inches from the heat, turning once, until the kielbasa is lightly browned, 6 to 8 minutes.

TIME-SAVERS

■ *Do-ahead: The potatoes can be cooked ahead. The zucchini and kielbasa can be cut up ahead. The skewers can be threaded a short time before cooking.*

Values are approximate per serving: Calories: 554 Protein: 19 gm Fat: 42 gm
Carbohydrates: 27 gm Cholesterol: 76 mg Sodium: 1346 mg

Step 8

Broiled Veal Chops
with Winter Vegetable Sauté

▼

*A light glaze of paprika-flavored olive oil helps keep these broiled chops juicy.
They're the simple centerpiece of a meal that also features a sautéed slaw of cabbage,
celery and onion seasoned with cumin seed and paprika. Ground cumin
can be substituted for the whole seeds, if necessary. Round out the meal with
steamed or boiled potatoes tossed with chopped fresh parsley.*

Working time: 35 minutes
Total time: 35 minutes

146

Broiled Veal Chops
with Winter Vegetable Sauté

4 Servings

4 teaspoons olive or other
    vegetable oil
4 teaspoons paprika
¾ teaspoon pepper
4 veal loin chops (½ inch thick,
    about 1½ pounds total)
1 large onion
2 large carrots

½ pound cabbage
1 rib celery
3 cloves garlic, minced or crushed
    through a press
¼ cup chicken broth
1 teaspoon cumin seed
Pinch of sugar
¼ teaspoon salt

Step 2

1 Preheat the broiler. Line a broiler pan with foil.

2 In a small bowl, combine 2 teaspoons of the olive oil, 2 teaspoons of the paprika and ½ teaspoon of the pepper. Brush the veal chops with the paprika oil and place them on the prepared broiler pan. Set aside.

3 In a food processor, coarsely chop the onion; remove and set aside. In the same work bowl, one at a time, shred the carrots, cabbage and celery.

Step 3

4 In a large nonstick skillet, warm the remaining 2 teaspoons oil over medium-high heat until hot but not smoking. Add the onion and garlic, and stir-fry until the onion begins to brown, about 5 minutes.

5 Add the carrots, cabbage, celery, chicken broth, cumin seed, sugar, salt and remaining 2 teaspoons paprika and ¼ teaspoon pepper. Cook, stirring, until the vegetables are just limp, 5 to 8 minutes.

6 Meanwhile, broil the veal chops 4 inches from the heat for 4 minutes. Turn and broil until cooked through, about 4 minutes.

7 Serve the chops with the vegetable sauté on the side.

TIME-SAVERS

■ **Do-ahead:** *The vegetables can be cut up ahead.*

Step 5

Values are approximate per serving: Calories: 305 Protein: 24 gm Fat: 17 gm
Carbohydrates: 14 gm Cholesterol: 83 mg Sodium: 293 mg

Bacon, Lettuce and Tomato Strata

Bacon, lettuce and tomato strata takes all of the elements of a BLT sandwich and puts them together in this classic American make-ahead dish. Not only is a strata suited to being made ahead, it actually benefits from sitting in the refrigerator overnight—although you could assemble it in the morning and and then put it in the oven when you get home in the evening.

▼

Working time: 30 minutes
Total time: 1 hour 20 minutes

Bacon, Lettuce and Tomato Strata

6 Servings

2 medium tomatoes	**5 eggs**
1 medium onion	**2 cups milk**
1 tablespoon vegetable oil	**1 tablespoon Dijon mustard**
10 slices whole wheat or white bread	**½ teaspoon salt**
	¼ teaspoon pepper
2 cups grated Cheddar cheese (about ½ pound)	**4 slices bacon (about ¼ pound)**
	2 leaves lettuce

Step 3

1 Slice the tomatoes ¼ inch thick. Coarsely chop the onion.

2 In a medium skillet, warm the oil over medium heat until hot but not smoking. Add the onion and sauté until wilted, 1 to 2 minutes.

3 Butter a shallow 9 x 13-inch baking dish. Spread half of the bread on the bottom of the prepared baking dish. Top with a layer of tomatoes. Top the tomatoes with cheese and continue layering in this manner, ending with cheese.

Step 3

4 In a large bowl, lightly beat the eggs. Add the sautéed onion, milk, mustard, salt and pepper. Pour the egg mixture over the ingredients in the baking dish. Cover and refrigerate for 2 hours or overnight.

5 Preheat the oven to 350°. Bake the strata, uncovered, for 50 minutes, or until puffed and golden and a knife inserted in the center comes out clean. Let stand 10 minutes before cutting.

6 Meanwhile, in a medium skillet, cook the bacon over medium heat until crisp, about 10 minutes. Drain on paper towels, crumble and set aside. Shred the lettuce. Serve the strata garnished with shredded lettuce and crumbled bacon.

TIME-SAVERS

■ *Microwave tip: In a small microwave-safe bowl, combine the chopped onion and the oil. Cover loosely and cook at 100% for 3 minutes, or until the onion is just tender. In a deep microwave-safe baking dish about 8 x 11 inches, layer the strata as desribed above in Steps 3 and 4, reducing the amount of milk to 1 cup. If possible, let the sirata sit for 2 hours before cooking. To cook, place the strata in the microwave, elevating if off the oven floor by placing it on an inverted glass pie plate or several custard cups. Cook at 100% for 10 minutes, rotating the dish after 5 minutes. Cook at 50% for 15 minutes, rotating the dish every 5 minutes. Let stand, covered, for 5 minutes. Cook the bacon on paper towels at 100% for 3 to 4 minutes. Serve the strata with shredded lettuce and crumbled bacon.*

Step 4

Values are approximate per serving: Calories. 424   Protein: 23 gm   Fat: 26 gm
Carbohydrates: 26 gm   Cholesterol: 234 mg   Sodium: 874 mg

Maple-Glazed Pork Chops with Roasted New Potatoes

▼

*It takes a little longer to bake pork chops than it does to pan-fry them,
but for this recipe there's only about ten minutes of hands-on work time before
you put them in the oven to cook. Butter-roasted red potatoes accompany the good-sized
chops, which are glazed at serving time with a sauce of maple syrup and cider
vinegar. Serve these chops with baked acorn squash and a mixed salad.*

Working time: 10 minutes
Total time: 40 minutes

Maple-Glazed Pork Chops with Roasted New Potatoes

4 Servings

4 center-cut loin pork chops (¾ inch thick, about 1¾ pounds total)
2 tablespoons flour
1 tablespoon olive or other vegetable oil
1 pound small red potatoes, unpeeled

2 teaspoons butter
¼ teaspoon pepper
⅓ cup maple syrup
3 tablespoons cider vinegar

Step 2

1 Preheat the oven to 425°.

2 Dredge the pork chops lightly in the flour, shaking off any excess.

3 In a large skillet, warm 2 teaspoons of the oil over medium-high heat until hot but not smoking. Add the pork chops and cook until browned, about 4 minutes per side.

4 Meanwhile, halve the potatoes. In a small saucepan or in the microwave, melt the butter. Combine the butter and remaining 1 teaspoon oil. Place the potatoes in a roasting pan or baking dish, drizzle the butter-oil mixture over them and sprinkle them with the pepper. Toss the potatoes to coat well.

Step 4

5 When the pork chops are browned, transfer them to a baking dish or casserole big enough to hold the chops in one layer; cover the dish with foil or a lid. Place the potatoes in the oven; 10 minutes later place the pork chops in the oven. Bake until the potatoes are tender and light golden and the chops are cooked through, 20 to 25 minutes total.

6 Meanwhile, add the maple syrup and vinegar to the meat drippings in the skillet and bring to a boil over medium-high heat, scraping up any browned bits on the bottom of the pan. Reduce the heat to low, cover and simmer until slightly thickened, about 10 minutes. Remove from the heat until the chops are done. Skim off any surface fat from the sauce if desired.

7 Serve the chops drizzled with the sauce and with the potatoes on the side.

Step 6

Values are approximate per serving: Calories: 666   Protein: 32 gm   Fat: 41 gm
Carbohydrates: 41 gm   Cholesterol: 119 mg   Sodium: 122 mg

Sloppy Josés

These saucy ground-beef sandwiches—south-of-the-border sloppy Joes—are spiced up with chili flavors: chili powder, hot pepper sauce and chili sauce. If you do not have any chili sauce on hand, use a combination of ketchup and tomato paste and add more hot pepper sauce and chili powder. If desired, top the sandwiches with shredded pepper jack cheese. Round out this casual meal with cole slaw and steak fries.

Working time: 20 minutes
Total time: 35 minutes

Sloppy Josés

4 Servings

1 medium onion	2 to 3 drops hot pepper sauce, to
1 small green bell pepper	taste
3 cloves garlic	1 tablespoon chili powder
2 teaspoons vegetable oil	1 tablespoon cumin
1 pound lean ground beef	¼ teaspoon salt
⅔ cup chili sauce	¼ teaspoon black pepper
1 tablespoon tomato paste	4 hamburger buns

1 In a food processor, coarsely chop the onion, green pepper and garlic.

Step 2

2 In a large skillet, warm the oil over medium-high heat until hot but not smoking. Add the onion-green pepper mixture, and cook, stirring, until the onion begins to turn color, about 5 minutes.

3 Add the beef and cook for 5 minutes, stirring to break up the meat.

4 Add the chili sauce, tomato paste, hot pepper sauce, chili powder, cumin, salt and black pepper. Bring the liquid to a boil. Reduce the heat to medium-low, cover and simmer for 15 minutes.

5 Meanwhile, toast the hamburger buns.

6 Serve the sloppy Josés over the open-face buns.

Step 3

TIME-SAVERS

■ *Microwave tip: Omit the oil. In a 3 quart microwave-safe casserole, combine the garlic, onion and bell pepper. Crumble in the beef. Cover loosely and cook at 100% for 5 minutes, stirring twice to break up the meat. Add the chili sauce, tomato paste, hot pepper sauce, chili powder, cumin, salt and black pepper. Re-cover and cook at 100% for 4 minutes, or until it comes to a boil. Cook at 50% for 10 minutes, stirring twice, to blend the flavors.*

■ *Do-ahead: The sloppy José mixture can be made well ahead and frozen. You might like to double or triple the recipe and freeze individual portions for quick microwaveable meals.*

Values are approximate per serving: Calories: 515 Protein: 26 gm Fat: 29 gm
Carbohydrates: 38 gm Cholesterol: 88 mg Sodium: 1085 mg

Step 4

Grilled Steaks with Red Wine-Mushroom Sauce

▼

A sophisticated wine-and-garlic marinade prepares these thick sirloin steaks for the grill. If it suits your schedule, let the steaks marinate in the refrigerator overnight. Serve the steaks with a simple vegetable sauté and mashed potatoes to soak up the flavorful mushroom sauce. Or, if you're serving this in hot weather, present it with grilled vegetables and thick peasant bread.

Working time: 20 minutes
Total time: 40 minutes

Grilled Steaks with Red Wine-Mushroom Sauce

4 Servings

4 cloves garlic, minced or crushed through a press	¼ teaspoon pepper
1 cup dry red wine	4 small New York sirloin steaks (about 1¾ pounds total)
2 tablespoons reduced-sodium soy sauce	4 scallions
1 tablespoon red wine vinegar	¾ pound mushrooms
1 teaspoon thyme	2 tablespoons butter
	2 tablespoons flour

1 In a shallow nonmetallic dish large enough to hold the steaks in a single layer, combine half of the garlic, the wine, soy sauce, vinegar, thyme and pepper. Place the steaks in the marinade and turn them over to thoroughly coat. Set them aside to marinate while you prepare the remaining ingredients.

Step 1

2 Preheat the broiler or start the charcoal. If broiling, line a broiler pan with foil.

3 Coarsely chop the scallions. Thinly slice the mushrooms.

4 In a medium skillet, melt the butter over medium-high heat. Add the remaining garlic, the scallions and mushrooms, and sauté until the scallions are limp and the mushrooms are beginning to release their liquid, 2 to 3 minutes. Stir in the flour and cook, stirring, until the flour is no longer visible, about 30 seconds.

5 Remove the steaks from the marinade, reserving the marinade. Stir the reserved marinade into the skillet and cook, stirring, until the mixture has come to a boil and thickened slightly, 1 to 2 minutes. Reduce the heat to low and simmer while you cook the steaks.

Step 4

6 Grill or broil the steaks 4 inches from the heat: 7 minutes per side for rare; 8 minutes per side for medium-rare; 9 minutes per side for well done. Let the steaks rest for 5 minutes before serving.

7 Serve the steaks topped with the red wine-mushroom sauce.

TIME-SAVERS

■ *Do-ahead: The marinade can be made and the steaks marinated ahead of time.*

Values are approximate per serving: Calories: 451   Protein: 41 gm   Fat: 27 gm
Carbohydrates: 11 gm   Cholesterol: 136 mg   Sodium: 451 mg

Step 5

Italian Sausage and Squash Stew

As a change from beef, lamb or veal stew, try this colorful mixture of fragrant Italian sausage, summer squash, rice and tomatoes. Zucchini and yellow squash are just two of the many varieties of summer squash you could use in this recipe. Try golden zucchini (such as Gold Rush), which has a brilliant yellow skin, or one of the scalloped summer squashes—greenish-white patty pan, yellow sunburst, or dark green scallopini.

Working time: 25 minutes
Total time: 50 minutes

Italian Sausage and Squash Stew

4 Servings

1 pound sweet Italian sausage
1 medium onion
1 medium zucchini
1 medium yellow squash
3 garlic cloves, minced or crushed
  through a press
½ cup raw rice
1 can (14 ounces) whole tomatoes,
  with their juice

1¾ cups low-sodium chicken broth
2 tablespoons tomato paste
1 teaspoon basil
1 teaspoon oregano
¼ teaspoon pepper
1 bay leaf
2 tablespoons butter, at room
  temperature
2 tablespoons flour

1 Cut the sausages into 1-inch chunks. Coarsely chop the onion.

2 In a large saucepan, cook the sausage over medium-high heat, stirring frequently, until evenly browned, 10 to 12 minutes.

3 Meanwhile, halve the zucchini and yellow squash lengthwise and then cut them crosswise into ¼-inch-thick half-rounds.

4 Add the onion and garlic to the saucepan and continue cooking, stirring frequently, until the onion has browned, about 5 minutes.

5 Add the rice, tomatoes and their juice, chicken broth, tomato paste, basil, oregano, pepper and bay leaf, and bring to a boil over medium-high heat. Reduce the heat to medium-low, cover and simmer for 15 minutes.

6 Meanwhile, using your fingers, thoroughly blend the butter and flour.

7 Uncover and return the stew to a boil over medium-high heat. Add the zucchini and yellow squash and cook until the vegetables are crisp-tender, about 5 to 7 minutes.

8 Pinching off about a tablespoon at a time, add the butter-flour mixture to the stew, stirring well after each addition. Cook until the stew has thickened slightly, 1 to 2 minutes.

9 Discard the bay leaf before serving.

TIME-SAVERS

■ **Do-ahead:** *The whole stew can be made ahead and reheated.*

Values are approximate per serving: Calories: 610 Protein: 22 gm Fat: 43 gm
Carbohydrates: 35 gm Cholesterol: 102 mg Sodium: 1142 mg

Step 1

Step 6

Step 7

Red-Glazed Pork Loin with Roasted Vegetables

Red currant jelly mixed with mustard, tomato paste and pepper makes a delicious sweet-savory glaze for this roasted pork loin. Potatoes and carrots, seasoned with a bit of basil, cook right in the pan alongside the pork. Although the roast cooks for an hour, preparation takes only about 20 minutes, leaving plenty of time for you to tend to the rest of the meal.

Working time: 20 minutes
Total time: 2 hours 5 minutes

Red-Glazed Pork Loin with Roasted Vegetables

6 Servings

¼ cup red currant jelly
2 cloves garlic, minced or crushed through a press
2 tablespoons tomato paste
1 tablespoon Dijon mustard
½ teaspoon dry mustard
½ teaspoon pepper
2-pound boneless pork loin

1½ pounds small red potatoes, unpeeled
5 medium carrots
2 tablespoons olive or other vegetable oil
½ teaspoon salt
½ teaspoon basil

Step 3

1 Preheat the oven to 450°. Line a roasting pan with foil.

2 In a small skillet or saucepan, melt the jelly over medium-low heat, about 5 minutes. Remove from the heat and stir in the garlic, tomato paste, Dijon mustard, dry mustard and ¼ teaspoon of the pepper.

3 Place the pork loin on the prepared roasting pan and brush with half the currant jelly mixture.

4 Roast the pork loin in the oven for 20 minutes.

5 Meanwhile, quarter the potatoes and cut the carrots into 1-inch lengths. In a large bowl, toss the potatoes and carrots with the olive oil, salt, basil and remaining ¼ teaspoon pepper.

6 Place the potatoes and carrots around the pork loin. Brush the pork with the remaining currant jelly mixture. Lower the oven temperature to 325° and continue roasting the pork and vegetables until the vegetables are tender and the pork is cooked through, about 1½ hours. Let the pork stand 5 minutes before slicing.

Step 5

TIME-SAVERS

■ *Microwave tip: In a small microwave-safe bowl, cook the jelly at 100% for 1 minute, or until melted. Combine it with the garlic, tomato paste, Dijon and dry mustards and ¼ teaspoon of the pepper. Place the pork loin in a shallow microwave-safe baking dish and surround with the potatoes and carrots. Loosely cover with waxed paper and cook at 50% for 20 minutes. Meanwhile, combine the oil, salt, basil and ¼ teaspoon pepper. Stir the vegetables and brush them with the herb-oil mixture. Brush the meat with the currant jelly mixture. Re-cover and cook at 50% for 20 minutes, or until the meat is cooked through and the vegetables are tender.*

■ *Do-ahead: The currant jelly mixture (Step 2) can be made and the vegetables cut up ahead.*

Values are approximate per serving: Calories: 618 Protein: 31 gm Fat: 38 gm
Carbohydrates: 37 gm Cholesterol: 106 mg Sodium: 417 mg

Step 6

Lentil Soup with Diced Ham and Carrots

Lentils have a satisfyingly hearty, almost meaty, flavor. And, unlike most dried beans or legumes, they take only about 30 minutes to cook. The lentils for this soup are cooked in chicken broth with diced carrots and celery. Cubes of baked or boiled ham—or smoked country ham if available—are then added to give the soup the old-fashioned flavor of a ham-bone broth.

Working time: 20 minutes
Total time: 55 minutes

Lentil Soup with Diced Ham and Carrots

4 Servings

1 medium red onion	1½ cups dried lentils
2 medium carrots	4 cups chicken broth
2 medium stalks celery	1 cup water
2 tablespoons olive or other vegetable oil	1 teaspoon oregano
	¼ teaspoon pepper
2 cloves garlic, minced or crushed through a press	¼ pound boiled, baked or smoked ham, unsliced

Step 1

1 In a food processor, coarsely chop the onion and set aside. In the same processor work bowl, coarsely chop the carrots, then add the celery and pulse to coarsely chop; remove and set aside.

2 In a medium saucepan, warm the oil over medium heat until hot but not smoking. Add the onion and garlic and cook, stirring occasionally, for 10 minutes.

3 Add the carrots, celery, lentils, chicken broth, water, oregano and pepper. Bring to a boil over medium-high heat. Reduce the heat to low, cover and simmer until the lentils are tender, about 30 minutes.

4 Meanwhile, cut the ham into small (about ½-inch) cubes.

Step 4

5 With a slotted spoon, remove about 1 cup of solids from the soup, transfer them to a food processor or blender and purée. Then stir the purée into the soup in the saucepan.

6 Add the ham to the soup and return it to a boil over medium-high heat. Serve hot

TIME-SAVERS

■ ***Do-ahead:*** *The vegetables and ham can be cut up ahead. The whole soup can be made well ahead and reheated.*

Step 5

Values are approximate per serving: Calories: 410   Protein: 30 gm   Fat: 12 gm
Carbohydrates: 49 gm   Cholesterol: 17 mg   Sodium: 1,450 mg

Southwestern Sausage Turnovers

These spicy meat-filled turnovers resemble pasties, once the favorite noontime meal of Cornish miners. In this departure from British tradition, a pastry made with cornmeal and cilantro, and a filling of sausage, chilies and cumin, carry out the Southwestern theme. The filled turnovers can be baked right away, as here, or frozen and baked later: Cook unthawed for 50 minutes in a 375° oven.

Working time: 30 minutes
Total time: 1 hour

6 Servings

½ cup cilantro or parsley sprigs
2¼ cups flour
½ cup yellow cornmeal
1 teaspoon salt
1 stick (4 ounces) chilled butter, cut into pieces
6 tablespoons chilled vegetable shortening, cut into pieces
4 to 6 tablespoons ice water
3 cloves garlic

1 small carrot
4 scallions
1 small all-purpose potato
1 can (4 ounces) chopped mild green chilies, drained
½ pound country sausage
1½ teaspoons cumin
1 teaspoon oregano
¼ teaspoon pepper
1 egg

Step 5

1 Mince the cilantro (or parsley).

2 In a food processor, combine the flour, cornmeal, ½ teaspoon of the salt and half of the cilantro (or parsley). Add the butter and shortening and pulse until the mixture resembles coarse meal. Add the ice water a tablespoon at a time until the dough forms a cohesive mass. Divide the dough into six portions and flatten each into a disk. Wrap in plastic wrap and refrigerate until chilled, at least 15 minutes.

3 Meanwhile, in the uncleaned food processor, mince the garlic. Add the carrot and coarsely chop. Remove and place in a bowl. Add the scallions to the processor and coarsely chop; add to the bowl.

4 Peel the potato, quarter it lengthwise and thinly slice crosswise. Add the potato to the other vegetables in the bowl.

Step 7

5 Add the chopped green chilies to the bowl. Crumble in the sausage. Add the remaining cilantro (or parsley), the cumin, oregano, remaining ½ teaspoon salt and the pepper. Mix gently to combine.

6 Preheat the oven to 375°. Line a baking sheet with foil and lightly grease the foil. In a small bowl, lightly beat the egg.

7 One at a time, roll out the disks of dough into 6- to 7-inch circles a scant ¼ inch thick. Dividing evenly, place some filling on one side of each pastry round, leaving a ½-inch border. Brush the edges of the pastry with water, then fold over to form semicircular turnovers. Seal the edges with the tines of a fork.

8 Place the turnovers on the baking sheet. Prick the dough with a fork and then brush the tops with the beaten egg. Bake for 30 to 35 minutes, or until golden. Serve hot or at room temperature.

Values are approximate per serving: Calories: 660 Protein: 12 gm Fat: 45 gm
Carbohydrates: 51 gm Cholesterol: 103 mg Sodium: 909 mg

Step 7

Mini-Patties
with Red Pepper Rice

▼

As a change from the usual "man-size" burger on a bun, try miniature beef patties smothered in a chunky mushroom sauce served alongside rice with red peppers. While children will be intrigued by the diminutive hamburgers and the colorful rice, adults will appreciate the subtle interplay of flavors. The beef patties are savory with mustard and onion; the mushroom sauce echoes the same flavors, but is softened with sour cream.

Working time: 20 minutes
Total time: 40 minutes

Mini-Patties
with Red Pepper Rice

4 Servings

2 cups water
1 cup raw rice
1 large red bell pepper
½ pound small mushrooms
1 medium onion
1 pound lean ground beef
⅓ cup fine unseasoned
 breadcrumbs
1 egg

¼ cup spicy brown mustard
1 tablespoon Worcestershire sauce
1 teaspoon oregano
½ teaspoon black pepper
2 teaspoons vegetable oil
3 tablespoons butter
2 tablespoons flour
1 cup beef broth
½ cup sour cream

1 In a medium saucepan, bring the water to a boil. Add the rice, reduce the heat to medium-low, cover and simmer until the rice is tender and all the liquid is absorbed, about 20 minutes.

Step 3

2 Meanwhile, cut the bell pepper into ¼-inch dice; stir the bell pepper into the rice 5 minutes before it is done. If the mushrooms are small, leave them whole; otherwise, halve or quarter them. Finely chop the onion.

3 Place half of the chopped onion in a medium bowl. Add the beef, breadcrumbs, egg, 3 tablespoons of the mustard, the Worcestershire sauce, oregano and ¼ teaspoon of the black pepper, and mix to thoroughly blend. Form into 12 small patties ¼ inch thick.

4 In a large skillet, preferably nonstick, warm the oil over medium-high heat until hot but not smoking. Add the patties and cook until browned, about 3 minutes per side. Transfer the patties to a plate and cover loosely to keep warm.

Step 4

5 Add the butter to the pan and warm over medium-high heat until melted. Add the remaining chopped onion and the mushrooms, and cook, stirring, until the mushrooms are just wilted, 2 to 3 minutes.

6 Stir in the flour and cook, stirring, until the flour is no longer visible, about 30 seconds. Stir in the beef broth, sour cream, the remaining 1 tablespoon mustard and ¼ teaspoon black pepper. Bring the mixture to a boil and return the patties (and any juices that have accumulated on the plate) to the pan. Baste with some of the sauce and cook to heat through, about 1 minute.

7 Serve the patties topped with some of the sauce and accompanied with the red pepper rice.

Values are approximate per serving: Calories: 745 Protein: 31 gm Fat: 44 gm
Carbohydrates: 55 gm Cholesterol: 175 mg Sodium: 661 mg

Step 6

Tomato-Grilled Pork Chops with Mediterranean Salad

Lean, well-trimmed pork must be marinated or basted to keep it moist during grilling. An herbed marinade of vegetable-juice cocktail, oil and vinegar does the trick here, and the same mixture then becomes a sauce for the chops. When you heat the reserved marinade, be sure to bring it to a full boil and simmer it for a few minutes to eliminate any danger of contamination from the raw pork.

Working time: 25 minutes
Total time: 40 minutes

4 Servings

1 can (6 ounces) vegetable-juice cocktail

3 cloves garlic, minced or crushed through a press

¼ cup red wine vinegar or cider vinegar

3 tablespoons olive or other vegetable oil

1½ teaspoons basil

1½ teaspoons oregano

½ teaspoon pepper

4 loin pork chops (¾ inch thick, about 1¾ pounds total)

1 cup canned white beans

2 cups (packed) fresh spinach leaves (about 2 ounces)

1 medium tomato

1 small red onion

1 teaspoon Dijon mustard

¼ teaspoon salt

1 tablespoon cornstarch

Step 2

1 In a shallow nonaluminum baking dish (big enough to hold the chops in one layer), combine the vegetable-juice cocktail, the garlic, 2 tablespoons of the vinegar, 1 tablespoon of the olive oil, 1 teaspoon each of the basil and oregano, and ¼ teaspoon of the pepper.

2 Add the pork chops and turn to coat all over with the marinade. Set aside to marinate while you prepare the grill.

3 Preheat the broiler or start the charcoal.

4 Rinse the beans under cold running water and drain well. Tear the spinach into bite-size pieces. Cut the tomato into thin wedges. Cut the onion into thin rings. Place the beans, spinach, tomato and onion in a medium bowl.

Step 7

5 In a small bowl, combine the mustard with the remaining 2 tablespoons vinegar, 2 tablespoons olive oil, ½ teaspoon basil, ½ teaspoon oregano, ¼ teaspoon pepper and the salt. Blend well.

6 Remove the chops from the baking dish, reserving the marinade. Grill or broil the chops 4 inches from the heat until browned all over and cooked through, 6 to 8 minutes per side.

7 Meanwhile, pour the marinade into a small saucepan and combine it with the cornstarch. Bring the mixture to a boil over medium-high heat, stirring constantly until slightly thickened, 2 to 3 minutes.

8 Just before serving, toss the salad with the vinaigrette.

TIME-SAVERS

■ ***Do-ahead:*** *The pork can be marinated and the vinaigrette made ahead.*

Values are approximate per serving: Calories: 512 Protein: 34 gm Fat: 36 gm
Carbohydrates: 12 gm Cholesterol: 110 mg Sodium: 471 mg

Step 8

Quick Chunky Chili

Chili is usually cooked for hours, but by using canned beans, you can cut the cooking time to 40 minutes. Instead of black beans (sometimes called turtle beans), you can use red, pink, pinto, or kidney beans. A wide assortment of canned beans is available in the Italian or Mexican food sections of most supermarkets. Rinsing the beans greatly reduces their sodium content.

Working time: 20 minutes
Total time: 45 minutes

6 Servings

1 can (16 ounces) black beans
1 medium onion
1 pound lean ground beef
3 cloves garlic, minced or crushed
    through a press
2 tablespoons chili powder
1½ teaspoons oregano
¼ teaspoon black pepper

1 can (14½ ounces) whole
    tomatoes, with their juice
2 cans (8 ounces each) tomato
    sauce
1 large green bell pepper
Chopped scallions, sour cream and
    grated Cheddar, for garnish
    (optional)

Step 4

1 Drain the beans in a colander, rinse under running water and drain again; set aside. Coarsely chop the onion.

2 In a large skillet over medium-high heat, brown the beef, stirring frequently, until it is no longer red, about 8 minutes.

3 Add the onion and garlic and continue cooking until the onion is translucent, about 3 minutes.

4 Add the chili powder, oregano and black pepper, and cook for 2 minutes longer.

5 Stir in the whole tomatoes with their juice, the tomato sauce and black beans. Bring the liquid to a boil over medium-high heat, breaking the tomatoes up with a spoon.

Step 5

6 Meanwhile, cut the green pepper into ½-inch pieces. When the chili has come to a boil, add the green pepper. Reduce the heat to medium-low, cover and simmer, stirring occasionally, for 25 minutes.

7 Serve the chili in bowls and, if desired, serve bowls of chopped scallions, sour cream and grated Cheddar on the side.

TIME-SAVERS

■ *Microwave tip: In a 3-quart microwave-safe casserole, combine the beef, onion, garlic, green pepper and spices. Loosely cover with waxed paper and cook at 100% for 8 minutes, stirring twice to break up the meat. Stir in the remaining ingredients, re-cover and cook at 100% for 7 minutes, or until boiling. Then cook at 50% for 10 minutes, stirring occasionally.*

■ *Do-ahead: The entire dish can be made ahead and reheated.*

Values are approximate per serving: Calories: 332 Protein: 20 gm Fat: 17 gm
Carbohydrates: 25 gm Cholesterol: 57 mg Sodium: 938 mg

Step 6

Beef-and-Onion Shepherd's Pie

▼

A crusty, golden crown of mashed sweet potatoes tops this hearty meat pie, which is more commonly made with a white-potato crust. Although this recipe calls for roast beef, you can also make it with lean uncooked beef: Just brown ½-inch cubes of meat in a bit of olive oil—cook them to medium or medium-rare—and add them at the same time that you would add the roast beef.

Working time: 45 minutes
Total time: 1 hour

Beef-and-Onion
Shepherd's Pie

6 Servings

1 pound sweet potatoes
1 tablespoon flour
2 tablespoons paprika
¾ teaspoon ground ginger
⅛ teaspoon allspice
¾ teaspoon salt
½ teaspoon pepper

3 medium onions
½ pound mushrooms
2 tablespoons vegetable oil
½ cup beef broth
1 pound roast beef (in 2 thick slices)
2 tablespoons butter
2 teaspoons brown sugar

Step 4

1 Preheat the oven to 425°. Line a baking sheet with foil.

2 With a sharp knife, cut 1 or 2 short slits in the sweet potatoes to act as steam vents. Bake the potatoes for 35 minutes, or until tender.

3 Meanwhile, in a small bowl, combine the flour, paprika, ¼ teaspoon of the ginger, the allspice, salt and pepper, and stir to blend.

4 Thinly slice the onions and mushrooms. In a large nonstick skillet, warm 1 tablespoon of the oil over medium-high heat until hot but not smoking. Add the onions and stir-fry until they begin to brown, about 5 minutes. Add the remaining 1 tablespoon oil and the mushrooms and cook until the mushrooms are softened, 2 to 3 minutes.

5 Stir in the seasoned flour and cook, stirring, until it is no longer visible, about 30 seconds. Add the beef broth and bring the mixture to a boil, stirring until thickened, about 2 minutes. Cut the roast beef into ½-inch cubes, add to the skillet and remove from the heat.

Step 5

6 When the potatoes are done, preheat the broiler. Halve the potatoes and scoop the flesh out into a medium bowl. Add the butter, brown sugar and remaining ½ teaspoon ginger, and mash into the potatoes with a potato masher or fork.

7 Transfer the beef mixture to an ovenproof skillet or shallow baking dish. Spoon the mashed potatoes around the rim of the skillet or dish on top of the beef mixture. Broil the pie for 3 to 4 minutes, or until the topping is lightly browned and the beef mixture is heated through.

TIME-SAVERS

■ *Microwave tip: To cook the sweet potatoes in the microwave, cut slits in them, arrange on a paper towel and cook at 100% for 8 minutes, or until tender, rearranging once.*

Values are approximate per serving: Calories: 314   Protein: 25 gm   Fat: 14 gm
Carbohydrates: 22 gm   Cholesterol: 72 mg   Sodium: 442 mg

Step 7

Grilled Beef Gyros
with Middle Eastern Salad

▼

Many American eateries have adopted a favorite Greek street food called gyros, pita pocket sandwiches made with shredded spit-roasted lamb. Here, grilled flank steak is substituted for the lamb and a mixture of lemon juice, olive oil, garlic and oregano is brushed onto the meat for a true Greek flavor. Lettuce, celery, carrot, bell pepper and a lemon sauce go into the pitas with the strips of steak.

Working time: 25 minutes
Total time: 35 minutes

Grilled Beef Gyros
with Middle Eastern Salad

4 Servings

¼ cup lemon juice
2 tablespoons olive or other vegetable oil
2 cloves garlic, minced or crushed through a press
1 teaspoon oregano
½ plus ⅛ teaspoon black pepper
1 pound flank steak
4 Romaine lettuce leaves
1 medium rib celery

1 medium carrot
1 small red bell pepper
⅓ cup mayonnaise
⅓ cup plain yogurt
¼ cup chopped parsley (optional)
2 teaspoons grated lemon zest (optional)
½ teaspoon salt
4 pita breads (about 6 inches in diameter)

Step 3

1 Preheat the broiler or start the charcoal. If broiling, line a broiler pan with foil.

2 In a small bowl, combine 2 tablespoons of the lemon juice, the olive oil, garlic, oregano and ⅛ teaspoon of the black pepper.

3 Brush half of the basting mixture on one side of the flank steak and broil or grill 4 inches from the heat for 8 minutes. Turn the steak over, brush with the remaining basting mixture and broil or grill for an additional 6 minutes, or until medium-rare. Set the steak aside on a plate to cool.

4 Meanwhile, shred the lettuce. Finely chop the celery, carrot and bell pepper. Put all of the vegetables in a medium bowl.

5 In a small bowl, combine the mayonnaise, yogurt, the remaining 2 tablespoons lemon juice, the parsley (if using), lemon zest (if using), salt and remaining ½ teaspoon black pepper.

6 Toss the vegetables with ⅓ cup of the dressing.

7 When ready to serve, thinly slice the steak on the diagonal. Cut the pita breads in half. Dividing evenly, stuff the pita breads with the salad. Top with slices of beef and some of the remaining dressing.

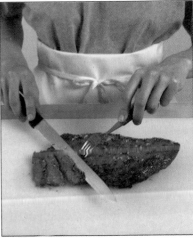
Step 7

TIME-SAVERS

■ *Do-ahead: The basting mixture (Step 2) and salad dressing (Step 5) can be made and the beef grilled ahead. The celery, carrot and bell pepper can be cut up ahead; do not shred the lettuce or dress the salad until shortly before serving.*

Values are approximate per serving: Calories: 589   Protein: 30 gm   Fat: 33 gm
Carbohydrates: 43 gm   Cholesterol: 70 mg   Sodium: 841 mg

Step 7

Savory Beef Stew
with Olives

▼

*Adding rich-tasting black olives is an effortless way to boost flavor in cooked
foods. In this unusual beef stew, the olives, along with tomatoes and lima beans,
impart a Spanish accent. Offer plenty of thick-crusted bread on the side or,
for an even heartier dish, add cooked rice or small soup pasta (such as orzo or pastina)
to the stew. If desired, use chick peas or kidney beans in place of the limas.*

Working time: 15 minutes
Total time: 50 minutes

Savory Beef Stew with Olives

4 Servings

1 pound stewing beef
1 medium onion
¼ cup flour
¼ teaspoon pepper
1 tablespoon olive oil
3 garlic cloves, minced or crushed
    through a press
1 can (16 ounces) whole tomatoes,
    with their juice

1 cup beef broth
¾ cup red wine or beef broth
1½ teaspoons oregano
1 bay leaf
1 package (10 ounces) frozen lima
    beans
1 cup drained pitted black olives

Step 1

1 If the beef is not already cut into uniform pieces, cut it into 1-inch cubes. Coarsely chop the onion.

2 In a plastic or paper bag, combine the flour and pepper and shake to mix. Add the beef and shake to coat lightly. Remove the beef.

3 In a large skillet or medium saucepan, warm the oil over medium-high heat until hot but not smoking. Add the beef and cook, stirring occasionally, until browned all over, about 10 minutes.

4 Add the onion and garlic and cook for 1 minute longer. Add the tomatoes and their juice (breaking up the tomatoes with a spoon), the beef broth, wine, oregano and bay leaf. Cover the pan and bring the liquid to a boil. Reduce the heat to low and simmer, covered, for 20 minutes, stirring occasionally.

Step 3

5 Add the lima beans and olives, increase the heat to medium-high, cover and bring to a boil. Reduce the heat to medium-low and simmer for 5 minutes longer.

TIME-SAVERS

■ **Do-ahead:** *The stew can be made ahead through Step 4; return to a boil and then proceed with the recipe. Or, make the stew completely ahead and then reheat gently.*

Values are approximate per serving: Calories: 498   Protein: 27 gm   Fat: 31 gm
Carbohydrates: 29 gm   Cholesterol: 82 mg   Sodium: 806 mg

Step 4

Honey-Apricot Spareribs

Mahogany brown and dripping with a thick, fruity sauce, these are everything spareribs should be. The ribs are broiled, then braised in a piquant blend of apricot jam, ketchup, soy sauce, ginger and garlic. If there's time, you can eliminate some of the fat from the meat by blanching the ribs in a large pot of boiling water for 2 to 3 minutes. Pat the ribs dry before basting and broiling them.

Working time: 25 minutes
Total time: 55 minutes

Honey-Apricot Spareribs

4 Servings

4 quarter-size slices (¼ inch thick) fresh ginger, unpeeled

3 cloves garlic, minced or crushed through a press

1 medium onion

¼ cup apricot jam

3 tablespoons reduced-sodium soy sauce

3 tablespoons honey

1 teaspoon chili powder

2 pounds spareribs

1 tablespoon vegetable oil

⅓ cup chicken broth

¼ cup orange juice

3 tablespoons ketchup

2 teaspoons grated orange zest (optional)

Step 4

1 Preheat the broiler. Line a broiler pan with foil.

2 In a food processor, mince the ginger and garlic. Add the onion and coarsely chop.

3 In a small bowl, combine 2 tablespoons of the apricot jam, 2 tablespoons of the soy sauce, 2 tablespoons of the honey and the chili powder.

4 Place the spareribs on the broiler pan and brush with half of the honey-apricot basting mixture. Broil 4 inches from the heat until golden brown, 7 to 10 minutes. Turn the spareribs over and brush them with the remaining basting mixture. Broil until golden brown (with some dark patches), 7 to 10 minutes.

5 Meanwhile, in a large skillet, warm the oil over medium-high heat until hot but not smoking. Add the ginger, garlic and onion, and stir-fry until the onion begins to brown, about 5 minutes.

Step 6

6 Add the chicken broth, orange juice, ketchup, orange zest (if using), and the remaining 2 tablespoons apricot jam, 1 tablespoon soy sauce and 1 tablespoon honey to the skillet. Bring the mixture to a boil, then reduce the heat to low, cover and simmer until the spareribs are finished cooking.

7 Cut the spareribs into sections. Increase the heat under the sauce to medium-high and add the ribs (and any pan juices from the broiler pan). Let the mixture return to a boil, then reduce the heat to medium-low, cover and simmer until the ribs are tender and cooked through, 20 to 25 minutes.

8 Serve the ribs with the sauce on the side.

Values are approximate per serving: Calories: 528 Protein: 28 gm Fat: 31 gm
Carbohydrates: 36 gm Cholesterol: 107 mg Sodium: 759 mg

Step 7

Beef and Sausage Balls in Spicy Tomato Sauce

Instead of the usual spaghetti, serve these hearty sausage-and-beef meatballs with other pasta shapes—ziti or penne, for instance. Or break with the pasta tradition and serve the meatballs and sauce over rice. For a casual Sunday supper or weekend lunch, surprise your family with a sub-shop special: hot meatball heroes on crusty Italian rolls. If you'd like a spicier dish, use hot instead of sweet sausage.

Working time: 25 minutes
Total time: 50 minutes

Beef and Sausage Balls in Spicy Tomato Sauce

4 Servings

½ **pound sweet Italian sausage**
½ **pound lean ground beef**
¼ **cup fine unseasoned breadcrumbs**
¼ **cup grated Parmesan cheese**
1 **medium onion**
1 **tablespoon olive or other vegetable oil**

2 **cloves garlic, minced or crushed through a press**
1 **can (16 ounces) crushed tomatoes**
1 **tablespoon tomato paste**
1 **bay leaf**
½ **teaspoon basil**
¼ **teaspoon black pepper**
¼ **teaspoon red pepper flakes**

Step 1

1 Remove the sausage from its casings.

2 In a medium bowl, combine the sausage with the beef, breadcrumbs and Parmesan. Form the mixture into meatballs about 1½ inches in diameter.

3 Coarsely chop the onion.

4 In a medium saucepan, warm the oil over medium heat until hot but not smoking. Add the meatballs and brown on all sides, about 8 minutes.

5 Add the onion and garlic and cook, stirring, until the onion is translucent, about 2 minutes.

6 Increase the heat to medium-high and add the tomatoes, tomato paste, bay leaf, basil, black pepper and red pepper flakes. Cover and return to a boil. Reduce the heat to medium-low, cover and simmer for 25 minutes, stirring occasionally.

7 Remove the bay leaf before serving.

Step 2

TIME-SAVERS

■ **Do-ahead:** *The meatballs can be formed ahead. The whole dish can be made ahead and gently reheated.*

Values are approximate per serving: Calories: 460   Protein: 23 gm   Fat: 35 gm
Carbohydrates: 13 gm   Cholesterol: 90 mg   Sodium: 811 mg

Step 6

Lamb Shish Kebab with Yogurt Dipping Sauce

▼

Chunks of lamb, along with bell pepper, red onion and cherry tomatoes, are skewered and broiled for this change-of-pace indoor barbecue. Serve the kebabs with warmed pita breads (or spear a big chunk of French bread on the end of each skewer as you serve it). A Greek-style salad—lettuce, cucumbers, tomatoes and feta cheese with a lemon-oregano vinaigrette—is the perfect partner for the kebabs.

Working time: 25 minutes
Total time: 35 minutes

Lamb Shish Kebab with Yogurt Dipping Sauce

4 Servings

3 tablespoons olive or other
  vegetable oil
¼ cup plus 2 tablespoons plain
  yogurt
3 tablespoons lemon juice
2 cloves garlic, minced or crushed
  through a press
1 teaspoon oregano
¼ teaspoon black pepper

1 large green bell pepper
2 small red onions
1 pound stewing lamb
8 cherry tomatoes
2 tablespoons sour cream
1½ teaspoons grated lemon zest
  (optional)
2 tablespoons chopped fresh mint
  or 1 teaspoon dried

1 Preheat the broiler. Line a broiler pan with foil.

2 In a small bowl, combine the oil, 2 tablespoons each of the yogurt and lemon juice, the garlic, oregano and ⅛ teaspoon of the black pepper.

3 Cut the bell pepper into 1-inch squares. Cut each onion into quarters. If the chunks of lamb are large, cut them into 1-inch pieces.

4 Thread the bell pepper, onions, lamb and cherry tomatoes on 4 large or 8 small skewers. Brush the kebabs with half the garlic-yogurt basting mixture. Broil 4 inches from the heat for 3 minutes. Turn the kebabs over, brush with the remaining basting mixture and broil for 6 minutes, or until the lamb is medium-rare.

5 Meanwhile, in a small bowl, combine the remaining ¼ cup yogurt, the remaining 1 tablespoon lemon juice, the sour cream, lemon zest (if using), mint and remaining ⅛ teaspoon black pepper.

6 Serve the kebabs with the yogurt dipping sauce on the side.

TIME-SAVERS

■ ***Microwave tip:*** *If you prefer more tender grilled vegetables, precook them in the microwave before grilling with the lamb. Place the cut-up vegetables (not the tomatoes) in a covered microwave-safe casserole with 2 tablespoons of water. Cook at 100% for 3 minutes.*

■ ***Do-ahead:*** *The meat and vegetables can be cut up and the basting mixture (Step 2) and dipping sauce (Step 5) made ahead.*

Values are approximate per serving: Calories: 300 Protein: 26 gm Fat: 18 gm
Carbohydrates: 7 gm Cholesterol: 81 mg Sodium: 89 mg

Step 3

Step 4

Step 5

Pork Chops
with Apples and Onions

Contrary to popular belief, most pork is not particularly high in fat. In fact, pork sold in today's health-conscious market is so lean that moist-heat cooking methods, such as braising, are required to keep the meat from drying out. In this recipe, pork chops are braised in broth and undiluted apple juice concentrate. You can use ordinary apple juice or cider, but the flavor will not be as intense.

Working time: 25 minutes
Total time: 45 minutes

Pork Chops
with Apples and Onions

4 Servings

2 medium onions	**4 pork chops, well trimmed (¾**
1 Granny Smith or other tart green	**inch thick, about 2 pounds total)**
apple, unpeeled	**½ cup beef broth**
3 tablespoons vegetable oil	**2 tablespoons frozen apple juice**
¼ cup flour	**concentrate**
½ teaspoon salt	**1 tablespoon Dijon mustard**
¼ teaspoon pepper	

Step 1

1 Cut the onions into ½-inch wedges. Cut the apple into ¼-inch wedges.

2 In a large skillet, warm 1 tablespoon of the oil over medium-high heat until hot but not smoking. Add the onions and apple and stir-fry until the onion and apple begin to brown, 2 to 3 minutes. Remove the onion and apple from the pan and set aside.

3 In a shallow bowl, combine the flour, salt and pepper. Dredge the pork chops in the seasoned flour.

4 Add the remaining 2 tablespoons oil to the skillet and warm over medium-high heat until hot but not smoking. Add the pork chops and cook until golden on both sides, about 4 minutes per side.

Step 2

5 Add the beef broth, apple juice concentrate and mustard and bring to a boil. Reduce the heat to medium-low, cover and simmer for 10 minutes.

6 Turn the pork chops over, add the sautéed onions and apple and continue simmering, covered, until the pork is cooked through, about 10 minutes longer. Remove the chops from the pan and serve topped with some of the onions and apple.

TIME-SAVERS

■ **Do-ahead:** *The onions and apple can be prepared (through Step 2) ahead of time.*

Step 6

Values are approximate per serving: Calories: 422 Protein: 35 gm Fat: 22 gm Carbohydrates: 20 gm Cholesterol: 96 mg Sodium: 593 mg

Garlic-Lemon Shrimp (page 191)

CHAPTER 4
SEAFOOD

Poached Salmon with Dill Butter

▼

The dill butter for this salmon dish can be made in advance and kept in the refriger-
ator or freezer. If you'd like, double or triple the herb butter recipe and save it
to use on baked potatoes, or to make a delicious variation on garlic bread. Serve the
salmon hot or at room temperature (with melted dill butter) accompanied
with plain or spinach fettuccine.

Working time: 20 minutes
Total time: 30 minutes

Poached Salmon with Dill Butter

4 Servings

1 lemon, halved, or ¼ cup lemon juice

Four salmon steaks (1 inch thick, 2 pounds total)

8 scallions, trimmed but left whole

8 sprigs fresh dill (optional)

¼ cup butter, softened to room temperature

2 tablespoons minced fresh dill or ¾ teaspoon dried

½ teaspoon salt

⅛ teaspoon pepper

Step 2

1 In a large skillet, bring 2 inches of water to a boil. Add the lemon halves, or lemon juice, and reduce the heat so that the water just simmers.

2 Add the salmon steaks (if they do not fit in a single layer, cook them in two batches), scallions and dill sprigs (if using). The fish should be completely covered by the water; add more water if necessary. When the water returns to a simmer (do not let the water boil), cook the salmon until it is firm and light pink in the center, 8 to 10 minutes.

3 Meanwhile, make the dill butter: In a small bowl, beat the butter until creamy and smooth. Beat in the chopped dill, salt and pepper.

Step 3

4 Using two slotted spatulas, carefully transfer the salmon to a serving platter or individual plates. Top each steak with one-quarter of the dill butter and two of the poached scallions.

TIME-SAVERS

■ *Microwave tip: Arrange the salmon in a microwave-safe baking dish in a single layer. The rounded end of the steaks should be toward the rim of the dish. Sprinkle on the lemon juice. Add the whole scallions and dill sprigs (if using). Cover loosely with plastic wrap and cook at 100% for 7 to 9 minutes, rotating the dish once if necessary. Let stand, covered, for 3 minutes.*

■ *Do-ahead: The dill butter can be made well ahead of time. The salmon can also be poached ahead of time and served at room temperature (with melted dill butter).*

Values are approximate per serving: Calories: 433 Protein: 46 gm Fat: 26 gm
Carbohydrates: 2 gm Cholesterol: 156 mg Sodium: 492 mg

Step 4

Mushroom-Smothered Baked Fish

▼

*The mushroom topping for these baked fillets is thickened with coarse breadcrumbs.
For the proper texture, the crumbs should be made with slightly stale bread.
If you have only fresh bread on hand, place a slice in the oven as it preheats (or in a
toaster oven set at 375°) for 5 minutes. For future use, store any stale bread that
accumulates in a plastic bag in the freezer. Then crumble it as needed for cooking.*

**Working time: 20 minutes
Total time: 35 minutes**

4 Servings

1 large carrot
1 rib celery
¼ pound mushrooms
1 slice firm-textured bread
2 tablespoons butter
1 tablespoon olive or other
  vegetable oil
1½ teaspoons oregano
½ teaspoon salt

¼ teaspoon pepper
3 tablespoons sour cream
3 tablespoons plain yogurt
4 scrod fillets or other mild-flavored
  white fish (about 1½ pounds
  total)
2 tablespoons grated Parmesan
  cheese

Step 4

1 Preheat the oven to 400°. Line a broiler pan with foil and lightly grease the foil.

2 In a food processor, finely chop the carrot. Add the celery and pulse briefly to coarsely chop; set aside. In the same work bowl, coarsely chop the mushrooms and set aside. Coarsely chop the bread.

3 In a medium skillet, warm the butter in the oil over medium-high heat until the butter is melted. Add the carrot, celery and mushrooms, and stir-fry until the vegetables begin to soften, 3 to 4 minutes.

4 Remove the skillet from the heat and stir in the breadcrumbs, oregano, salt and pepper. In a small bowl, blend the sour cream and yogurt.

5 Place the fish on the foil-lined pan. Coat the fish with the sour cream-yogurt mixture. Spread the mushroom-breadcrumb mixture evenly over the fish. Sprinkle with the Parmesan.

6 Bake the fish for 15 to 18 minutes, or until it just flakes when tested with a fork.

Step 5

TIME-SAVERS

■ *Microwave tip: Prepare the vegetables and bread as described in Step 2. Place the butter, oil, carrot, celery and mushrooms in a shallow microwave-safe dish. Cover loosely and cook at 100% for 3 minutes. Stir in the breadcrumbs, oregano, salt and pepper. Arrange the fish in a microwave-safe baking dish. Top as directed in Step 5. Cover loosely with waxed paper and cook at 100% for 8 minutes, rotating the dish once.*

■ *Do-ahead: The mushroom-breadcrumb mixture can be prepared ahead of time.*

Values are approximate per serving: Calories: 302 Protein: 34 gm Fat: 14 gm
Carbohydrates: 10 gm Cholesterol: 96 mg Sodium: 538 mg

Step 5

Garlic-Lemon Shrimp

▼

Grilling these garlic-lemon shrimp in their shells will keep them moist, but if you prefer deveined shrimp, you'll have to shell them first. Since the shrimp kebabs require very little time on the barbecue, plan to grill another component of the meal while you have the fire going. Try vegetable kebabs, or toast thick slices of French bread to go along with the shrimp. For an easy dessert, grill skewers of butter-and-rum-basted fruit chunks.

Working time: 35 minutes
Total time: 35 minutes

Garlic-Lemon Shrimp

4 Servings

¼ **cup (packed) fresh dill sprigs or 2 teaspoons dried**
3 scallions
3 tablespoons butter
3 cloves garlic, minced or crushed through a press
1 tablespoon grated lemon zest (from about 2 lemons; optional)

¼ **teaspoon salt**
¼ **teaspoon pepper**
½ **cup lemon juice**
1 pound medium shrimp
2 teaspoons flour

Step 3

1 Preheat the broiler or start the charcoal. If broiling, line a broiler pan with foil.

2 Finely chop the dill and scallions.

3 In a small saucepan, warm 2 tablespoons of the butter over medium heat until it is melted. Add the dill, scallions, garlic, lemon zest (if using), salt and pepper. Stir in the lemon juice.

4 If desired, shell and devein the shrimp. Thread the shrimp on skewers (if broiling, place the skewers on the broiler pan) and brush them with the garlic-lemon basting mixture.

Step 4

5 Grill or broil the shrimp 4 inches from the heat until they begin to turn pink, 2 to 3 minutes.

6 Turn the shrimp over, brush with more basting mixture and broil until the shrimp are cooked through, 2 to 3 minutes.

7 Meanwhile, thoroughly blend the remaining 1 tablespoon butter with the flour. Return the remaining basting mixture to medium-high heat and bring to a boil. Add the butter-flour mixture bit by bit, stirring well after each addition, and cook until the sauce has thickened slightly, 2 to 3 minutes.

8 Serve the shrimp with the sauce on the side.

TIME-SAVERS

■ **Do-ahead:** *The basting mixture (Steps 2 and 3) can be made and the shrimp shelled and deveined ahead of time.*

Step 7

Values are approximate per serving: Calories: 193 Protein: 19 gm Fat: 10 gm
Carbohydrates: 6 gm Cholesterol: 163 mg Sodium: 367 mg

Rich Red Snapper Chowder with Carrots

The name chowder usually conjures up images of cubed potatoes and plump clams in a milky broth. This dense, chunky stew, however, takes chowder in another direction. It begins with a highly flavorful fish, red snapper, which is pan-browned; then seasoned flour is browned in the same skillet to further flavor and enrich the stew. Fresh hot biscuits are the ideal accompaniment.

Working time: 25 minutes
Total time: 40 minutes

Rich Red Snapper Chowder
with Carrots

4 Servings

1 pound red snapper	**4 medium carrots**
⅓ cup flour	**4 ribs celery**
⅜ teaspoon black pepper	**2 cups chicken broth**
1 tablespoon butter	**1½ teaspoons thyme**
2 tablespoons olive or other	**Pinch of cayenne pepper**
vegetable oil	**¼ cup chopped parsley (optional)**

1 Cut the fish into 1-inch chunks.

2 In a small shallow bowl, combine the flour and ⅛ teaspoon of the black pepper. Dredge the fish lightly in the seasoned flour, reserving the excess.

3 In a large skillet, preferably nonstick, warm the butter in 1 tablespoon of the oil over medium-high heat until the butter is melted. Add the fish and cook until golden brown all over, about 7 minutes. Be careful when turning the fish to keep the pieces intact.

Step 3

4 Meanwhile, in a food processor, coarsely chop the carrots; remove and set aside. In the same processor work bowl, pulse briefly to coarsely chop the celery.

5 When the fish is done, remove it to a plate and cover loosely to keep warm.

6 Add the remaining 1 tablespoon oil to the skillet. Stir in the reserved dredging mixture and cook, stirring, over medium heat until the flour is dark brown, 4 to 5 minutes.

Step 6

7 Gradually add the chicken broth, stirring constantly to keep the mixture smooth. Add the thyme, the remaining ¼ teaspoon black pepper and the cayenne.

8 Bring the mixture to a boil over medium-high heat. Add the carrots, celery and parsley (if using). Reduce the heat to low, cover and simmer until the vegetables are tender, about 5 minutes.

9 Stir the cooked fish into the stew and cook until the fish is heated through, about 2 minutes.

TIME-SAVERS

■ **Do-ahead:** *The vegetables and fish can be cut up ahead.*

Values are approximate per serving: Calories: 289   Protein: 27 gm   Fat: 12 gm
Carbohydrates: 18 gm   Cholesterol: 50 mg   Sodium: 656 mg

Step 8

Herb-Coated Sole
on a Vegetable Nest

Here is a handsome presentation for delicate sole fillets: Serve them on
a bed of sautéed shredded vegetables. Potatoes, red bell pepper and onion are
shredded in the food processor; the herbed breadcrumb coating for the
fish is made in the same processor work bowl for quick cleanup. Serve the sole on
its "nest," accompanied with a simple side salad.

Working time: 20 minutes
Total time: 40 minutes

Herb-Coated Sole
on a Vegetable Nest

4 Servings

1 medium onion
½ pound small red potatoes, unpeeled
3 cloves garlic
1 large red bell pepper
1 tablespoon plus 2 teaspoons olive or other vegetable oil
¼ cup low-sodium chicken broth
¼ cup chopped parsley (optional)

1¾ teaspoons oregano
¼ teaspoon red pepper flakes
¼ teaspoon salt
½ teaspoon black pepper
1 slice firm-textured white bread
2 tablespoons chopped chives or scallion greens
1 pound sole fillets or other firm-fleshed white fish

Step 1

1 In a food processor, shred the onion; add the potatoes and shred. Remove the onion-potato mixture and set aside. In the same work bowl, mince the garlic; add the bell pepper and coarsely chop.

2 In a large nonstick skillet, warm 1 tablespoon of the oil over medium-high heat until hot but not smoking. Add the onion-potato mixture and stir-fry until the vegetables begin to brown, about 4 minutes.

3 Add the garlic, bell pepper, chicken broth, 2 tablespoons of the parsley (if using), 1 teaspoon of the oregano, the red pepper, salt and ¼ teaspoon of the black pepper, and cook, stirring, until the bell pepper begins to soften, about 2 minutes. Transfer the vegetables to an 11 x 7-inch baking dish.

4 Preheat the oven to 375°.

Step 6

5 In the same processor work bowl, finely chop the bread. Add the remaining ¾ teaspoon oregano, ¼ teaspoon black pepper and the chives, and pulse on and off to distribute the ingredients.

6 Arrange the fish on top of the vegetables in the baking dish. Sprinkle the fish with the herbed breadcrumbs and drizzle with the remaining 2 teaspoons oil. Bake the fish for 15 minutes, or until it just flakes when tested with a fork. Remove from the oven and preheat the broiler.

7 Broil the fish 4 inches from the heat for about 2 minutes, or until the top is just browned. Serve sprinkled with the remaining 2 tablespoons parsley (if using).

Values are approximate per serving: Calories: 237 Protein: 24 gm Fat: 8 gm
Carbohydrates: 18 gm Cholesterol: 55 mg Sodium: 267 mg

Step 6

Scallop-Asparagus Stir-Fry with Curried Rice

Because they are relatively expensive, it's a good idea to stretch scallops by combining them with other tasty ingredients for a satisfying meal. Asparagus and bell pepper, along with a generous serving of well-seasoned rice, accomplish this nicely. If you must pare down preparation time, the stir-fried scallops and vegetables can also be served with plain rice, pasta or bread.

Working time: 35 minutes
Total time: 40 minutes

Scallop-Asparagus Stir-Fry with Curried Rice

4 Servings

1 small onion
1 tablespoon vegetable oil
3 tablespoons curry powder
1 cup raw rice
1¼ cups chicken broth
1 cup water
¼ teaspoon salt
¼ teaspoon sugar
¾ pound asparagus
4 scallions
1 large red bell pepper

4 quarter-size slices (¼ inch thick) fresh ginger, unpeeled
1 pound sea scallops
3 tablespoons cornstarch
¼ teaspoon black pepper
2 tablespoons Oriental sesame oil
3 cloves garlic, minced or crushed through a press
2 tablespoons reduced-sodium or regular soy sauce
¼ teaspoon red pepper flakes

Step 3

1 Coarsely chop the onion.

2 In a medium saucepan, warm the vegetable oil over medium-high heat until hot but not smoking. Add the onion and stir-fry until it begins to brown, about 4 minutes.

3 Add 2 tablespoons of the curry powder and stir to completely incorporate. Add the rice, 1 cup of the chicken broth, the water, salt and sugar, and bring to a boil over high heat. Reduce the heat to low, cover and cook until the rice is tender, 15 to 20 minutes.

4 Meanwhile, cut the asparagus and scallions into 2-inch sections. Cut the bell pepper into thin strips 2 inches long. Sliver the ginger.

5 Cut any large scallops in half. In a bowl, combine the cornstarch and black pepper. Dredge the scallops in the cornstarch mixture.

Step 5

6 In a large skillet, warm 1 tablespoon of the sesame oil over medium-high heat until hot but not smoking. Add the garlic, scallions and ginger, and stir-fry for about 3 minutes.

7 Add the remaining 1 tablespoon sesame oil and the scallops and stir-fry until the scallops begin to brown, about 4 minutes.

8 Add the asparagus, bell pepper, the remaining ¼ cup chicken broth, the soy sauce, remaining 1 tablespoon curry powder and the red pepper flakes. Bring the mixture to a boil, stirring constantly. Reduce the heat to low, cover and simmer, stirring occasionally, until the scallops are cooked through, about 7 minutes.

9 Serve the scallop mixture over the curried rice.

Values are approximate per serving: Calories: 449   Protein: 28 gm   Fat: 13 gm
Carbohydrates: 56 gm   Cholesterol: 37 mg   Sodium: 935 mg

Step 8

Skillet-Baked Trout
with Lemon-Caper Sauce

There are many species of trout—including Dolly Varden, brown, rainbow, lake, steelhead and brook—but only a few of them are available commercially. Rainbow and brook trout are the most common species sold in fish markets, and rainbows are found in most supermarkets. If you can't fit four whole fish in your skillet at once, brown them two at a time, then transfer them to a shallow ovenproof dish for baking.

Working time: 20 minutes
Total time: 35 minutes

Skillet-Baked Trout
with Lemon-Caper Sauce

4 Servings

3 slices bacon
½ cup flour
½ cup cornmeal
¼ teaspoon salt
½ teaspoon pepper
4 small whole brook trout (about
  ½ pound each)
2 tablespoons olive or other
  vegetable oil

2 tablespoons butter
3 tablespoons lemon juice
2 tablespoons capers, drained
2 teaspoons grated lemon zest
  (optional)
¼ cup chopped parsley (optional)

Step 3

1 Preheat the oven to 425°.

2 In a large ovenproof skillet, cook the bacon over medium heat until crisp, about 10 minutes. Drain the bacon on paper towels and set aside. Pour off all but 1 tablespoon of bacon fat from the skillet.

3 Meanwhile, in a shallow container, combine the flour, cornmeal, salt and pepper. Dredge the fish in the seasoned flour-cornmeal mixture. Discard the excess.

4 Add 1 tablespoon of the oil to the bacon fat in the skillet and warm over medium-high heat until hot but not smoking. Add the fish and cook until browned on both sides, about 2 minutes per side, adding the remaining 1 tablespoon oil, if necessary, to prevent sticking.

Step 4

5 Place the skillet in the oven and bake for 15 minutes, or until the fish just flakes when tested with a fork. Remove the trout to individual dinner plates.

6 Return the skillet to the stovetop. Over medium-high heat, add the butter, lemon juice, capers, lemon zest and parsley (if using). Cook, stirring, for 1 minute to heat through.

7 Pour the lemon-caper sauce over the fish and crumble the bacon on top.

TIME-SAVERS

■ *Do-ahead: The dredge (Step 3) can be made ahead.*

Values are approximate per serving: Calories: 388 Protein: 26 gm Fat: 25 gm
Carbohydrates: 13 gm Cholesterol: 86 mg Sodium: 390 mg

Step 6

Spicy Fish Ragout over Lemon Rice

▼

This spicy stew features big chunks of fish and vegetables in a white wine-tomato broth that is seasoned with three kinds of pepper—cayenne, red pepper flakes and black pepper. The ragout is served over rice for a one-dish meal. Best of all, the whole meal takes just about half an hour to cook. If scrod fillets are not available, halibut, pollock or any other firm-fleshed white fish can be used instead.

Working time: 30 minutes
Total time: 30 minutes

Spicy Fish Ragout over Lemon Rice

4 Servings

2 cups water
1 cup raw rice
2 tablespoons lemon juice
1 tablespoon butter
2 teaspoons grated lemon zest (optional)
⅜ teaspoon cayenne pepper
¼ pound mushrooms
3 plum tomatoes or 4 whole canned tomatoes, well drained
1 large green bell pepper
2 medium onions
2 tablespoons olive or other vegetable oil

3 cloves garlic, minced or crushed through a press
½ cup bottled clam juice or chicken broth
½ cup dry white wine or chicken broth
4 tablespoons tomato paste
¼ teaspoon red pepper flakes
½ teaspoon salt
½ teaspoon black pepper
1 pound fillets of scrod or other firm-fleshed white fish

Step 2

1 In a medium saucepan, bring the water to a boil. Add the rice, lemon juice, butter, lemon zest (if using) and ¼ teaspoon of the cayenne. Reduce the heat to medium-low, cover and simmer until the rice is tender and all the liquid is absorbed, about 20 minutes.

2 Meanwhile, cut the mushrooms into ¼-inch slices. Coarsely chop the tomatoes. Cut the bell pepper into 1-inch squares. Coarsely chop the onions.

3 In a large skillet, warm the oil over medium-high heat until hot but not smoking. Add the onions and garlic, and stir-fry until the onions begin to brown, about 5 minutes.

4 Add the mushrooms, tomatoes, bell pepper, clam juice, wine, tomato paste, red pepper flakes, salt, black pepper and the remaining ⅛ teaspoon cayenne. Bring the mixture to a boil.

Step 4

5 Meanwhile, cut the fish into 1-inch chunks.

6 When the mixture has come to a boil, add the fish. Reduce the heat to low, cover and simmer until the fish just flakes when tested with a fork, about 7 minutes.

7 Uncover the skillet, increase the heat to high and cook for 1 to 2 minutes to reduce the liquid slightly.

8 Serve the ragout over the rice.

Values are approximate per serving: Calories: 426 Protein: 27 gm Fat: 11 gm
Carbohydrates: 49 gm Cholesterol: 59 mg Sodium: 624 mg

Step 6

Tuna Salad Niçoise

Salade Niçoise is a specialty of the French Riviera city of Nice. It typically contains boiled potatoes, tuna, green beans, hard-cooked eggs and olives in a robust vinaigrette. (Anchovies are also traditional; add a few, if you like them.) This substantial salad makes a wonderful summer supper and is also fine picnic fare. To fully appreciate the fresh flavors of the vegetables and dressing, serve the salad at room temperature.

Working time: 20 minutes
Total time: 35 minutes

Tuna Salad Niçoise

6 Servings

1 pound small red potatoes, unpeeled
2 eggs
¾ pound green beans or 1 package (10 ounces) frozen green beans, thawed
1 pint cherry tomatoes
¼ cup white wine vinegar or cider vinegar
⅓ cup olive or other vegetable oil

1 tablespoon Dijon mustard
1 clove garlic, minced or crushed through a press
1 teaspoon basil
½ teaspoon salt
¼ teaspoon pepper
1 can (6 ounces) pitted black olives, drained
1 can (6½ ounces) water-packed tuna, drained

1 Quarter the potatoes.

2 Place the potatoes and the eggs in a large saucepan and cover with cold water. Bring to a boil over medium-high heat. Reduce the heat to medium and simmer, uncovered, until the potatoes just test tender, about 20 minutes. Remove the eggs after 15 minutes of cooking, cool them under cold running water and then peel them.

3 Meanwhile, cut the beans into 2-inch lengths. Halve the cherry tomatoes. Finely chop the hard-cooked eggs.

4 When the potatoes are tender, add the beans to the saucepan and continue cooking the potatoes and beans for about 2 minutes longer, or until the beans are just crisp-tender. Drain the potatoes and beans.

5 In a small bowl, whisk together the vinegar, oil, mustard, garlic, basil, salt and pepper. Place the still warm potatoes and beans in a serving bowl and pour the dressing over them. Toss to coat well.

6 Add the cherry tomatoes and olives to the bowl. Flake the tuna into the bowl with a fork. Toss gently to combine all the ingredients. Sprinkle the chopped egg on top.

TIME-SAVERS

■ *Microwave tip: To thaw the frozen green beans, remove them from the package, place on a microwave-safe plate and cook at 100% for 3 minutes.*

■ *Do-ahead: The eggs can be cooked ahead of time; but cook the potatoes closer to the time that you will assemble the salad, as it is best to dress them while they are still warm. The vinaigrette can be made (Step 5) ahead and the whole salad can be assembled in advance.*

Values are approximate per serving: Calories: 289   Protein: 13 gm   Fat: 17 gm
Carbohydrates: 22 gm   Cholesterol: 82 mg   Sodium: 635 mg

Step 2

Step 3

Step 5

Carolina Shrimp Pie

▼

Freshly caught seafood abounds in the coastal Carolinas, and many great shrimp recipes come from that region. This one is a hearty shrimp casserole, a sort of pot pie made with bread cubes and crumbs instead of a pastry crust. The bread should be dry, so if you have only fresh bread on hand, place it in the oven for five minutes during the preheating time. You can also dry the bread in a toaster oven.

Working time: 35 minutes
Total time: 1 hour

Carolina Shrimp Pie

4 Servings

5 slices firm-textured white bread
1 egg
¾ cup milk
4 scallions
1 large green bell pepper
1 pound shrimp
4 tablespoons butter
2 cloves garlic, minced or crushed
   through a press

1 tablespoon sherry (optional)
2 teaspoons Worcestershire sauce
3 drops hot pepper sauce
½ teaspoon salt
¼ teaspoon black pepper
3 tablespoons fine unseasoned
   breadcrumbs

Step 2

1 Preheat the oven to 375°. Butter a 1-quart baking dish.

2 Cut the bread into cubes. In a medium bowl, beat the egg and milk together. Add the bread cubes and toss to coat well. Set aside.

3 Coarsely chop the scallions. Dice the bell pepper. Shell, devein and coarsely chop the shrimp.

4 In a medium skillet, warm 3 tablespoons of the butter over medium-high heat until melted. Add the scallions, bell pepper and garlic, and cook until the vegetables are softened and the garlic is beginning to brown, about 7 minutes.

Step 3

5 Scrape the scallion-pepper mixture into the bowl with the bread cubes. Add the shrimp, sherry (if using), Worcestershire sauce, hot pepper sauce, salt and black pepper, and toss to combine.

6 Transfer the mixture to the prepared baking dish and sprinkle the fine breadcrumbs on top. On the stovetop or in the microwave, melt the remaining 1 tablespoon butter. Drizzle butter over the breadcrumbs.

7 Bake for about 25 minutes, or until the top of the pie is golden.

TIME-SAVERS

■ *Microwave tip: Prepare and assemble the ingredients as directed. Place the casserole on an inverted plate in the microwave. Cover loosely with waxed paper and cook at 100% for 4 minutes, then at 50% for 3 to 5 minutes, or until the shrimp are cooked through.*

■ *Do-ahead: The vegetables, bread cubes and shrimp can be cut up ahead. The casserole can be assembled a short time ahead, refrigerated and then baked just before serving.*

Values are approximate per serving: Calories: 369 Protein: 26 gm Fat: 18 gm
Carbohydrates: 25 gm Cholesterol: 234 mg Sodium: 792 mg

Step 6

Fillets with Shallot-Ginger Glaze

▼

The secret to many a sauce—including this golden shallot-ginger glaze for fish—is the cornstarch. This humble ingredient thickens cooking liquids, producing a luxurious sauce without added fat. For best results, blend cornstarch with a small amount of cold liquid; then add it to the rest of the sauce and simmer and stir gently for a few minutes.

Working time: 15 minutes
Total time: 35 minutes

Fillets with
Shallot-Ginger Glaze

4 Servings

6 shallots or 1 medium onion
4 quarter-size slices (¼ inch thick)
  fresh ginger, unpeeled
1 garlic clove
4 sole fillets or other firm-fleshed
  white fish (about 1½ pounds
  total)
3 tablespoons butter
1 tablespoon olive or other
  vegetable oil

½ cup chicken broth
4 teaspoons cornstarch
⅓ cup white wine or chicken broth
1 tablespoon lemon juice
2 teaspoons grated lemon zest
  (optional)
¼ teaspoon pepper

Step 3

1 In a food processor, mince the shallots, ginger and garlic.

2 Preheat the broiler. Line a broiler pan with foil and lightly grease the foil. Place the fish on the broiler pan.

3 In a medium skillet, warm the butter over medium-high heat until it is melted. Add the shallot-ginger mixture and cook, stirring, until the mixture is just golden, 8 to 10 minutes. Remove the skillet from the heat.

Step 4

4 Spoon half the shallot-ginger mixture over the fish. Drizzle the olive oil on top. Broil the fish 4 inches from the heat until it just flakes when tested with a fork, about 6 minutes.

5 Meanwhile, in a small bowl, blend together the ½ cup chicken broth and cornstarch. Return the skillet to medium heat and stir in the wine, lemon juice, lemon zest (if using) and the pepper. Bring to a boil, add the broth and cornstarch, and return to a boil, stirring constantly. Reduce the heat to medium-low and simmer, stirring occasionally, for 1 minute.

6 Serve the fish with some of the sauce spooned on top.

TIME-SAVERS

■ ***Do-ahead:*** *The shallot-ginger mixture can be made ahead through Step 3.*

Step 5

Values are approximate per serving: Calories: 303 Protein: 33 gm Fat: 14 gm
Carbohydrates: 6 gm Cholesterol: 105 mg Sodium: 355 mg

Baked Stuffed Shrimp with Tomato Tartar Sauce

▼

Although stuffed shrimp may seem like a dish you would only order in a restaurant, it is in fact quite easy to prepare at home. The technique for butterflying the shrimp is the same as that for deveining them; you just make a deeper cut. To speed dinner preparations, the stuffing can be made in advance; but the tomato tartar sauce should be mixed at the last minute so the tomato will not thin the mayonnaise too much.

Working time: 35 minutes
Total time: 35 minutes

4 Servings

1 slice fresh bread
4 scallions
¼ cup parsley sprigs
1 garlic clove
¼ cup grated Parmesan cheese
½ teaspoon pepper
2 tablespoons butter
1 pound large or medium shrimp

1 medium plum tomato
¼ cup mayonnaise
¼ cup plain yogurt
1 teaspoon lemon juice
1 teaspoon dry mustard
1 teaspoon Dijon mustard
¼ teaspoon salt

1 Preheat the oven to 425°. Line a baking sheet with foil.

2 In a food processor, combine the bread, 2 of the scallions, the parsley and garlic, and pulse on and off to form coarse crumbs. Add the Parmesan and ¼ teaspoon of the pepper and pulse just until mixed; set aside.

3 Melt the butter on the stovetop or in the microwave.

4 Shell the shrimp, leaving the tails on if desired. Devein the shrimp, cutting them as deeply as possible without actually cutting through them; spread the two sides of the shrimp apart to butterfly them slightly.

5 Place the shrimp, butterflied-side up, on the foil-lined baking sheet and flatten them out. Place a heaping tablespoon of the stuffing on each shrimp, mounding it slightly, then drizzle the shrimp with the melted butter.

6 Bake the shrimp for about 11 minutes, or just until firm.

7 Meanwhile, finely chop the tomato and the remaining 2 scallions. Combine them in a small bowl with the mayonnaise, yogurt, lemon juice, dry and Dijon mustards, salt and remaining ¼ teaspoon pepper, and stir well.

8 Serve the shrimp with the tomato tartar sauce.

TIME-SAVERS

■ **Do-ahead:** *The shrimp can be deveined and butterflied ahead of time, and the stuffing mixture (Step 2) made ahead.*

Values are approximate per serving: Calories: 307 Protein: 23 gm Fat: 20 gm
Carbohydrates: 8 gm Cholesterol: 168 mg Sodium: 582 mg

Step 2

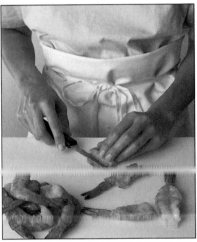
Step 4

Step 5

New England Crab Chowder with Nutmeg Croutons

▼

This delectable seafood stew, which owes its inspiration to New England clam chowder, combines chunks of crabmeat with potato, carrots and celery in a lightly creamy broth. Fragrant triangles of nutmeg-buttered toast nicely complement the sweetness of the crab—in fact, you might want to double the recipe for the nutmeg butter and make extra croutons.

Working time: 30 minutes
Total time: 45 minutes

New England Crab Chowder with Nutmeg Croutons

4 Servings

1 medium all-purpose potato
2 medium carrots
2 cloves garlic
5 scallions
1 rib celery
3 tablespoons plus 4 teaspoons butter
3 tablespoons flour

2 cups chicken broth
¼ teaspoon pepper, preferably white
¾ teaspoon nutmeg
1 can (6 ounces) crabmeat
2 slices firm-textured white bread
2 cups milk

Step 1

1 Peel the potato and cut it into ½-inch cubes. In a food processor, coarsely chop the carrots; remove and set aside. Add the garlic and mince; add the scallions and coarsely chop; remove and set aside. Add the celery and coarsely chop.

2 In a large saucepan, warm 3 tablespoons of the butter over medium-high heat until it is melted. Add the garlic-scallion mixture and cook, stirring, until the scallions are wilted, about 2 minutes.

3 Stir in the flour and cook, stirring, until the flour is no longer visible, about 1 minute. Slowly pour in the chicken broth, stirring constantly. Bring the mixture to a boil and then add the potato, carrots, pepper and ¼ teaspoon of the nutmeg. Let the mixture return to a boil, then reduce the heat to medium-low, cover and simmer until the potato is tender, about 15 minutes.

Step 5

4 Meanwhile, drain the crabmeat and pick out any pieces of shell or cartilage. Toast the bread.

5 In a small saucepan or skillet, combine the remaining 4 teaspoons butter with the remaining ½ teaspoon nutmeg and cook over low heat until fragrant, about 1 minute. Brush the toast with the nutmeg butter and cut into triangles.

6 Increase the heat under the soup to medium-high and bring to a boil. Add the crab, celery and milk, and cook until just heated through, about 3 minutes. Serve the soup with the nutmeg croutons.

TIME-SAVERS

■ *Do-ahead: The vegetables can be cut up (keep the potato cubes in a bowl of cold water to keep them from discoloring) and the nutmeg butter (Step 5) made ahead. The entire chowder can be made ahead and gently reheated.*

Step 6

Values are approximate per serving: Calories: 354 Protein: 18 gm Fat: 18 gm
Carbohydrates: 30 gm Cholesterol: 89 mg Sodium: 907 mg

Broiled Halibut
with Avocado Salad

▼

*Thai cusine is recalled in this dish, which features juicy halibut steaks,
velvety avocado cubes and diced bell pepper in a sweet-and-savory peanut sauce.
Peanut butter gives the sauce richness; ginger, garlic, lemon juice and
zest, soy sauce and honey provide a delicious counterpoint. Garnish the
plates with slim wedges of melon and lime twists.*

Working time: 20 minutes
Total time: 30 minutes

Broiled Halibut with Avocado Salad

4 Servings

3 quarter-size slices (¼ inch thick) fresh ginger, unpeeled
2 cloves garlic
¼ cup (packed) parsley sprigs (optional)
2 medium shallots or 1 small onion
¼ cup lemon juice
2 tablespoons butter
4 small halibut steaks (about 2¼ pounds total)
1 avocado

1 large red bell pepper
2 tablespoons reduced-sodium soy sauce
1 tablespoon olive or other vegetable oil
3 tablespoons creamy peanut butter
2 teaspoons honey
1 tablespoon grated lemon zest (optional)
¼ teaspoon black pepper

Step 3

1 Preheat the broiler. Line a broiler pan with foil.

2 In a food processor, mince the ginger. Add the garlic and parsley (if using), and mince. Add the shallots and finely chop.

3 For the dressing, in a small saucepan or skillet, combine the ginger, garlic, parsley, shallots and lemon juice. Bring to a boil over medium-high heat, reduce the heat to low and simmer, uncovered, for 5 minutes. Remove from the heat and set aside to cool slightly.

4 Meanwhile, melt the butter on the stovetop or in the microwave. Place the halibut on the broiler pan and brush with the melted butter.

5 Broil the fish 4 inches from the heat for 5 minutes. Turn the fish over and broil for 4 minutes, or until cooked through.

Step 6

6 Meanwhile, cube the avocado. Dice the bell pepper.

7 To the dressing mixture, add the soy sauce, olive oil, peanut butter, honey, lemon zest (if using) and black pepper, and stir until smooth. When the fish is done, add any juices that have accumulated on the broiler pan to the dressing.

8 Divide the avocado, bell pepper and fish among 4 dinner plates and drizzle the dressing over all.

TIME-SAVERS

■ *Do-ahead: The dressing (Steps 2, 3 and 7) can be made and the bell pepper cut up ahead. The avocado can be cut up, but toss it with 2 teaspoons of lemon juice to keep it from discoloring.*

Step 7

Values are approximate per serving: Calories: 472 Protein: 48 gm Fat: 26 gm
Carbohydrates: 12 gm Cholesterol: 82 mg Sodium: 536 mg

Lobster with Three Sauces

Although lobster is already a special treat, you can enhance the sense of occasion by serving it with some unusual dipping sauces: an herbed lemon-sour cream sauce, a three-mustard mayonnaise and a subtle tarragon vinaigrette. These small lobsters, weighing 1 to 1¼ pounds, are sometimes called chicken lobsters. If you can't find any this size, use larger lobsters and let two diners share each one.

Working time: 20 minutes
Total time: 30 minutes

4 Servings

¼ cup (packed) fresh basil leaves or
   2 teaspoons dried
2 scallions
1 tablespoon butter
3 cloves garlic, minced or crushed
   through a press
½ cup sour cream
¾ teaspoon pepper
1 tablespoon lemon juice
1¼ teaspoons grated lemon zest
   (optional)
3 tablespoons mayonnaise

2 tablespoons plain yogurt
2 tablespoons plus 1 teaspoon
   Dijon mustard
2 tablespoons spicy brown mustard
¼ teaspoon dry mustard
¼ cup white wine vinegar or cider
   vinegar
¼ cup olive or other vegetable oil
1¼ teaspoons tarragon
½ teaspoon salt
4 small lobsters (1 to 1¼ pounds
   each)

Step 1

1 For the lemon-herb sauce: Finely chop the basil and scallions. In a small skillet, warm the butter over medium heat until it is melted. Add 2 cloves of the garlic and cook until fragrant, about 1 minute. Add the scallions and basil, and cook, stirring, until the scallions begin to soften, about 2 minutes. Remove the skillet from the heat and stir in the sour cream, ¼ teaspoon of the pepper, the lemon juice and the lemon zest (if using). Remove to a small serving dish.

2 For the creamy mustard sauce: In a small serving dish, combine the mayonnaise, yogurt, 2 tablespoons of the Dijon mustard, the spicy brown mustard, dry mustard and ¼ teaspoon of the pepper.

3 For the tarragon wine vinaigrette: In a small serving dish, combine the vinegar, olive oil, tarragon, salt, the remaining 1 clove garlic, 1 teaspoon Dijon mustard and ¼ teaspoon pepper.

4 In a pot large enough to hold the lobsters, bring 5 inches of water to a boil. (Or use the largest pot you have and cook the lobsters in batches.)

Step 2

5 Add the lobsters to the boiling water. Cover and return to a boil. Reduce the heat to low and simmer until the lobsters are cooked through, about 10 minutes. Drain the lobsters well and serve them with the three sauces.

TIME-SAVERS

■ *Do-ahead: All of the sauces can be made ahead. The lobsters can be cooked ahead and served at room temperature or chilled.*

Values are approximate per serving: Calories: 428 Protein: 26 gm Fat: 33 gm
Carbohydrates: 9 gm Cholesterol: 108 mg Sodium: 1150 mg

Step 3

Sole Stuffed with Shrimp

▼

Seafood-stuffed fish fillets—like those you might order at an elegant restaurant—can be easily prepared at home. Impressive and rich-tasting (though surprisingly moderate in calories and fat), the fillets in this recipe are stuffed with a mixture of sautéed vegetables and whole baby shrimp. If you cannot find baby shrimp, cook ¼ pound of medium shrimp in boiling water until pink; then shell, devein and coarsely chop them.

Working time: 25 minutes
Total time: 45 minutes

Sole Stuffed with Shrimp

4 Servings

1 clove garlic	**4 sole fillets (about 1½ pounds)**
1 small onion	**⅔ cup bottled clam juice or chicken**
1 medium carrot	**broth**
1 rib celery	**1 tablespoon cornstarch**
1 tablespoon butter	**¼ cup heavy cream**
1½ teaspoons thyme	**¼ teaspoon salt**
¼ pound cooked baby shrimp	**¼ teaspoon pepper**

Step 3

1 Preheat the oven to 375°. Lightly grease a baking dish big enough to hold four rolled fillets in one layer (about 8 x 8).

2 In a food processor, mince the garlic. Add the onion and coarsely chop; set aside. In the same processor work bowl, one at a time, finely chop the carrot and celery; set aside.

3 In a medium skillet, warm the butter over medium-high heat until it is melted. Add the garlic-onion mixture and sauté until the onion begins to soften, about 3 minutes. Add the carrot, celery and 1 teaspoon of the thyme. Cook until the vegetables begin to soften, about 4 minutes. Remove from the heat and stir in the shrimp.

4 Place 3 tablespoons of the stuffing on each fillet and loosely roll up. Place the rolls and any leftover stuffing in the prepared dish and pour in the clam juice (or chicken broth). Cover with foil and bake for 20 minutes, or until the fish just flakes when tested with a fork.

5 Meanwhile, in a small bowl, blend the cornstarch, heavy cream, remaining ½ teaspoon thyme, the salt and pepper.

Step 4

6 Remove the fish rolls to a plate and cover loosely to keep warm. Transfer the cooking juices and the extra stuffing to a saucepan. Bring the mixture to a boil over medium-high heat. Add the cornstarch mixture and cook, stirring, until thickened slightly, about 3 minutes. Serve the fish rolls topped with the sauce.

TIME-SAVERS

■ *Microwave tip: In a small casserole, cook the butter, garlic, onion, carrot, celery and 1 teaspoon thyme, covered, at 100% for 3 minutes. Stir in the shrimp. Stuff the fillets as directed above, then arrange in a shallow baking dish. Add the clam juice, cover loosely and cook at 100% for 9 minutes, rotating the dish once. Meanwhile, combine the ingredients for the cream sauce (Step 5); add the cooking liquid and extra stuffing, cover with waxed paper and cook at 100% for 3 to 4 minutes, until slightly thickened, stirring once.*

Values are approximate per serving: Calories: 292 Protein: 40 gm Fat: 11 gm
Carbohydrates: 7 gm Cholesterol: 169 mg Sodium: 548 mg

Step 4

Red Snapper
with Vegetable Julienne

One of the ingredients in the vegetable julienne that accompanies this red snapper is a leek. A member of the onion family, a leek looks like a very large scallion but has a milder onion flavor. Since leeks can be quite sandy, they must be washed carefully: Trim the leek and halve it lengthwise, then rinse it under cold running water, separating the layers, until it is clean. If necessary, substitute several large scallions for the leek.

Working time: 20 minutes
Total time: 45 minutes

Red Snapper
with Vegetable Julienne

4 Servings

1 small onion
1½ cups chicken broth
¼ cup dry white wine or chicken broth
¼ teaspoon black pepper
1 bay leaf
4 small red snapper fillets, or other firm-fleshed white fish (about 1¼ pounds total)

2 ribs celery
1 medium yellow or green bell pepper
1 large leek (white and tender green parts only), thoroughly washed
1 large carrot
3 tablespoons milk
2 tablespoons cornstarch

Step 1

1 Quarter the onion. In a large skillet, bring the broth, wine, black pepper, bay leaf and onion quarters to a boil over medium-high heat.

2 Add the fish, reduce the heat to low, cover and simmer until the fish just flakes when tested with a fork, about 10 minutes.

3 Meanwhile, cut the celery, bell pepper, leek and carrot into matchsticks about ¼ inch wide and 3 inches long.

4 With a slotted spatula, carefully remove the fish to a plate and cover loosely to keep warm. Discard the bay leaf. Bring the broth to a boil over medium-high heat and cook uncovered to reduce it to 1 cup, about 5 minutes.

Step 4

5 Add the vegetables to the broth, reduce the heat to low, cover and simmer until the vegetables are crisp-tender, about 11 minutes.

6 Meanwhile, blend the milk and cornstarch.

7 Return the broth to a boil over medium-high heat and stir in the cornstarch mixture. Cook until thickened slightly, 1 to 2 minutes.

8 Serve the fish topped with the sauce and vegetables.

TIME-SAVERS

■ *Microwave tip: Thinly slice the onion and celery. In a shallow microwave-safe baking dish, arrange the onion, celery, bell pepper, leek, carrot, black pepper and bay leaf. Place the fish on top of the vegetables. Pour in 1 cup of broth and the wine. Cover the dish with plastic wrap and cook at 100% for 12 minutes, rotating the dish once. Remove the fish and cover loosely to keep warm; discard the bay leaf. Uncover the dish and cook the vegetables at 100% for 6 minutes, or until the vegetables are tender. Stir in the cornstarch mixture and cook at 100% for 3 minutes, or until the sauce is thickened.*

Step 5

Values are approximate per serving: Calories: 206 Protein: 31 gm Fat: 3 gm
Carbohydrates: 12 gm Cholesterol: 54 mg Sodium: 497 mg

Garlic Shrimp with Cuban Black Bean Salad

▼

A perfect summertime lunch, this tropical-tasting shrimp and black bean platter is flavorful and filling, almost a meal in itself. It can be served warm, at room temperature or chilled, and the black bean salad that accompanies the sautéed shrimp can be made in minutes if you chop the vegetables in a food processor. For a variation, use cannellini, pinto or kidney beans instead of black beans.

Working time: 40 minutes
Total time: 40 minutes

Garlic Shrimp with Cuban Black Bean Salad

4 Servings

6 cloves garlic
1 medium red onion
1 large green bell pepper
1 medium red bell pepper
2 ribs celery
2 tablespoons chopped chives or
  scallion greens
¼ cup olive or other vegetable oil

¼ cup lemon juice
1½ teaspoons grated lemon zest
  (optional)
½ teaspoon salt
¼ teaspoon red pepper flakes
¼ teaspoon black pepper
1 can (15 ounces) black beans
1 pound medium shrimp

Step 1

1 In a food processor, mince the garlic; remove and set aside. In the same processor work bowl, one at a time, coarsely chop the onion, green bell pepper, red bell pepper and celery. Chop the chives (or scallion greens) by hand.

2 In the same work bowl, combine the chives (or scallion greens), 2 tablespoons of the olive oil, the lemon juice, lemon zest (if using), salt, red pepper flakes and black pepper. Process the dressing to blend.

3 In a large skillet, warm 1 tablespoon of the olive oil over medium-high heat until hot but not smoking. Add 1 teaspoon of the minced garlic, the onion, green and red bell peppers and celery, and stir-fry until the vegetables are crisp-tender, 3 to 4 minutes.

4 Drain the beans, rinse under cold running water and drain well. Stir the drained black beans into the skillet and cook until heated through, about 1 minute. Transfer the vegetables and beans to a serving bowl or platter. Pour the dressing over the mixture and toss to thoroughly combine; set aside.

Step 4

5 Shell and devein the shrimp.

6 Add the remaining 1 tablespoon olive oil to the skillet and warm over medium-high heat until hot but not smoking. Add the remaining garlic and stir-fry until it begins to brown, about 2 minutes. Add the shrimp and cook until the shrimp turns pink and is opaque throughout, about 4 minutes.

7 Serve the shrimp on a bed of black bean salad.

TIME-SAVERS

■ *Do-ahead: The vegetables can be cut up, the shrimp shelled and deveined, and the dressing (Step 2) made ahead.*

Values are approximate per serving: Calories: 345 Protein: 26 gm Fat: 16 gm
Carbohydrates: 26 gm Cholesterol: 140 mg Sodium: 841 mg

Step 6

Scallop and Vegetable Brochettes with Garlic Butter

Sea scallops are ideal for grilling on skewers because they are usually uniform in size, and their firmness keeps them from falling apart as they cook. Cherry tomatoes, for the same reasons, are also well suited for brochettes. Here, summer squash and green bell peppers complement the scallops and tomatoes. Lemon-garlic butter, seasoned with red pepper flakes and parsley, makes a delicious basting sauce.

Working time: 20 minutes
Total time: 30 minutes

Scallop and Vegetable Brochettes with Garlic Butter

4 Servings

3 tablespoons butter	2 teaspoons grated lemon zest
3 cloves garlic, minced or crushed	(optional)
through a press	1 large yellow squash
1 teaspoon lemon juice	1 large green bell pepper
¼ teaspoon red pepper flakes	1 pound sea scallops
3 tablespoons chopped parsley	16 cherry tomatoes

1 Preheat the broiler or start the charcoal. If broiling, line a broiler pan with foil.

2 In a small skillet or saucepan, warm the butter over medium heat until it is melted. Add the garlic and cook until the garlic flavor is released, about 3 minutes. Remove from the heat and stir in the lemon juice, red pepper flakes, parsley and lemon zest (if using).

Step 3

3 Halve the squash lengthwise, then cut crosswise into ½-inch half-rounds. Cut the bell pepper into 1-inch squares. Cut any large scallops in half so they are all approximately the same size.

4 Alternating ingredients, thread the squash, bell pepper, scallops and tomatoes on skewers. (If broiling, place the skewers on the broiler pan.) Brush the skewers with half the garlic butter and grill or broil 4 inches from the heat.

5 Turn the skewers over, brush with the remaining garlic butter and grill or broil until the scallops are cooked through and the vegetables are tender, about 4 minutes.

Step 4

TIME-SAVERS

■ ***Microwave tip:*** *To make the garlic butter, combine all of the ingredients listed in Step 2 in a small bowl. Cook at 100% for 1 minute.*

■ ***Do-ahead:*** *All of the ingredients can be prepared ahead. If using wooden (not metal) skewers, the brochettes can be assembled ahead and kept tightly covered until time to cook.*

Step 4

Values are approximate per serving: Calories: 205   Protein: 20 gm   Fat: 10 gm
Carbohydrates: 9 gm   Cholesterol: 61 mg   Sodium: 276 mg

Salmon and Corn Chowder

This satiny chowder contains a variety of tastes and textures. The creamy broth holds meaty chunks of fresh salmon, sweet corn kernels and crunchy diced bell pepper; a crumble of smoky bacon is the last-minute topping. You could substitute canned salmon for the fresh, but choose mild pink salmon rather than the oilier red salmons. The canned salmon will not need to be cooked, just heated through.

Working time: 30 minutes
Total time: 60 minutes

Salmon and Corn Chowder

4 Servings

1 pound red potatoes, unpeeled	1 medium green bell pepper
1 medium onion	¼ cup (packed) fresh dill sprigs or
3 slices bacon	2 teaspoons dried
2 cloves garlic, minced or crushed	½ pound salmon fillet
through a press	2 cups frozen corn
2 tablespoons flour	¼ teaspoon black pepper
2½ cups chicken broth	1 cup milk

1 Cut the potatoes into ½-inch dice. Coarsely chop the onion.

2 Cut the bacon slices crosswise into ½-inch-wide strips. In a medium saucepan, cook the bacon over medium heat, stirring frequently, until crisp, about 10 minutes. Drain the bacon on paper towels.

Step 2

3 Pour off all but 1 tablespoon of fat from the saucepan. Add the onion and garlic, and stir-fry over medium-high heat until the onion begins to brown, about 5 minutes.

4 Stir in the flour and cook, stirring, until the flour is no longer visible, about 30 seconds. Add the chicken broth and potatoes, and bring to a boil over medium-high heat. Reduce the heat to medium-low, cover and simmer until the potatoes are tender, about 15 minutes.

5 Meanwhile, dice the bell pepper. Finely chop the dill. Cut the salmon into ½-inch cubes.

6 Return the soup to a boil over medium-high heat. Add the bell pepper, corn and black pepper, and cook until the bell pepper is crisp-tender, about 5 minutes.

Step 4

7 Remove about half of the soup to a food processor and purée, then return the purée to the saucepan. Return the chowder to a boil, add the salmon and milk, and cook until heated through and the fish just flakes when tested with a fork, about 5 minutes.

8 Stir in the dill. Serve the soup garnished with the bacon.

TIME-SAVERS

■ **Do-ahead:** *The soup can be made ahead through Step 6.*

Values are approximate per serving: Calories: 379   Protein: 22 gm   Fat: 12 gm
Carbohydrates: 47 gm   Cholesterol: 46 mg   Sodium: 777 mg

Step 7

Skillet Potato Pie with Eggs and Cheese (page 267)

CHAPTER 5
ONE-DISH MEALS

Stovetop Chicken with Spanish Rice

The Spanish one-pot dish arroz con pollo (rice with chicken) is the inspiration for this skillet dinner. The olives add a typically Spanish flavor to the casserole, as does the olive oil, especially if you use a flavorful extra-virgin one. Just add some crusty bread, a tossed green salad and a light dessert, and the meal is complete.

Working time: 15 minutes
Total time: 45 minutes

228

Stovetop Chicken with Spanish Rice

4 Servings

1 medium onion	1 can (14½ ounces) whole
1 large green bell pepper	tomatoes, with their juice
2 tablespoons olive or other	1¾ cups chicken broth
vegetable oil	1 bay leaf
2½ pounds chicken parts	2 teaspoons paprika
2 cloves garlic, minced or crushed	¼ teaspoon black pepper
through a press	½ cup pitted black or
1 cup raw rice	pimiento-stuffed green olives

Step 2

1 Cut the onion into thin slices. Cut the bell pepper into thin strips.

2 In a flameproof casserole or Dutch oven, warm 1 tablespoon of the oil over medium-high heat until hot but not smoking. Add the chicken and brown all over, about 10 minutes. Remove the chicken to a plate and set aside.

3 Add the remaining 1 tablespoon oil to the casserole. Add the onion, bell pepper and garlic and cook, stirring frequently, until the onion is translucent, about 5 minutes.

Step 4

4 Add the rice and cook for 2 minutes, stirring to coat the rice with the oil. Add the chicken, the tomatoes and their juice, chicken broth, bay leaf, paprika and black pepper. Bring the mixture to a boil. Reduce the heat to medium-low, cover and simmer for 20 minutes, stirring occasionally so the chicken cooks evenly.

5 Discard the bay leaf. Stir in the olives and serve.

TIME-SAVERS

■ ***Do-ahead:*** *The whole dish can be made ahead and reheated.*

Step 5

Values are approximate per serving: Calories: 715   Protein: 42 gm   Fat: 39 gm
Carbohydrates: 47 gm   Cholesterol: 145 mg   Sodium: 886 mg

Hot Pepper Quiche

Quiche was once the dish of choice at brunches and informal dinner parties. It fell from favor for a while, but here is a good reason to revive it: a vegetable-filled version with upbeat Mexican seasonings. Tomatoes, bell pepper, yellow squash and corn are set in a savory custard of eggs, pepper jack cheese (Monterey jack studded with bits of jalapeño) and zesty spices. Serve the quiche with mixed greens and corn muffins.

Working time: 25 minutes
Total time: 1 hour 20 minutes

Hot Pepper Quiche

6 Servings

1 bunch scallions (6 to 8)
1 plum tomato or 2 whole canned tomatoes, well drained
1 medium green bell pepper
1 small yellow squash
¼ pound pepper jack cheese
1 package (10 ounces) frozen corn, thawed
1 tablespoon butter
3 cloves garlic, minced or crushed through a press

1 tablespoon olive or other vegetable oil
2 tablespoons flour
1 tablespoon chili powder
1 tablespoon cumin
½ teaspoon salt
Pinch of cayenne pepper
4 eggs
⅓ cup milk
One 9-inch pie crust, storebought or homemade

Step 4

1 Coarsely chop the scallions and the tomato. Thinly slice the bell pepper and the squash. Grate the pepper jack cheese. Place the thawed corn on paper towels to drain.

2 Preheat the oven to 375°. Line a baking sheet with foil.

3 In a large skillet, warm the butter over medium heat until it is melted. Add the scallions and garlic, and cook, stirring, until the scallions are softened, about 5 minutes.

4 Add the olive oil. Add the bell pepper and squash, and cook, stirring, until the vegetables are softened, about 4 minutes.

5 Add the tomato, corn, flour, chili powder, cumin, salt and cayenne, and cook, stirring, until the flour is no longer visible, about 30 seconds. Remove from the heat.

Step 6

6 In a medium bowl, beat the eggs with the milk. Add the sautéed vegetables and the grated cheese and stir to combine.

7 Turn the quiche mixture into the pie crust. Place the pie crust on the prepared baking sheet. Bake for 50 minutes, or until the filling is set and the top is golden. Let cool for 10 minutes before slicing.

TIME-SAVERS

■ *Microwave tip: Prepare the ingredients and preheat the oven as described in Steps 1 and 2. In a medium microwave-safe bowl, combine the butter, garlic, oil, scallions, bell pepper and squash. Cover and cook at 100% for 7 minutes, or until the vegetables are tender. Stir in the tomato, corn, flour, chili powder, cumin, salt and cayenne until well combined. Proceed with the recipe as directed in Steps 6 and 7.*

Values are approximate per serving: Calories: 391   Protein: 14 gm   Fat: 25 gm
Carbohydrates: 31 gm   Cholesterol: 169 mg   Sodium: 579 mg

Step 7

Rustic Pizza Pie

An Italian "pizza rustica" is quite different from the flat, cheese-and-tomato-topped round of dough we know as pizza. It is a deep, double-crusted pie, made with shortcrust pastry or yeast dough; the filling is usually a hearty blend of cheese and vegetables. In this American adaptation, eggs, cream cheese, ricotta and Parmesan provide a rich backdrop for spinach, corn and smoked cheese.

Working time: 30 minutes
Total time: 1 hour 10 minutes

Rustic Pizza Pie

8 Servings

1 package rapid-rise yeast
¾ cup hot (125° to 130°) water
¼ cup olive or other vegetable oil
½ teaspoon salt
About 3½ cups plus ⅓ cup flour
1 package (10 ounces) frozen
  chopped spinach, thawed
¼ pound smoked cheese, such as
  mozzarella, Gouda or Edam
1 medium onion
3 cloves garlic, minced

1 whole egg plus 2 egg yolks
2 cups (1 pound) ricotta cheese
½ cup plus 1 tablespoon grated
  Parmesan cheese
1 package (3 ounces) cream cheese,
  at room temperature
1 can (8¾ ounces) corn, drained
1 teaspoon basil
1 teaspoon oregano
¼ teaspoon pepper
1 tablespoon milk

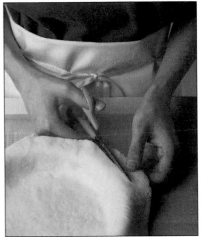
Step 7

1 Preheat the oven to 425°. Lightly grease an 8-inch round cake pan.

2 In a food processor, dissolve the yeast in the water. With the processor running, add 3 tablespoons of the oil, the salt and 3¼ cups of the flour, and process until it forms a ball. If the dough is sticky, add up to ¼ cup more flour. If it is too dry, add 2 to 3 tablespoons water.

3 Divide the dough into two balls, one two times the size of the other. Roll the larger of the two portions out to an 11- to 12-inch circle ¼ inch thick. Roll the smaller piece out to a 9-inch circle. Cover both dough circles with a towel.

4 Use your hands to squeeze the thawed spinach dry. Cut the smoked cheese into small dice. Coarsely chop the onion.

5 In a medium skillet, warm the remaining 1 tablespoon oil over medium-high heat until hot but not smoking. Add the onion and garlic, and sauté until the onion begins to brown, about 3 minutes.

Step 7

6 In a medium bowl, beat the whole egg and 1 of the egg yolks with the ricotta. Add the onion-garlic mixture, ½ cup of the Parmesan, the smoked cheese and cream cheese, and beat to blend. Stir in the remaining ⅓ cup flour, the corn, spinach, basil, oregano and pepper.

7 Fit the larger circle of dough into the cake pan; trim to ½ inch all the way around. Spoon the filling into the pan. Place the small circle of dough on top. Pinch the edges of the dough together to seal.

8 Lightly beat the remaining egg yolk with the milk. Brush the pizza with the egg glaze. Sprinkle on the remaining 1 tablespoon Parmesan. Cut two or three 1-inch steam vents in the crust. Bake for 20 minutes, or until the crust is golden. Let stand about 20 minutes before serving.

Values are approximate per serving: Calories: 547 Protein: 23 gm Fat: 26 gm
Carbohydrates: 55 gm Cholesterol: 141 mg Sodium: 476 mg

Step 7

Roasted Salmon with Carrots, Mushrooms and New Potatoes

▼

Roasting fish may seem like an odd concept until you taste this hearty combination of juicy salmon chunks cooked with vegetables—it's as satisfying as any beef stew. You'll need a thick salmon fillet or steak to enable you to cut the sizable cubes the recipe requires; the fish may be relatively expensive, but with the generous amount of vegetables, just one pound of salmon serves four.

Working time: 10 minutes
Total time: 50 minutes

Roasted Salmon with Carrots, Mushrooms and New Potatoes

4 Servings

¼ cup olive or other vegetable oil
¼ cup chopped parsley (optional)
2 cloves garlic, minced or crushed
   through a press
¾ teaspoon salt
¼ teaspoon pepper

8 small red potatoes (about
   1 pound), unpeeled
2 large carrots
3 scallions
½ pound small mushrooms
1-pound salmon fillet

1 Preheat the oven to 450°.

2 In a medium bowl, combine the oil, parsley (if using), garlic, salt and pepper.

3 Quarter the potatoes (or, if they are large, cut them into ¾-inch cubes). Cut the carrots on the diagonal into ½-inch slices. Cut the scallions (white and tender green parts) into 2-inch sections. If the mushrooms are large, halve them.

Step 3

4 Scatter the potatoes, carrots, scallions and mushrooms over the bottom of a shallow 1½-quart baking dish. Drizzle 2 tablespoons of the garlic oil over them and toss gently to coat. Place the dish in the oven and roast until the potatoes are almost done and beginning to brown, about 30 minutes; stir the vegetables once or twice to ensure even cooking.

5 Meanwhile, cut the salmon into 1½-inch cubes. Add the salmon to the bowl of garlic oil and toss gently to coat.

Step 4

6 Lower the oven temperature to 375°. Gently stir the vegetables in the baking dish, scatter the salmon on top and roast until the vegetables are tender and the salmon just flakes when tested with a fork, about 10 minutes longer.

TIME-SAVERS

■ **Do-ahead:** *The garlic oil (Step 2) can be made and the vegetables and fish cut up ahead.*

Values are approximate per serving: Calories: 413 Protein: 27 gm Fat: 21 gm
Carbohydrates: 29 gm Cholesterol: 62 mg Sodium: 491 mg

Step 5

Zucchini-Beef Moussaka

This hearty Greek dish is usually made with lamb and eggplant; beef and zucchini present a pleasant variation. A custardlike sauce containing sour cream and a touch of Parmesan tops the casserole. The seasonings are characteristically Greek: garlic, oregano and cinnamon (which adds a subtle spiciness). For a Greek-inspired side salad, just add some olives and crumbled feta cheese to your favorite greens.

Working time: 25 minutes
Total time: 1 hour

Zucchini-Beef Moussaka

4 Servings

1 large tomato or 2 whole canned tomatoes, drained	½ teaspoon salt
1 medium onion	¼ teaspoon pepper
3 cloves garlic, minced or crushed through a press	1 large zucchini
1 pound ground beef	2 tablespoons cornstarch
3 tablespoons tomato paste	¾ cup grated Parmesan cheese
1 teaspoon cinnamon	1 egg
1 teaspoon oregano	⅔ cup sour cream
	2 tablespoons flour

Step 3

1 Preheat the oven to 375°.

2 Coarsely chop the tomato and onion. In a medium saucepan over medium heat, combine the tomato, onion, garlic, ground beef, tomato paste, cinnamon, oregano, salt and pepper. Bring the mixture to a boil, breaking up the meat with a spoon. Reduce the heat to low, cover and simmer for 10 minutes.

3 Meanwhile, cut the zucchini into ⅛-inch-thick rounds. In a plastic or paper bag, shake the cornstarch and zucchini together to coat.

4 In a shallow 1½-quart baking dish, layer half the meat-tomato mixture, half the zucchini and ¼ cup of the Parmesan. Top with the remaining meat-tomato mixture, zucchini and ¼ cup of the Parmesan.

Step 4

5 In a small bowl, lightly beat the egg. Blend in the sour cream, flour and remaining ¼ cup Parmesan.

6 Spoon the sour cream mixture evenly over the top of the casserole and bake for 30 minutes, or until the top is light golden and the moussaka is heated through.

TIME-SAVERS

■ *Microwave tip:The microwave version of this dish will be a bit more liquidy (serve it over rice), but the time savings is substantial. In a 2-quart microwave-safe casserole, combine the chopped tomato, onion, sliced zucchini, garlic, ground beef, tomato paste, cinnamon, oregano, salt and pepper. Cover and cook at 100% for 6 minutes, stirring once halfway through to break up the ground beef. Meanwhile, prepare the topping as directed in Step 5. Stir the cornstarch and ½ cup Parmesan into the casserole. Spoon the topping over the casserole and cook at 50% until the topping is set and the casserole is heated through, about 12 minutes.*

Values are approximate per serving: Calories: 591 Protein: 30 gm Fat: 44 gm
Carbohydrates: 18 gm Cholesterol: 178 mg Sodium: 770 mg

Step 6

Dilled Chicken Bake with Potatoes and Carrots

▼

Chic restaurants have lately been serving updated "comfort food," making much of their trendy re-interpretations of dishes Mom used to make. Here is the real thing—not a fancied-up version, but an old-fashioned dinner of cut-up chicken, potatoes and carrots browned on top of the stove, then baked in a casserole. A generous sprinkling of dill adds a fragrant touch.

Working time: 15 minutes
Total time: 55 minutes

Dilled Chicken Bake with Potatoes and Carrots

1 Servings

2½ pounds chicken parts
1½ pounds all-purpose potatoes
2 large carrots
1 medium onion
2 cloves garlic, minced or crushed
    through a press
1 tablespoon dried dill

1 teaspoon salt
½ teaspoon pepper
2 tablespoons flour
⅔ cup chicken broth
2 tablespoons chopped fresh dill
    (optional)

1 Preheat the oven to 375°.

2 In a large flameproof casserole or Dutch oven, cook the chicken skin-side down over medium heat for 5 minutes to render some of its fat. Increase the heat to medium-high and continue cooking until browned on all sides, about 5 minutes per side.

Step 2

3 Meanwhile, peel the potatoes and cut them into 1½-inch chunks. Cut the carrots into 1½-inch pieces. Cut the onion into ½-inch wedges.

4 Remove the chicken to a plate and cover loosely to keep warm. Warm the pan drippings in the casserole over medium-high heat until hot but not smoking. Add the onion and garlic and cook until golden, about 3 minutes.

5 Add the potatoes and carrots and cook, stirring, until the vegetables are well coated with the pan drippings, about 1 minute.

Step 3

6 Return the chicken (and any juices that have accumulated on the plate) to the casserole and remove the pan from the heat. Stir in the dried dill, salt and pepper. Cover and bake for 10 minutes.

7 Remove the casserole from the oven, stir to redistribute the chicken and vegetables, re-cover and bake for another 15 minutes, or until the vegetables are tender and the chicken is cooked through.

8 With a slotted spoon, transfer the ingredients to a platter. Stir the flour into the drippings in the casserole and cook over medium-high heat, stirring, until the flour is no longer visible, about 30 seconds.

9 Stir in the chicken broth and cook, stirring, until the gravy is slightly thickened, 1 to 2 minutes.

10 Serve the chicken and vegetables garnished with the fresh dill, if desired, and pass the gravy separately.

Values are approximate per serving: Calories: 568   Protein: 40 gm   Fat: 30 gm
Carbohydrates: 34 gm   Cholesterol: 145 mg   Sodium: 878 mg

Step 6

Turkey-Potato Skillet Pie

This delicious variation on shepherd's pie is both a substantial and healthful dinner. Low-fat turkey replaces the traditional lamb or beef, and the skins are left in the mashed potatoes both for fiber and for the cook's convenience. If you'd like to substitute leftover cooked turkey for the ground turkey, chop it and stir it into the vegetable filling just before covering it with the mashed potato topping.

Working time: 40 minutes
Total time: 50 minutes

Turkey-Potato Skillet Pie

6 Servings

1½ pounds boiling potatoes
3 cloves garlic, peeled
4 stalks celery
2 medium onions
1 medium green bell pepper
2 tablespoons olive or other
  vegetable oil
1 pound ground turkey
½ cup chicken broth

1 teaspoon cornstarch
1 tablespoon Dijon mustard
¾ teaspoon thyme
¼ teaspoon salt
½ teaspoon black pepper
2 tablespoons butter
1 egg, lightly beaten
3 tablespoons grated Parmesan
  cheese (optional)

1 Place the unpeeled potatoes (halved if large) and 2 of the garlic cloves in a large saucepan with water to cover. Bring the water to a boil, cover and cook until the potatoes are tender, 15 to 18 minutes.

Step 3

2 Meanwhile, in a food processor, mince the remaining clove of garlic. Add the celery, onions and bell pepper and coarsely chop. In a large broilerproof skillet, preferably cast iron, warm the oil over medium-high heat until hot but not smoking. Add the chopped vegetables and cook, stirring frequently, until the onions just begin to brown, about 10 minutes.

3 Add the turkey, breaking it up with a spoon, and cook until the turkey turns opaque, about 5 minutes.

4 In a small bowl, combine the broth and cornstarch. Add the mustard, thyme, salt and ¼ teaspoon of the black pepper. Stir the broth mixture into the skillet. Bring the liquid to a boil, stirring, until the mixture thickens slightly, about 1 minute. Set aside.

5 Preheat the broiler.

Step 6

6 Drain the cooked potatoes. In a shallow bowl, mash the potatoes and the garlic. Stir in the butter, beaten egg, remaining ¼ teaspoon black pepper and the Parmesan (if using). Stir one-third of the potato mixture into the turkey filling.

7 Spoon the mashed potatoes on top of the turkey mixture in the skillet. Place the skillet under the broiler, 4 inches from the heat, and broil until golden, about 10 minutes.

TIME-SAVERS

■ ***Do-ahead:*** *The whole dish can be assembled ahead, brought back to room temperature and then broiled just before serving.*

Values are approximate per serving: Calories: 304 Protein: 18 gm Fat: 15 gm
Carbohydrates: 24 gm Cholesterol: 101 mg Sodium: 401 mg

Step 7

Beef Stew with Parmesan Biscuit Topping

▼

The enticing aroma of cheese biscuits baking atop this one-dish meal is matched by the delicious, rich flavors of the stew underneath. Although the recipe does not take long to make, you can cut down on last-minute preparations by making the stew the night before and then reheating it briefly while you mix the biscuit dough. If your family doesn't like lima beans, use a second cup of corn instead.

Working time: 25 minutes
Total time: 1 hour

242

Beef Stew with Parmesan Biscuit Topping

6 Servings

2 cups beef broth
1 cup plus 2 tablespoons water
2 tablespoons tomato paste
2 tablespoons Dijon mustard
2 cloves garlic, minced or crushed
   through a press
1 teaspoon basil
½ teaspoon pepper
1 pound small red potatoes,
   unpeeled
1½ pounds stewing beef
2 medium carrots

1 medium onion
2 cups flour
¼ cup grated Parmesan cheese
2 teaspoons baking powder
½ teaspoon salt
4 tablespoons cold butter, cut into
   tablespoons
⅔ cup milk
¼ cup chopped parsley (optional)
1 tablespoon cornstarch
1 cup frozen baby lima beans
1 cup frozen corn

Step 2

1 In a large ovenproof skillet or Dutch oven, bring the beef broth, 1 cup of the water, the tomato paste, mustard, garlic, basil and ¼ teaspoon of the pepper to a boil over medium-high heat.

2 Meanwhile, cut the potatoes into ½-inch-thick slices. Cut the beef into bite-size pieces. Add the potatoes and beef to the skillet. Cover, return to a boil, reduce the heat to medium-low and simmer for 10 minutes.

3 Meanwhile, cut the carrots into 1-inch pieces. Cut the onion into thin wedges. Add the carrots and onion to the skillet. Cover, increase the heat to medium-high and return to a boil. Reduce the heat to medium-low and simmer the stew while you make the biscuit dough.

4 Preheat the oven to 425°.

Step 3

5 Make the biscuit dough: In a food processor, combine the flour, Parmesan, baking powder, salt and remaining ¼ teaspoon pepper. Pulse briefly to combine. Cut in the butter until the mixture resembles coarse meal. Pour in the milk and process just until the dough balls up. Add the parsley (if using) and pulse just to combine.

6 In a small bowl, combine the cornstarch with the remaining 2 tablespoons water. Increase the heat under the stew to medium-high and return it to a boil. Stir in the lima beans and corn. Stir in the cornstarch mixture and cook, stirring, until the stew thickens slightly, about 3 minutes.

7 Using about ½ cup of dough for each, form the dough into 6 biscuits and place on top of the stew. Place the skillet in the oven and bake for 14 minutes, or until the biscuits are golden on top.

Values are approximate per serving: Calories: 692 Protein: 33 gm Fat: 32 gm
Carbohydrates: 67 gm Cholesterol: 104 mg Sodium: 1044 mg

Step 7

Sausage and Spinach Risotto

A classic risotto is truly a labor of love. In the standard Italian recipe, boiling broth is slowly added to the rice, which is constantly stirred to render it creamy and tender. Here, the flavors of a risotto are preserved, but the rice simmers in a covered pot — along with spinach and country sausage — requiring virtually no attention. A true risotto is made with a short-grain rice, but long-grain rice should be used here.

Working time: 20 minutes
Total time: 55 minutes

Sausage and Spinach Risotto

4 Servings

1 medium red onion
1 large yellow, red or green bell pepper
¾ pound country sausage
1 cup raw rice

2 cups chicken broth
¼ teaspoon black pepper
1 package (10 ounces) frozen spinach, thawed
½ cup grated Parmesan cheese

1 Coarsely chop the onion and bell pepper.

2 Remove the sausage from its casings. In a large skillet, cook the sausage over medium heat for 5 minutes, breaking it up with a spoon.

Step 2

3 Add the onion and cook until the sausage and onion begin to brown, about 5 minutes.

4 Add the bell pepper and rice and cook, stirring, for about 1 minute to coat the rice with fat.

5 Add the chicken broth and black pepper, and bring to a boil over medium-high heat. Reduce the heat to low, cover and simmer for 15 minutes.

6 Add the spinach and stir to evenly distribute it. Re-cover and cook 15 minutes longer.

Step 4

7 Stir in the Parmesan and serve.

TIME-SAVERS

■ *Microwave tip: Thaw the spinach in the microwave by removing it from the box, placing it on a saucer or plate and cooking at 100% for about 3 minutes. Squeeze the excess moisture from the spinach and set aside. In a 2½-quart microwave-safe casserole, combine the onion and bell pepper with the crumbled sausage. Cover and cook at 100% for 5 minutes, stirring once. Add the rice, stirring to coat the rice with fat. Add 1½ cups of chicken broth and the black pepper. Re-cover and cook at 100% for 9 minutes, or until the liquid comes to a boil. Cook at 50% for 15 minutes, or until the rice is just tender and the liquid is absorbed. Stir the spinach and Parmesan into the rice, re-cover and let stand for 5 minutes.*

■ *Do-ahead: The risotto can be prepared ahead through Step 6. Add about ¼ cup of chicken broth or water to the risotto, then reheat it in the microwave before stirring in the Parmesan.*

Step 6

Values are approximate per serving: Calories: 613 Protein: 21 gm Fat: 39 gm
Carbohydrates: 44 gm Cholesterol: 66 mg Sodium: 1303 mg

Poached Chicken and Vegetables

▼

The idea behind this simple one-dish meal is similar to that of a New England boiled dinner. Chicken, sausage and vegetables are poached together, which not only cooks the ingredients but also produces a flavorful broth. Serve the meats, vegetables and some of the broth together in shallow soup bowls, and save the rest of the broth for another use. For a lower calorie count, the chicken should be skinned before eating.

Working time: 15 minutes
Total time: 45 minutes

Poached Chicken and Vegetables

4 Servings

5 cups chicken broth
2 cups water
½ teaspoon thyme
½ pound sweet Italian sausage
2½ pounds chicken parts
8 small red potatoes, unpeeled
  (about 1 pound)

3 medium carrots
1 medium red onion
1 package (10 ounces) frozen corn,
  thawed

Step 2

1 In a large saucepan or flameproof casserole, bring the chicken broth, water and thyme to a boil over medium-high heat.

2 Meanwhile, remove the sausage casings and break the sausage into 1-inch chunks.

3 Add the sausage and chicken to the boiling broth. Reduce the heat to medium-low, cover and simmer for 25 minutes, stirring occasionally.

4 Meanwhile, halve the potatoes. Cut the carrots into 2-inch lengths. Cut the onion into ½-inch wedges.

5 Increase the heat to medium-high and return the broth to a boil. Add the potatoes, carrots and onion, reduce the heat to medium-low, cover and simmer until the potatoes are tender, about 15 minutes.

6 Add the corn to the broth and cook until heated through, 1 to 2 minutes. To serve, divide the meats and vegetables among 4 shallow soup bowls. Spoon in ½ cup broth.

Step 4

TIME-SAVERS

■ *Microwave tip: Thaw the corn in the microwave by placing the package on a plate and cooking at 100% for 3 minutes. (If the package is foil-wrapped, first remove the foil.) Cut the potatoes into quarters rather than halves. Place the potatoes, carrot pieces and 2 cups of chicken broth in a microwave-safe 4-quart casserole. Cook at 100% for 10 minutes, stirring once. Add the onion and cook at 100% for 5 minutes. Add the chicken, sausage and thyme and cook at 100% for 20 minutes. Add the remaining 3 cups broth, only 1 cup of water and the corn, and cook at 100% for 7 minutes or until the broth comes to a boil..*

■ *Do-ahead: The potatoes, carrots and onion can be cut up ahead of time. The entire dish can also be made ahead of time and reheated on the stovetop or in the microwave.*

Values are approximate per serving: Calories: 557 Protein: 44 gm Fat: 24 gm
Carbohydrates: 43 gm Cholesterol: 138 mg Sodium: 1043 mg

Step 5

Topsy-Turvy Pizza

This casual one-dish supper is made like a fruit cobbler. The sausage
and tomato filling is cooked in a skillet, then topped with cheesy biscuit dough and
baked. You can use either sweet or spicy Italian sausage in this recipe.
Serve the "pizza" directly from the skillet and accompany it with a tossed
green salad simply dressed with oil and vinegar.

Working time: 25 minutes
Total time: 45 minutes

Topsy-Turvy Pizza

6 Servings

1 medium onion
3 cloves garlic
¼ pound mushrooms
1 tablespoon olive or other
 vegetable oil
½ pound Italian sausage
1 can (8 ounces) tomato sauce
½ cup chopped pitted black olives
 (optional)

1 teaspoon basil
½ teaspoon oregano
¼ teaspoon pepper
1 cup flour
1 teaspoon baking powder
3 tablespoons butter
1½ cups grated part-skim
 mozzarella cheese
About ¼ cup milk

1 In a food processor, coarsely chop the onion, garlic and mushrooms.

2 In a 9-inch ovenproof skillet, warm the oil over medium-high heat until hot but not smoking. Add the onion, garlic and mushrooms and cook, stirring, until the onion begins to brown, about 5 minutes.

3 Remove the sausages from their casings and add to the skillet. Cook, breaking up the sausage with a spoon, until the meat loses its pinkness, about 5 minutes. Drain any excess fat from the pan.

4 Preheat the oven to 425°.

5 Add the tomato sauce, olives (if using), basil, oregano and pepper. Bring the mixture to a boil. Reduce the heat to medium-low and simmer, uncovered, while you make the topping.

6 In the same food processor work bowl (there is no need to clean it), combine the flour and baking powder. With the machine running, add the butter, a chunk at a time, and process until the mixture resembles cornmeal. Pulse in ½ cup of the mozzarella. With the machine on, add just enough milk so the mixture forms a soft dough.

7 Turn the dough out onto a lightly floured work surface and roll out to a circle 9 inches in diameter (and about ¼ inch thick).

8 Off the heat, sprinkle the remaining 1 cup mozzarella over the tomato mixture in the skillet. Lay the circle of dough on top. Place the skillet in the oven and bake for 20 minutes, or until the top is golden.

TIME-SAVERS

■ *Do-ahead: The "pizza" sauce (Steps 1 through 5) can be made ahead. Bring it back to a simmer while you make the biscuit topping.*

Values are approximate per serving: Calories: 339 Protein: 16 gm Fat: 20 gm
Carbohydrates: 23 gm Cholesterol: 55 mg Sodium: 752 mg

Step 3

Step 7

Step 8

Chicken with Potatoes, Peppers and Zucchini

Unlike most casseroles, this aromatic chicken dinner is baked in stages—or layers. First potatoes and onions, drizzled with herbed olive oil, are baked for 5 minutes. Then bell peppers, zucchini and tomatoes are layered over the potatoes with more of the fragrant oil and the dish goes back into the oven. Finally, browned chicken pieces are placed on top and the casserole is baked until the vegetables are meltingly tender.

Working time: 25 minutes
Total time: 1 hour

Chicken with Potatoes, Peppers and Zucchini

6 Servings

1¼ pounds small red potatoes, unpeeled
2 medium onions
3 cloves garlic, minced or crushed through a press
¼ cup olive or other vegetable oil
2 teaspoons oregano
1½ teaspoons thyme
½ teaspoon red pepper flakes
1 teaspoon salt
¾ teaspoon black pepper
1 medium yellow or red bell pepper

1 medium green bell pepper
4 small plum tomatoes or 6 canned whole tomatoes, well drained
1 medium zucchini
1 bay leaf
1 teaspoon butter
4 chicken breast halves (about 2 pounds total)
¼ cup dry white wine or chicken broth
2 teaspoons basil

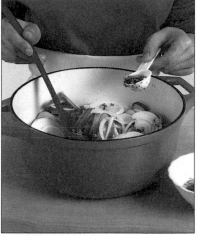

Step 4

1 Preheat the oven to 425°.

2 Thinly slice the potatoes and onions.

3 In a small bowl, combine the garlic, 3 tablespoons of the oil, 1½ teaspoons of the oregano, the thyme, red pepper flakes and ½ teaspoon each of the salt and black pepper.

4 Place the potatoes and onions in a casserole or Dutch oven, drizzle 2 tablespoons of the herbed oil over them and toss to coat. Bake the casserole, uncovered, while you prepare the rest of the vegetables.

Step 5

5 Cut the bell peppers into thin strips. Cut the tomatoes into thin slices (or coarsely chop the canned tomatoes). Cut the zucchini into thin rounds. Add the peppers, tomatoes and zucchini to the casserole and drizzle the remaining herbed oil over them. Add the bay leaf, return the casserole to the oven and continue to bake while you brown the chicken.

6 In a large skillet, warm the butter in the remaining 1 tablespoon oil over medium-high heat until the butter is melted. Add the chicken, skin-side down, and cook until browned, about 5 minutes per side. Add the chicken to the casserole, cover and return to the oven.

7 To the skillet the chicken was browned in, add the wine, basil, remaining ½ teaspoon oregano, ½ teaspoon salt and ¼ teaspoon black pepper. Bring the mixture to a boil, scraping up any browned bits clinging to the pan. Pour this mixture over the chicken in the casserole, re-cover and bake for 20 to 25 minutes longer, or until the chicken is cooked through and the vegetables are meltingly soft. Remove the bay leaf before serving.

Values are approximate per serving: Calories: 401   Protein: 28 gm   Fat: 21 gm
Carbohydrates: 24 gm   Cholesterol: 79 mg   Sodium: 462 mg

Step 7

Alsatian Sausage and Cabbage Casserole

This cold-weather warmer is based on choucroute garnie, a hearty winter
dish from Alsace. An authentic Alsatian choucroute garnie is made with sauerkraut
and sausages, bacon, smoked pork and other smoked meats. This simpler version is
lighter in fat and sodium: Cabbage replaces some of the sauerkraut, and chicken is
used instead of some of the heavier meats. Beer is the perfect accompaniment.

Working time: 35 minutes
Total time: 1 hour 5 minutes

Alsatian Sausage and Cabbage Casserole

6 Servings

½ **pound sauerkraut**
1 **pound small red potatoes, unpeeled**
1 **teaspoon olive or other vegetable oil**
4 **slices bacon**
2 **medium onions**
½ **pound green cabbage**
1 **pound kielbasa, or other precooked smoked sausage**

½ **pound skinless, boneless chicken breast**
3 **cloves garlic, minced**
¼ **cup chopped parsley (optional)**
1 **teaspoon cumin seed or ½ teaspoon ground cumin**
½ **teaspoon pepper**
1 **bay leaf**
1 **cup dry white wine or low-sodium chicken broth**

1 Preheat the oven to 400°. Soak the sauerkraut in a bowl of cold water while you prepare the remaining ingredients.

2 Cut the potatoes into ¼-inch slices. Layer them in a shallow 2-quart casserole. Sprinkle the oil on top and toss the potatoes to lightly coat them. Bake, uncovered, for 20 minutes (they will be half-cooked, but will cook further in Step 9).

3 Meanwhile, in a large skillet, preferably nonstick, cook the bacon over medium heat until crisp, about 10 minutes. Drain the bacon on paper towels; crumble and set aside. Reserve 2 tablespoons of the fat in the skillet.

4 Meanwhile, coarsely chop the onions. Very finely shred the cabbage. Cut the kielbasa and the chicken into ¾-inch chunks.

5 Add the onions and garlic to the bacon fat in the skillet and cook over medium-high heat until browned, 3 to 4 minutes. Add the cabbage and cook, stirring, until slightly wilted, about 3 minutes. Remove the skillet from the heat.

6 Drain the sauerkraut, rinse under cold running water and drain well. Squeeze the sauerkraut dry with your hands and add it to the skillet. Stir in the bacon, parsley (if using), cumin and pepper.

7 Remove the potatoes from the oven but leave the oven on. Stir the potatoes to redistribute them. Add half of the sauerkraut-cabbage mixture, all of the kielbasa and chicken, and the bay leaf. Pour in the wine. Top with the remaining sauerkraut-cabbage mixture.

8 Cover the casserole and bake for 30 minutes, or until the potatoes are tender and the chicken is cooked through. Remove the bay leaf before serving.

Values are approximate per serving: Calories: 427 Protein: 23 gm Fat: 28 gm
Carbohydrates: 22 gm Cholesterol: 79 mg Sodium: 1077 mg

Step 2

Step 6

Step 7

Noodle-Stuffed Butternut Squash

Bread and rice are often used for making stuffing, so why not pasta? Here,
a combination of cooked egg noodles, savory ham, mellow Swiss cheese, onion and bell
peppers is used to fill butternut squash halves for an unusual, hearty main
dish. Instead of the egg noodles, you could use any small pasta shapes, such as elbow
macaroni, or long, thin pasta, such as spaghetti, broken into 2- to 3-inch lengths.

Working time: 35 minutes
Total time: 55 minutes

4 Servings

2 medium butternut squash (about 2½ pounds each)	**1 tablespoon butter**
1 medium onion	**1½ teaspoons olive or other vegetable oil**
1 medium red or green bell pepper	**2 cloves garlic, minced or crushed through a press**
¼ pound ham, preferably smoked, unsliced	**¾ teaspoon basil**
½ cup grated Swiss cheese	**¼ teaspoon salt**
¼ pound egg noodles	**¼ teaspoon black pepper**

1 Preheat the oven to 400°. Line a baking sheet with foil.

2 Halve the butternut squash lengthwise and remove the seeds and strings. Place the squash halves cut-side down on the baking sheet and bake for 30 minutes, or until tender. Preheat the broiler.

3 Meanwhile, coarsely chop the onion and bell pepper. Cut the ham into ½-inch cubes. Grate the cheese. Bring a large pot of water to a boil.

4 Scoop out the flesh of the cooled squash, leaving a scant ½-inch-thick shell. Coarsely chop the squash flesh.

5 Add the noodles to the boiling water and cook until al dente, 6 to 8 minutes, or according to package directions.

6 Meanwhile, in a large skillet, warm the butter in the oil over medium-high heat until the butter is melted. Add the onion and garlic, and stir-fry until the onion begins to brown, about 5 minutes. Add the bell pepper, basil, salt and black pepper to the skillet and cook until the bell pepper begins to soften, about 3 minutes.

7 Drain the noodles. Remove the skillet from the heat and stir in the ham, half of the cheese, the chopped squash and the drained noodles. Spoon the noodle stuffing into the squash shells and sprinkle with the remaining cheese.

8 Broil the stuffed squash 4 inches from the heat for 5 minutes, or until the cheese is bubbling and golden.

TIME-SAVERS

■ *Microwave tip: To cook the squash halves, place them in a shallow microwave-safe baking dish with ¼ cup water. Cover with plastic wrap and cook at 100% for 15 to 20 minutes, or until tender; rotate once or twice.*

Values are approximate per serving: Calories: 481   Protein: 20 gm   Fat: 13 gm
Carbohydrates: 80 gm   Cholesterol: 64 mg   Sodium: 653 mg

Step 3

Step 4

Step 7

Mini Cassoulet

In a true cassoulet—the French country version of baked beans—white beans are slowly baked with confit (goose or duck preserved in fat) and other meats. And making one is an all-day affair. In this quick version, canned beans, a game hen, spicy country sausage, vegetables and herbs are cooked in under an hour to produce a manageable—and delectable—one-pot meal.

Working time: 20 minutes
Total time: 55 minutes

Mini Cassoulet

4 Servings

1 teaspoon vegetable oil
1 Cornish game hen (about 1½
pounds), quartered, or 1½
pounds chicken parts
3 medium carrots
1 medium onion
½ pound country sausage
3 cloves garlic, minced or crushed
through a press

2 tablespoons flour
2 cups chicken broth
1½ teaspoons thyme
¼ teaspoon pepper
1 bay leaf
1 can (19 ounces) white kidney
beans
1 can (19 ounces) red kidney beans

Step 1

1 In a large skillet, warm the oil over medium heat until hot but not smoking. Add the Cornish hen quarters (or chicken parts) and brown all over, about 20 minutes.

2 Meanwhile, cut the carrots into 1-inch lengths. Thinly slice the onion.

3 Remove the hen to a plate and cover loosely to keep warm. Remove the sausage from its casings and crumble it into the skillet. Cook the sausage over medium heat for 5 minutes.

4 Add the onion and garlic and cook, stirring occasionally, until the onion begins to brown, about 5 minutes. Sprinkle the flour into the skillet and cook, stirring, until the flour is no longer visible, about 30 seconds.

Step 3

5 Return the Cornish hen to the skillet. Add the chicken broth, thyme, pepper, bay leaf and carrots. Bring to a boil over medium-high heat. Reduce the heat to low, cover and simmer for 10 minutes, or until the hen is nearly cooked through.

6 Meanwhile, rinse the canned white and red kidney beans under running water and drain well. Measure out about half the beans and coarsely purée them in the food processor.

7 Add the beans (puréed and whole) to the skillet and cook over medium heat until the hen is cooked through, about 10 minutes.

8 Remove the bay leaf before serving.

TIME-SAVERS

■ ***Do-ahead:*** *The whole dish can be made ahead and reheated.*

Values are approximate per serving: Calories: 749   Protein: 45 gm   Fat: 44 gm
Carbohydrates: 42 gm   Cholesterol: 125 mg   Sodium: 1307 mg

Step 7

Broccoli and Smoked Turkey Gratin with Two Cheeses

The term "gratin" most commonly refers to a dish with a golden topping of cheese and breadcrumbs. In this case, the cheese is not just the topping; it is also combined with the broccoli and smoked turkey in the casserole itself. The interplay of mellow Swiss and sharp Romano is unusual and good, and smoked turkey supplies yet another satisfying flavor. However, if smoked turkey is not available, try smoked chicken or ham.

Working time: 25 minutes
Total time: 55 minutes

Broccoli and Smoked Turkey Gratin with Two Cheeses

6 Servings

2 cups grated Swiss cheese (about 8 ounces)
3 tablespoons butter
¼ cup flour
1 cup milk
½ teaspoon nutmeg
¼ teaspoon pepper
¼ cup grated Romano or Parmesan cheese

2 tablespoons Dijon mustard
1 package (10 ounces) frozen chopped broccoli, thawed
¾ pound smoked turkey, unsliced
1 bunch scallions (6 to 8)
1 tablespoon fine unseasoned breadcrumbs

Step 1

1 Preheat the oven to 375°. Lightly butter a shallow 11 x 7-inch baking dish. Coarsely grate the Swiss cheese.

2 In a medium saucepan, warm the butter over medium heat until melted. Stir in the flour and cook, stirring, until the flour is no longer visible, about 1 minute. Stir in the milk, nutmeg and pepper, and cook, stirring, until the mixture is thickened, about 3 minutes.

3 Stir 1½ cups of the Swiss cheese, the Romano and mustard into the saucepan. Remove from the heat.

4 Squeeze the thawed broccoli with your hands to remove any excess moisture. Cut the turkey into ¾-inch cubes. Coarsely chop the scallions.

5 Stir the broccoli, turkey and scallions into the saucepan. Pour this mixture into the prepared baking dish. Sprinkle the top with the breadcrumbs and the remaining ½ cup grated Swiss cheese.

Step 4

6 Bake for about 30 minutes, or until light golden on top.

TIME-SAVERS

■ ***Microwave tip:*** *To make the whole dish in the microwave, prepare the recipe as directed, using a microwave-safe baking dish. Loosely cover with waxed paper and place the dish on an inverted plate. Cook at 100% for 3 minutes. Cook at 50% for 8 minutes, rotating the dish once about halfway through. Uncover and cook at 50% for 3 minutes, or until the center is heated through.*

■ ***Do-ahead:*** *The Swiss cheese can be grated and the broccoli, turkey and scallions cut up in advance. The whole dish can be baked ahead and served at room temperature or gently reheated.*

Step 5

Values are approximate per serving: Calories: 343 Protein: 26 gm Fat: 21 gm
Carbohydrates: 12 gm Cholesterol: 84 mg Sodium: 937 mg

Tex-Mex Lattice-Topped Pie

Hidden under the impressive lattice crust is a family-pleasing mix of chili-spiced ground beef and Cheddar cheese (the savory crust is made with Cheddar, too). Notice that the lattice is simply crisscrossed, not woven over-and-under. It's a timesaving step, but you can make a true lattice if you're so inclined. Some cooks find it easiest to weave the strips of dough on a sheet of waxed paper and then transfer the lattice to the pie.

Working time: 45 minutes
Total time: 1 hour

Tex-Mex Lattice-Topped Pie

8 Servings

1¾ cups flour	2 medium pickled jalapeño peppers
¾ cup cornmeal	1 tablespoon olive oil
½ teaspoon salt	4 cloves garlic, minced
6 tablespoons cold butter, cut into pieces	1 pound lean ground beef
4 tablespoons cold shortening	2 tablespoons chili powder
1½ cups shredded Cheddar cheese	2 teaspoons cumin
About 6 tablespoons ice water	1½ teaspoons oregano
1 large onion	1 egg yolk
4 large plum tomatoes	1 tablespoon milk
5 scallions	3 large romaine lettuce leaves
	½ cup sour cream

Step 4

1 In a large bowl, combine the flour, cornmeal and salt. Cut in the butter and shortening. Stir in 1 cup of the Cheddar cheese. Sprinkle in 4 to 6 tablespoons of the ice water and toss with a fork; the dough should barely hold together. Form the dough into two disks, one twice as large as the other; wrap well and chill while you prepare the filling.

2 Chop the onion, tomatoes and scallions. Mince the jalapeños.

3 In a large skillet, warm the oil over medium-high heat. Add the onion and garlic, and stir-fry for 5 minutes. Crumble in the beef and cook until it is no longer pink, 3 to 5 minutes. Add the jalapeños, the chili powder, cumin and oregano, and cook until fragrant, about 1 minute. Remove the skillet from the heat and stir in ⅓ cup each of the tomatoes and scallions.

4 Preheat the oven to 425°. On a floured surface, roll the larger of the two disks of dough into an 11-inch circle. Fit the dough into a 9-inch pie plate, leaving an even overhang all around. Roll out the remaining dough into a 10-inch circle and cut the circle into 8 strips.

Step 5

5 Spoon the filling into the pie shell and sprinkle with the remaining ½ cup Cheddar. Place 4 strips of dough across the pie. Place the remaining 4 strips of dough perpendicular to the first set. Crimp the ends of the lattice strips to seal them to the rim of the pie crust.

6 Beat the egg yolk and milk together to make an egg glaze. Brush the glaze over the top of the pie and bake the pie for 17 to 20 minutes, or until the crust is golden.

7 Meanwhile, shred the lettuce. Serve the pie with the remaining tomatoes and scallions, the shredded lettuce and sour cream.

Values are approximate per serving: Calories: 597   Protein: 21 gm   Fat: 40 gm
Carbohydrates: 37 gm   Cholesterol: 121 mg   Sodium: 484 mg

Step 5

Chinese Pork and Rice Casserole

In addition to the more familiar stir-fries, Chinese cuisine includes numerous casseroles, such as this one-pot meat-and-rice dish. Although this is made with pork, ground beef or turkey could easily be substituted; and regular green cabbage can be used if Chinese cabbage is not available. A side dish of sliced cucumbers and radishes, topped with scallion slivers, form a crisp and cooling counterpoint to the main dish.

Working time: 25 minutes
Total time: 50 minutes

Chinese Pork and Rice Casserole

4 Servings

4 quarter-size slices (¼ inch thick) fresh ginger, unpeeled
3 cloves garlic
4 scallions
2 medium carrots
4 cups chopped Chinese or Napa cabbage (about ¾ pound)
2 tablespoons Oriental sesame oil
¾ pound lean ground pork

1 cup raw rice
½ pound small mushrooms
1 cup beef broth
1 cup water
2 tablespoons reduced-sodium or regular soy sauce
2 tablespoons chopped parsley (optional)

Step 3

1 In a food processor, finely chop the ginger and garlic. Add the scallions and coarsely chop. Remove from the food processor and set aside.

2 In the same processor work bowl, coarsely chop the carrots. Remove and set aside. Add the Chinese cabbage and coarsely chop.

3 In a large skillet, warm 1 tablespoon of the sesame oil over medium-high heat until hot but not smoking. Add the ginger, garlic, scallions and ground pork and stir-fry, breaking up the meat, until the pork is no longer pink, about 5 minutes.

Step 4

4 Add the remaining 1 tablespoon oil and the rice. Reduce the heat to medium and cook, stirring, until the rice is completely coated with the oil.

5 Add the carrots, Chinese cabbage, whole mushrooms (halved if they are not small), beef broth, water and soy sauce and bring to a boil over medium-high heat. Reduce the heat to low, cover and simmer until the rice is tender, about 20 minutes. Stir in the parsley (if using).

TIME-SAVERS

■ **Do-ahead:** *The vegetables can be chopped ahead of time.*

Step 5

Values are approximate per serving: Calories: 431   Protein: 23 gm   Fat: 16 gm
Carbohydrates: 49 gm   Cholesterol: 58 mg   Sodium: 592 mg

Spinach-Cheese Pizza

Inspired by the Greek spinach and cheese pie called spanakopita, this pizza's
crust is topped with ricotta redolent with garlic, lemon zest and plenty of oregano.
Fresh spinach, shredded mozzarella, and a dusting of Parmesan are
layered over the ricotta. For a super-quick pie, pick up a prepared pizza crust
from the supermarket dairy case instead of making the crust from scratch.

Working time: 40 minutes
Total time: 1 hour 45 minutes

Spinach-Cheese Pizza

6 Servings

⅔ cup lukewarm water
1½ teaspoons active dry yeast (½ package)
2¼ cups plus 2 tablespoons flour
¾ teaspoon salt
¼ cup olive or other vegetable oil
4 cloves garlic
1 container (15 ounces) part-skim ricotta cheese
1 tablespoon lemon juice
2 teaspoons grated lemon zest

1 teaspoon oregano
½ teaspoon pepper
1 egg
1 pound fresh spinach, stemmed, or 1 package (10 ounces) frozen leaf spinach, thawed
1 tablespoon cornmeal
½ pound shredded part-skim mozzarella cheese
3 tablespoons grated Parmesan cheese

Step 6

1 Place the water in a small bowl and sprinkle the yeast on top. Set aside until the yeast is dissolved, about 5 minutes.

2 In a large bowl, combine 2¼ cups of the flour and the salt. Make a well in the center and add the yeast mixture and 2 tablespoons of the oil. Blend until a cohesive dough is formed.

3 Place the dough on a floured work surface. Sprinkle the remaining 2 tablespoons flour over the dough and knead until smooth and elastic, about 5 minutes. Place the dough in an oiled bowl and turn to coat it with oil. Cover the bowl with a damp towel and set aside in a warm place until almost doubled in bulk, about 1 hour.

4 Meanwhile, in a food processor, mince the garlic. Add the ricotta, lemon juice, lemon zest, oregano and pepper, and process to purée. Add the egg and pulse to blend.

Step 7

5 Steam the fresh or frozen spinach in a steamer until just limp, 3 to 4 minutes. Remove the spinach to paper towels to drain. (If using frozen spinach, squeeze to remove as much moisture as possible.)

6 When the dough has risen, preheat the oven to 475°. Lightly dust a baking sheet with the cornmeal. Punch the dough down, then roll it out on a lightly floured surface to a 12-inch round. Transfer the dough round to the baking sheet.

7 Spread the ricotta mixture over the dough, leaving a 1-inch border all around. Cover the ricotta with the spinach leaves and drizzle the spinach with the remaining 2 tablespoons oil. Sprinkle the mozzarella and Parmesan on top and bake for 17 to 20 minutes, or until the edges of the dough are browned.

Values are approximate per serving: Calories: 521 Protein: 26 gm Fat: 25 gm
Carbohydrates: 47 gm Cholesterol: 81 mg Sodium: 642 mg

Step 7

Skillet Potato Pie with Eggs and Cheese

▼

This marvelously homey dish should be served directly from the skillet, preferably a large cast-iron one. To round out the meal, serve a tossed green salad with a light vinaigrette. To make preparation faster and easier, buy potatoes that are small enough to go through the feed tube of a food processor without having to be cut to size.

Working time: 40 minutes
Total time: 50 minutes

Skillet Potato Pie with Eggs and Cheese

4 Servings

9 small red potatoes (about 1½ pounds), unpeeled
4 slices bacon
1 medium onion
5 eggs
2 tablespoons milk
½ teaspoon thyme

½ teaspoon salt
¼ teaspoon pepper
2 tablespoons chopped parsley (optional)
1 cup grated Cheddar cheese (about ¼ pound)

1 Preheat the oven to 375°.

2 With the slicing blade of a food processor, cut the potatoes into ⅛-inch-thick slices.

3 In a large ovenproof skillet, cook the bacon over medium heat until crisp, about 10 minutes. Reserving the fat in the skillet, drain the bacon on paper towels; crumble and set aside.

4 Meanwhile, coarsely chop the onion. Add the onion to the skillet and sauté over medium heat until softened but not browned, about 7 minutes.

5 Add the potato slices and gently toss them with the onions. Cook over medium-high heat, turning frequently, until the potatoes are tender, about 15 minutes.

6 In a medium bowl, beat the eggs with the milk, thyme, salt, pepper and parsley (if using). Stir in the Cheddar.

7 Pour the egg-cheese mixture over the potatoes and sprinkle the crumbled bacon on top.

8 Place the skillet in the oven and bake until the eggs are set, 8 to 10 minutes. Serve hot, directly from the skillet.

TIME-SAVERS

■ *Microwave tip: Cook the bacon on paper towels at 100% for 3 to 4 minutes. Crumble and set aside. In a large microwave-safe casserole, toss the potatoes and finely chopped onion with 2 tablespoons of olive oil. Loosely cover with plastic wrap and cook at 100% for 12 to 14 minutes, stirring once, or until the potatoes are tender. Pour in the egg-cheese mixture and stir. Re-cover and cook at 50%, rotating the dish once, for 4 to 6 minutes, or until the eggs are just set. Let stand 3 minutes.*

Values are approximate per serving: Calories: 481   Protein: 21 gm   Fat: 28 gm
Carbohydrates: 34 gm   Cholesterol: 385 mg   Sodium: 606 mg

Step 2

Step 5

Step 7

Pennsylvania German-Style Broccoli (page 281).

CHAPTER 6
SIDE DISHES

Bayou Beans and Rice

In Louisiana's Cajun country, red beans and rice is traditionally cooked up
on Monday, using the remains of Sunday's ham as a flavorful base. In this lightened
version, the beans and rice pick up plenty of flavor from garlic, scallions, bell
peppers, herbs and spices. For an authentic touch, make sure there are bottles of
hot pepper sauce and vinegar on the table.

Working time: 20 minutes
Total time: 25 minutes

Bayou Beans and Rice

4 Servings

1½ cups low-sodium chicken broth
1 cup water
1 teaspoon oregano
1 teaspoon thyme
¼ teaspoon hot pepper flakes
1 cup raw rice
2 tablespoons olive or other vegetable oil
5 cloves garlic, minced or crushed through a press

½ teaspoon salt (optional)
¼ teaspoon black pepper
Pinch of cayenne pepper
1 bunch scallions (6 to 8)
1 medium red bell pepper
1 medium green bell pepper
1 can (19 ounces) red kidney beans

Step 3

1 In a medium saucepan, combine 1 cup of the chicken broth, the water, ½ teaspoon each of the oregano and thyme, and ⅛ teaspoon of the hot pepper flakes. Bring the mixture to a boil, add the rice, reduce the heat to medium-low, cover and simmer until the rice is tender and all the liquid is absorbed, about 20 minutes.

2 Meanwhile, in another medium saucepan, combine the remaining ½ cup chicken broth, the oil, garlic, salt (if using), black pepper, the remaining ½ teaspoon each oregano and thyme, the remaining ⅛ teaspoon hot pepper flakes and the cayenne. Bring the mixture to a boil, then reduce the heat to low, cover and simmer while you prepare the remaining ingredients.

3 Coarsely chop the scallions and bell peppers. Drain the beans, then rinse them under running water and drain well.

Step 4

4 Add the bell peppers to the seasoned broth and bring the mixture to a boil over medium-high heat. Add the beans, cook for about 1 minute, then remove from the heat, cover and set aside until ready to serve.

5 Stir the scallions into the rice when it is done. Serve the rice topped with the beans.

TIME-SAVERS

■ **Do-ahead:** *The bell-pepper-and-bean mixture can be made ahead and gently reheated.*

Values are approximate per serving: Calories: 373 Protein: 12 gm Fat: 8 gm
Carbohydrates: 63 gm Cholesterol: 0 mg Sodium: 493 mg

Step 5

Bell Peppers Stuffed with Corn, Beans and Rice

Although these stuffed peppers are designed to be a low-calorie entrée, they could just as easily be a hearty vegetable side dish. If you can't get red and yellow peppers, use all green ones (although their flavor is slightly less sweet). If, on the other hand, the produce section of your supermarket leans toward the exotic, look for orange, purple or chocolate-brown bell peppers and serve an even more colorful meal.

Working time: 15 minutes
Total time: 50 minutes

Bell Peppers Stuffed with Corn, Beans and Rice

4 Servings

2 plum tomatoes or 2 whole canned tomatoes, well drained
1 small onion
¼ cup packed fresh basil leaves or 1 teaspoon dried
1½ cups low-sodium chicken broth
3 cloves garlic, minced or crushed through a press
2 tablespoons lemon juice
3 teaspoons grated lemon zest (optional)

1 teaspoon oregano
¼ teaspoon black pepper
½ cup frozen corn
¾ cup raw rice
4 large bell peppers, preferably a mixture of red, green and yellow
1 cup canned black beans, rinsed and well drained
3 tablespoons grated Parmesan cheese

Step 4

1 Coarsely chop the tomatoes and onion. Mince the basil.

2 In a medium saucepan, bring the chicken broth to a boil over medium-high heat. Add the tomatoes, onion, basil, garlic, lemon juice, lemon zest (if using), oregano, black pepper, corn and rice. Let the mixture return to a boil, then reduce the heat to low, cover and simmer until the rice is tender and has absorbed all the liquid, about 20 minutes.

3 Preheat the oven to 350°.

4 Meanwhile, cut an opening in the tops of the bell peppers and remove the stems, seeds and ribs, leaving the rest of the pepper intact. Stand them upright in a baking dish. (If necessary, shave a small piece off the bottoms of the peppers so they will stand upright.)

5 Stir the black beans into the cooked rice.

Step 5

6 Dividing evenly, stuff the peppers with the rice mixture. Top with the Parmesan cheese. Bake for 15 minutes, or until the cheese is almost golden.

TIME-SAVERS

■ **Microwave tip:** *Prepare the peppers as directed, but place them in a microwave-safe casserole. Cover and cook at 100%, rotating once, for 8 minutes, or until heated through.*

■ **Do-ahead:** *The corn, bean and rice mixture can be made ahead. The whole dish can be assembled ahead and then cooked later, either in a conventional oven or in the microwave.*

Step 6

Values are approximate per serving: Calories: 259 Protein: 10 gm Fat: 3 gm
Carbohydrates: 49 gm Cholesterol: 3 mg Sodium: 231 mg

Pepper-Walnut
Rice Skillet

Instead of serving either rice or pasta as a side dish, try combining the two for an interesting blend of textures and tastes. Here, the starches are cooked pilaf-style (sautéed with onion and garlic until golden before they are cooked in broth). Just about any small pasta will do for this recipe. And, depending on your preferences—and what's in the pantry—you can substitute pecans, almonds, or even pine nuts for the walnuts.

Working time: 25 minutes
Total time: 40 minutes

Pepper-Walnut
Rice Skillet

4 Servings

1 **medium onion**	1½ **cups chicken broth**
2 **tablespoons butter**	1 **cup water**
1 **tablespoon olive or other**	¾ **teaspoon crumbled sage**
vegetable oil	¼ **teaspoon black pepper**
1 **clove garlic, minced or crushed**	1 **medium green bell pepper**
through a press	1 **medium yellow bell pepper**
1 **cup raw rice**	1 **cup walnut pieces (about 4**
1 **cup small pasta shells or elbow**	**ounces)**
macaroni	

Step 3

1 Coarsely chop the onion.

2 In a large skillet, warm 1 tablespoon of the butter in the oil over medium-high heat until the butter is melted. Add the onion and garlic and stir-fry until the mixture begins to brown, about 3 minutes.

3 Add the remaining 1 tablespoon butter, the rice and pasta, and cook, stirring, until the rice begins to turn golden, about 3 minutes.

4 Add the chicken broth, water, sage and black pepper, and bring the mixture to a boil over medium-high heat. Reduce the heat to low, cover and simmer for 10 minutes.

5 Meanwhile, cut the bell peppers into bite-size pieces.

Step 5

6 Add the bell peppers to the skillet and mix in thoroughly. Re-cover and cook over low heat, stirring occasionally, until the rice and pasta are cooked through and the peppers are crisp-tender, about 12 minutes.

7 Meanwhile, finely chop the walnuts. In an ungreased skillet, cook the walnuts over medium heat, shaking frequently, until they are lightly toasted, 2 to 3 minutes.

8 Stir the toasted walnuts into the rice mixture just before serving.

TIME-SAVERS

■ ***Do-ahead:*** *The vegetables can be prepared and the walnuts toasted in advance. The whole dish can be made ahead and reheated in the microwave.*

Step 7

Values are approximate per serving: Calories: 557 Protein: 12 gm Fat: 28 gm
Carbohydrates: 66 gm Cholesterol: 16 mg Sodium: 437 mg

Layered Vegetable Casserole

Flash-cooked vegetables—steamed or blanched and served still crisp—are so popular today that we sometimes forget how delicious our garden favorites are when slowly baked. Onions and garlic become mild and sweet, and the flavors of bell peppers and tomatoes are intensified. To make this side dish a one-pot meal, cook chicken breasts or thighs on top of the vegetables for the last 20 to 25 minutes of baking.

Working time: 20 minutes
Total time: 1 hour 10 minutes

Layered Vegetable Casserole

8 Servings

1 tablespoon butter
2 tablespoons olive or other vegetable oil
1 clove garlic, minced or crushed through a press
1 pound plum tomatoes
½ pound small mushrooms
2 medium onions
1 large yellow bell pepper
1 large green bell pepper
⅔ cup grated Parmesan cheese
½ cup fine unseasoned breadcrumbs
2 tablespoons oregano
½ teaspoon black pepper

1 Preheat the oven to 375°.

2 In a small skillet, warm the butter in the oil over medium heat. Add the garlic and cook, stirring occasionally, until it begins to brown, about 3 minutes. Remove from the heat.

Step 3

3 Thinly slice the tomatoes. Halve the mushrooms if they are large. Thinly slice the onions. Cut the bell peppers into thin strips.

4 In a medium bowl, combine the Parmesan, breadcrumbs, oregano and black pepper.

5 Place the onions in the bottom of a shallow 3-quart baking dish or casserole. Sprinkle with some of the breadcrumb mixture. Follow with layers of the bell peppers, mushrooms and tomatoes, sprinkling some of the breadcrumb mixture on top of each layer as you go. Top the casserole with any remaining breadcrumb mixture.

Step 5

6 Drizzle the garlic oil over the entire casserole. Cover and bake for 30 minutes.

7 Uncover and bake for 20 minutes longer, or until the vegetables are tender.

TIME-SAVERS

■ *Microwave tip: Combine the butter, oil and garlic in a small custard cup. Cook at 100% for 30 seconds to 1 minute, until the butter is melted and the garlic is fragrant. Prepare all of the vegetables as instructed. In a shallow microwave-safe casserole, place the onion layer, some of the breadcrumb mixture and the bell pepper layers, and drizzle with half the garlic oil. Cover with waxed paper and cook at 100% for 8 minutes. Finish assembling the casserole with the mushrooms, tomatoes, remaining breadcrumb mixture and garlic oil. Cook, uncovered, at 100% for 9 minutes, or until the vegetables are crisp-tender.*

Values are approximate per serving: Calories: 133 Protein: 5 gm Fat: 8 gm
Carbohydrates: 12 gm Cholesterol: 9 mg Sodium: 192 mg

Step 6

Orange-Filled Baked Acorn Squash

Acorn squash halves, with the contrasting colors of their deep-green shells and their orange-gold flesh, make a particularly attractive side dish. In this recipe, the squash is baked, brushed with melted butter and then filled with a sour cream sauce containing chunks of orange, orange zest and juice. The sauce is seasoned with the unusual combination of nutmeg and basil.

Working time: 15 minutes
Total time: 40 minutes

Orange-Filled Baked Acorn Squash

1 Servings

2 medium acorn squash (about 1¾ pounds each)

3 oranges

½ cup sour cream

1 teaspoon brown sugar

2 tablespoons chopped fresh basil or 1 teaspoon dried

¼ teaspoon nutmeg

½ teaspoon salt

1 tablespoon butter

Step 2

1 Preheat the oven to 400°. Line a baking pan with foil.

2 Halve the acorn squash lengthwise and remove the strings and seeds. Place the squash cut-side down on the prepared baking pan and bake for 30 minutes.

3 Meanwhile, grate one of the oranges to yield 2 teaspoons of zest. Juice the orange and measure out ¼ cup. Peel the remaining 2 oranges, removing as much of the bitter white pith as possible. Coarsely chop the oranges and set aside.

4 In a small bowl, combine the sour cream, orange juice, orange zest, brown sugar, basil, nutmeg and salt.

5 Melt the butter on the stovetop or in the microwave.

6 Turn the squash cut-side up, brush with the melted butter and bake for about 5 minutes longer, or until the squash is tender.

Step 4

7 Stir the chopped orange into the sour cream mixture. Dividing evenly, spoon the mixture into the acorn squash halves and serve.

TIME-SAVERS

■ *Microwave tip: To cook the squash, place it, cut-side down, in a shallow microwave-safe baking dish. Cover loosely and cook at 100% for 12 minutes, rotating the dish (or rearranging the squash) once about halfway through.*

■ *Do-ahead: The oranges can be prepared and the sour cream mixture made (Step 4) ahead of time. Do not combine the sour cream mixture with the chopped oranges until just before serving.*

Step 6

Values are approximate per serving: Calories: 196 Protein: 3 gm Fat: 9 gm
Carbohydrates: 29 gm Cholesterol: 20 mg Sodium: 323 mg

Pennsylvania German-Style Broccoli

*Pennsylvania German cooks, like their German forebears, often serve vegetables
with pungent warm dressings. Here, steamed broccoli is tossed with a hot vinaigrette
that's flavored with bacon, vinegar, mustard and black pepper. This dish can
also be made with frozen broccoli: Use two ten-ounce packages of whole broccoli spears,
thawed and well drained, but not steamed.*

Working time: 15 minutes
Total time: 25 minutes

6 Servings

4 slices bacon	4 teaspoons spicy brown mustard
1 pound broccoli	¾ teaspoon sugar
4 scallions	¾ teaspoon salt
1 medium red bell pepper	½ teaspoon black pepper
⅓ cup cider vinegar	2 tablespoons vegetable oil

1 In a medium skillet, cook the bacon over medium heat until crisp, about 10 minutes. Drain the bacon on paper towels, crumble and set aside. Pour off all but 3 tablespoons of bacon fat from the pan; set the pan aside.

2 Meanwhile, cut the broccoli into bite-size pieces. Steam the broccoli pieces in a vegetable steamer until they are crisp-tender, about 8 minutes.

3 Meanwhile, coarsely chop the scallions and bell pepper and place them in a serving bowl.

4 Add the cooked broccoli to the serving bowl.

5 Warm the bacon fat in the skillet over medium heat. Add the vinegar, mustard, sugar, salt and black pepper. Cook, stirring constantly to scrape up the pan drippings. Remove from the heat and stir in the oil. Pour the hot dressing over the vegetables and toss to combine.

6 Sprinkle the crumbled bacon over the broccoli and serve.

TIME-SAVERS

■ **Microwave tip:** *To cook the broccoli, place it in a microwave-safe dish with 1 tablespoon of water. Cover and cook at 100% for 5 minutes, or until crisp-tender.*

■ **Do-ahead:** *The bacon can be cooked and the dressing (Steps 1 and 5) made ahead and reheated.*

Step 1

Step 2

Step 5

Values are approximate per serving: Calories: 137   Protein: 3 gm   Fat: 12 gm
Carbohydrates: 5 gm   Cholesterol: 8 mg   Sodium: 421 mg

Spicy Broccoli and Corn Custards

These steamed custards belong to a family of molded dishes called timbales, which make elegant accompaniments to a meal. Here, cottage cheese and sour cream are blended into a rich custard, to which corn and broccoli—in their easy-to-use frozen forms—are added. Baking the timbales in a water-filled pan tempers the oven's heat to protect the delicate custard from overcooking.

Working time: 15 minutes
Total time: 55 minutes

Spicy Broccoli and Corn Custards

4 Servings

1 package (10 ounces) frozen chopped broccoli, thawed	½ teaspoon salt
	¼ teaspoon black pepper
1 package (10 ounces) frozen corn, thawed	Pinch of cayenne pepper
	2 tablespoons chopped chives or scallion greens
1 cup cottage cheese	
3 eggs	3 tablespoons grated Parmesan cheese
⅔ cup sour cream	
1 tablespoon chili powder	

1 Preheat the oven to 325°. Lightly butter four 1-cup ramekins or custard cups.

2 Place the thawed frozen broccoli and corn on several layers of paper towel to drain; squeeze them in the towels if necessary to remove excess moisture.

3 In a food processor, puree the cottage cheese. Add the eggs, one at a time, and process until blended. Blend in the sour cream, chili powder, salt, black pepper and cayenne.

4 In a medium bowl, stir together the broccoli, corn, cottage cheese-egg mixture and chives.

Step 4

5 Dividing evenly, spoon the mixture into the prepared ramekins. Sprinkle the tops with the Parmesan.

6 Place the ramekins in a roasting pan and add hot water to come halfway up the sides of the ramekins. Place the roasting pan in the oven and bake for 45 minutes, or until a knife inserted in the center of the custard comes out clean. Serve warm, in the ramekins.

Step 5

TIME-SAVERS

■ *Microwave tip: To thaw the broccoli and corn, remove any foil. Place the vegetables on a microwave-safe plate and cook at 100% for 6 minutes.*

■ *Microwave tip: To make the whole dish in the microwave, prepare the recipe as directed (but do not butter the ramekins). Place the filled ramekins in a circular pattern on a large microwave-safe plate. Cook at 50% until a knife inserted near the center of a custard comes out clean, 8 to 10 minutes, rotating the plate once halfway through.*

■ *Do-ahead: The custards can be made a short while ahead and served at room temperature.*

Values are approximate per serving: Calories: 296   Protein: 18 gm   Fat: 16 gm
Carbohydrates: 23 gm   Cholesterol: 187 mg   Sodium: 662 mg

Step 6

Orange-Glazed Beets

▼

Fresh beets have a wonderfully complex flavor, earthy and sweet, but they can be tricky to cook. Depending on the age of the beets when picked, they may require as little as twenty minutes or as much as an hour (or more) to reach tenderness. If time is at a premium, you can prepare this dish with well-drained canned sliced beets: Make the orange glaze as directed, then add the beets and cook just until heated through.

Working time: 35 minutes
Total time: 1 hour

Orange-Glazed Beets

4 Servings

2 pounds small beets
3 tablespoons butter
1 can (6 ounces) frozen orange juice
  concentrate
2 teaspoons grated orange zest
  (optional)

1 tablespoon sugar
½ teaspoon salt
¼ teaspoon pepper
2 scallions

1 Bring a large saucepan of water to a boil.

2 Meanwhile, trim the beets.

3 Place the beets in the boiling water and cook at a low boil for 25 minutes. Remove the beets to a plate to cool.

Step 2

4 Meanwhile, in a large skillet, warm the butter over medium heat until it is melted. Add the orange juice concentrate, orange zest (if using), sugar, salt and pepper, and bring to a boil. Reduce the heat to low, cover and simmer for 10 minutes.

5 Peel the beets and cut them into thin rounds.

6 Return the orange glaze to a boil over medium-high heat, add the beets and let the mixture return to the boil. Reduce the heat to medium-low, cover and simmer, stirring occasionally, until the beets are heated through, 2 to 3 minutes.

7 Meanwhile, coarsely chop the scallions. Just before serving, toss the scallions with the beets.

Step 5

TIME-SAVERS

■ ***Microwave tip:*** *Combine the trimmed beets and ½ cup water in a casserole. Cover and cook at 100% for 20 minutes, stirring twice. Let the beets cool; then peel and slice. Return the sliced beets to the casserole and stir in the butter, orange juice concentrate, zest, sugar, salt and pepper. Cover and cook at 100% for 5 minutes, stirring twice.*

■ ***Do-ahead:*** *The beets can be cooked and the orange glaze (Step 4) prepared ahead.*

Values are approximate per serving: Calories: 245   Protein: 4 gm   Fat: 9 gm
Carbohydrates: 40 gm   Cholesterol: 23 mg   Sodium: 478 mg

Step 6

Creamy Herb-Stuffed Mushrooms

Stuffed mushroom caps make an unusual side dish, an elegant first course, or even a vegetarian entrée if you double the recipe. The filling—made with the mushroom stems, cottage cheese, Parmesan, shallots and garlic—is topped with breadcrumbs and a drizzle of olive oil. If you can buy mushrooms loose, rather than in packages, look for good-sized ones to save on preparation time and make impressive portions.

Working time: 25 minutes
Total time: 40 minutes

Creamy Herb-Stuffed Mushrooms

4 Servings

16 large mushrooms (about 1 pound)
4 medium shallots or 1 small onion
3 cloves garlic
3 tablespoons butter
1 teaspoon oregano
½ cup cottage cheese
2 tablespoons grated Parmesan
2 tablespoons chopped parsley (optional)
¼ teaspoon pepper
2 tablespoons fine unseasoned breadcrumbs
1 tablespoon olive oil

1 Preheat the oven to 400°. Lightly butter a baking dish just large enough to hold the mushrooms.

2 Remove the stems from the mushrooms and place the caps, rounded-side down, in the buttered baking dish.

3 In a food processor, finely chop the shallots (or onion) and garlic; remove and set aside. In the same processor work bowl, coarsely chop the mushroom stems.

4 In a medium skillet, warm 1 tablespoon of the butter over medium heat until melted. Add the shallots and garlic and sauté until the shallots are translucent, about 2 minutes.

5 Add the remaining 2 tablespoons butter, the mushroom stems and the oregano. Sauté until the mushrooms are limp, 3 to 5 minutes. Remove the skillet from the heat.

6 In a medium bowl, combine the cottage cheese, Parmesan, parsley (if using), pepper and the shallot-mushroom mixture.

7 Dividing evenly, stuff the mushroom caps with about 1½ tablespoons of the cottage cheese mixture. Sprinkle with the breadcrumbs and drizzle with the oil. Bake for 15 minutes, or until the topping starts to brown.

TIME-SAVERS

■ *Microwave tip: Combine the chopped mushroom stems, shallots and garlic with 1 tablespoon of butter in a microwave-safe bowl. Cover with plastic wrap and cook at 100% for 4 minutes, stirring once. Prepare the stuffing and fill the mushrooms as instructed above. Arrange the mushroom caps in a microwave-safe baking dish. Cover loosely with waxed paper and cook at 100% for 9 minutes, rotating the dish once. If desired, brown the mushroom caps under the broiler before serving.*

Values are approximate per serving: Calories: 196   Protein: 8 gm   Fat: 15 gm
Carbohydrates: 11 gm   Cholesterol: 29 mg   Sodium: 270 mg

Step 2

Step 6

Step 7

Spicy Corn and Green Chili Pudding

▼

The next time you're setting up a buffet for a casual party or planning a picnic menu, include this spicy corn pudding. It's a great partner for barbecued poultry, hamburgers or steaks. You don't need to bake the pudding at the last minute: If necessary, make it up to an hour ahead of time and cover the pan loosely with foil to keep it warm.

Working time: 15 minutes
Total time: 1 hour

Spicy Corn and
Green Chili Pudding

6 Servings

½ **pound Monterey jack cheese**
¾ **cup yellow cornmeal**
2 **tablespoons chili powder**
½ **teaspoon baking powder**
½ **teaspoon salt**
½ **teaspoon black pepper**
Pinch of cayenne pepper

3 **eggs**
1 **cup sour cream**
1 **cup milk**
2 **cans (4 ounces each) chopped
   mild green chilies, drained**
1 **package (10 ounces) frozen corn,
   thawed**

1 Preheat the oven to 375°. Butter a shallow 1½-quart casserole or baking dish.

2 Shred the cheese.

3 In a medium bowl, stir together the cornmeal, chili powder, baking powder, salt, black pepper and cayenne.

4 In a large bowl, beat the eggs. Beat in the sour cream and milk.

5 Stir the green chilies, corn and 1½ cups of the cheese into the egg mixture. Stir in the cornmeal mixture.

6 Pour the batter into the prepared dish and sprinkle the remaining cheese on top. Bake for 45 to 50 minutes, or until the pudding is set and the top is golden.

Step 2

Step 4

Step 5

Values are approximate per serving: Calories: 408 Protein: 18 gm Fat: 24 gm
Carbohydrates: 31 gm Cholesterol: 162 mg Sodium: 750 mg

Paprika Vegetables

This vegetable medley derives its warm, rich taste from paprika—a spice that is made by drying and grinding different types of red bell peppers. Paprika may be sweet or pungent, depending on whether the peppers' seeds are ground along with the flesh. The paprika in the supermarket is likely to be a sweet Spanish variety; you may also find Hungarian paprika, which comes in sweet, medium-hot and hot versions.

Working time: 20 minutes
Total time: 30 minutes

Paprika Vegetables

6 Servings

⅓ cup olive or other vegetable oil
¼ cup white wine vinegar or cider vinegar
1 tablespoon tomato paste
3 garlic cloves, minced or crushed through a press
1 to 2 teaspoons paprika, to taste
1 teaspoon oregano

½ teaspoon salt
¼ teaspoon black pepper
1 small head cauliflower (about 2¼ pounds)
1 large zucchini (about ½ pound)
1 large red bell pepper
2 medium carrots

1 In a small saucepan, combine the olive oil, vinegar, tomato paste, garlic, paprika, oregano, salt and black pepper. Warm over medium heat, then reduce the heat to low, cover and simmer while you prepare the vegetables.

2 Cut the cauliflower into florets. Halve the zucchini lengthwise and then cut crosswise into ¼-inch-thick half-rounds. Cut the bell pepper into 1-inch squares. Cut the carrots on the diagonal into ¼-inch-thick slices.

3 Steam the vegetables in a vegetable steamer until just crisp-tender, about 10 minutes.

4 Transfer the hot vegetables to a serving bowl and toss with the hot paprika vinaigrette.

TIME-SAVERS

■ **Do-ahead:** *The dressing and vegetables can be prepared in advance, or the whole dish made ahead and served at room temperature.*

Step 1

Step 2

Step 4

Values are approximate per serving: Calories: 149 Protein: 2 gm Fat: 12 gm
Carbohydrates: 10 gm Cholesterol: 0 mg Sodium: 224 mg

Sesame-Garlic Zucchini

This deeply flavored, sesame-garlic zucchini dish is a delicious accompaniment to broiled steak, hamburgers or chicken, and also makes a good light meal on its own. Serve double portions as a lunch or supper main dish, along with a big basket of warm, crisp-crusted bread. For a more colorful presentation, use half yellow squash and half zucchini; another time, try this recipe with baby eggplants.

▼

Working time: 20 minutes
Total time: 25 minutes

Sesame-Garlic Zucchini

4 Servings

4 medium zucchini (about 1¾
   pounds total)
5 cloves garlic
3 medium scallions
2 tablespoons Oriental sesame oil

3 tablespoons reduced-sodium or
   regular soy sauce
1 tablespoon red wine vinegar or
   cider vinegar

1 Halve the zucchini lengthwise. With a sharp paring knife, cut the zucchini flesh in a diamond pattern without piercing the skin.

2 Place the zucchini halves in a vegetable steamer, cover and steam until tender, 7 to 9 minutes.

3 Meanwhile, in a food processor, mince the garlic. Add the scallions and mince.

4 In a small skillet, warm the sesame oil over medium-high heat until hot but not smoking. Add the garlic-scallion mixture and cook until the garlic is fragrant and the scallions are slightly softened, about 3 minutes.

5 Remove the skillet from the heat and add the soy sauce and vinegar.

6 When the zucchini are done, place them on a serving platter and spoon the sesame-garlic mixture over them. Serve hot, warm or at room temperature.

TIME-SAVERS

■ *Microwave tip: Arrange the zucchini in a shallow microwave-safe baking dish. Cover with plastic wrap and cook at 100% for 7 minutes, or until just tender, rearranging once. Proceed with the recipe as directed above.*

■ *Do-ahead: The sesame-garlic mixture (Steps 3 through 5) can be made ahead. The whole dish can be cooked ahead and served at room temperature.*

Values are approximate per serving: Calories: 103   Protein: 3 gm   Fat: 7 gm
Carbohydrates: 9 gm   Cholesterol: 0 mg   Sodium: 457 mg

Step 1

Step 4

Step 6

Quick Winter Vegetable Sauté

This hot, savory sauté makes good use of sturdy winter vegetables. The onion, cabbage, carrots and broccoli can be shredded in seconds in a food processor—and there's no need to clean the processor bowl between vegetables. Although the mild sweetness of the caraway nicely complements these winter vegetables, if you don't care for its flavor, substitute dill or toasted sesame seeds.

Working time: 10 minutes
Total time: 20 minutes

Quick Winter Vegetable Sauté

4 Servings

1 large stalk broccoli
1 medium onion
½ small head of cabbage (about ½ pound)
2 medium carrots
2 tablespoons butter
2 tablespoons olive or other vegetable oil

2 cloves garlic, minced or crushed through a press
1 teaspoon caraway seeds, crushed
½ teaspoon salt
½ teaspoon pepper

Step 3

1 In a food processor, with the shredding blade, shred the onion and set aside.

2 Remove the florets from the broccoli stalk and reserve the stalk. Cut the florets into bite-size pieces and set aside.

3 Then shred the cabbage, carrots and broccoli stalk, removing the shredded vegetables to a large bowl as the food processor gets too full.

4 In a large skillet, warm the butter in the olive oil over medium-high heat until the butter is melted. Add the shredded onion and garlic and stir-fry for about 2 minutes.

5 Add the broccoli florets, the rest of the shredded vegetables, the caraway seeds, salt and pepper. Cook, stirring frequently, until the broccoli is crisp-tender and the rest of the vegetables are tender, 5 to 8 minutes.

Step 4

TIME-SAVERS

■ **Do-ahead:** *All of the vegetables can be cut up ahead*

Values are approximate per serving: Calories: 167 Protein: 3 gm Fat: 13 gm
Carbohydrates: 12 gm Cholesterol: 16 mg Sodium: 371 mg

Step 5

Hoppin' John Salad

The Southern dish called Hoppin' John is made by cooking black-eyed peas
(also known as cowpeas) and rice with bacon or ham. Traditionally served on New
Year's Day, Hoppin' John is believed to bring good luck in the coming year.
Here, the bacon is replaced by a lemon-mustard dressing, the black-eyed peas and rice
are combined with colorful vegetables, and the dish is served at room temperature.

Working time: 15 minutes
Total time: 25 minutes

6 Servings

1 cup water
½ cup raw rice
1 package (10 ounces) frozen black-eyed peas, thawed
4 plum tomatoes or 2 medium tomatoes
3 ribs celery
1 large yellow or red bell pepper
6 scallions

3 tablespoons lemon juice
1 tablespoon yellow mustard
1 clove garlic, minced or crushed through a press
4 teaspoons grated lemon zest (optional)
½ teaspoon black pepper
⅓ cup olive or other vegetable oil

Step 1

1 In a medium saucepan, bring the water, rice and black-eyed peas to a boil over medium-high heat. Reduce the heat to medium-low, cover and simmer until the rice and black-eyed peas are tender and all the liquid is absorbed, 15 to 20 minutes. Remove from the heat and set aside to cool slightly.

2 Meanwhile, coarsely chop the tomatoes, celery, bell pepper and scallions, and place in a large salad bowl.

3 In a small bowl, combine the lemon juice, mustard, garlic, lemon zest (if using) and black pepper. Whisk in the olive oil.

Step 3

4 Add the rice and black-eyed peas to the vegetables. Add the dressing and toss to combine.

TIME-SAVERS

■ **Do-ahead:** *Any of the salad components— black-eyed peas and rice, chopped vegetables or dressing—can be prepared ahead. Or the whole salad can be assembled ahead.*

Step 4

Values are approximate per serving: Calories: 249 Protein: 6 gm Fat: 13 gm
Carbohydrates: 29 gm Cholesterol: 0 mg Sodium: 60 mg

Waldorf Salad with Red Cabbage and Cider Dressing

▼

Waldorf salad may have been temporarily passé, but a little jazzing up—with red cabbage, three types (and colors) of apples and a lighter, zestier dressing—has made this American classic more appealing to modern tastes. Serve this onetime side salad as a vegetarian main dish, or add diced cooked turkey or chicken to transform it to a more substantial entrée.

Working time: 15 minutes
Total time: 15 minutes

Waldorf Salad with Red Cabbage and Cider Dressing

6 Servings

1 large Granny Smith or other tart
  green apple, cored but unpeeled
1 large Delicious or other red apple,
  cored but unpeeled
1 large Golden Delicious apple,
  cored but unpeeled
2 tablespoons lemon juice
2 cups shredded red cabbage
  (about ¼ pound)

2 stalks celery
⅓ cup mayonnaise
⅓ cup plain yogurt
2 tablespoons cider or apple juice
1 teaspoon Dijon mustard
⅔ cup raisins
½ cup chopped walnuts

1 Dice the apples. Place them in a salad bowl and toss them with the lemon juice.

2 Finely shred the cabbage. Dice the celery.

Step 1

3 In a small bowl, combine the mayonnaise, yogurt, cider and mustard.

4 Add the cabbage, celery, raisins, walnuts and dressing to the apples in the salad bowl and toss to combine.

TIME-SAVERS

■ ***Do-ahead:*** *The dressing (Step 3) can be made and the celery and cabbage cut up ahead. The whole salad can also be made ahead.*

Step 2

Values are approximate per serving: Calories: 270 Protein: 3 gm Fat: 16 gm
Carbohydrates: 32 gm Cholesterol: 8 mg Sodium: 120 mg

Step 4

Tangy Pea Salad

▼

This layered salad is based on an old-fashioned Midwestern dish called peas and cheese. The salad was originally made with a boiled dressing (something like a sweetly tangy white sauce) but in this updated version, a mixture of mayonnaise and yogurt is used to cut preparation time and calories. Bring the salad to the table in a glass bowl, if possible, to show off the layers before you toss and serve it.

Working time: 15 minutes
Total time: 15 minutes

Tangy Pea Salad

6 Servings

2 packages (10 ounces each) frozen
    peas, thawed
¼ cup mayonnaise
¼ cup plain yogurt
1 tablespoon cider vinegar
1½ tablespoons pickle relish
1 teaspoon dry mustard

2 cups shredded iceberg lettuce
    (about 4 large leaves)
2 cups shredded Romaine lettuce
    (about 6 large leaves)
1 medium red onion
½ cup chopped parsley (optional)
½ pound shredded Cheddar cheese

Step 3

1 Thaw the peas in the microwave or under running water.

2 In a small bowl, combine the mayonnaise, yogurt, vinegar, pickle relish and mustard.

3 Shred the lettuces. Halve the onion lengthwise, then cut crosswise into very thin half-rounds; separate the half-rounds into individual pieces.

4 In a deep salad bowl, layer the salad in the following manner: half of each of the lettuces, 6 tablespoons of the parsley (if using), all of the onion, 1 package of peas, the remaining lettuce, all of the Cheddar, the remaining package of peas.

5 Pour the dressing over the salad and sprinkle the remaining 2 tablespoons parsley (if using) on top. Do not toss the salad until ready to serve.

Step 4

TIME-SAVERS

■ *Microwave tip: To thaw the peas, remove them from their boxes and place them in a medium microwave-safe bowl. Cook them at 100% for 5 minutes, stirring once halfway through to break them up.*

■ *Do ahead: The individual components can be prepared ahead. The salad can also be entirely assembled ahead of time; in fact, this type of salad is designed to be made a whole day ahead—the dressing is poured on top, but not mixed with the other ingredients, so that it will not wilt them.*

Values are approximate per serving: Calories: 245 Protein: 11 gm Fat: 20 gm
Carbohydrates: 5 gm Cholesterol: 46 mg Sodium: 328 mg

Step 5

Two-Bean Salad with Gruyère and Toasted Pecans

For a picnic with Parisian flair, pair this sophisticated bean salad with a simple roast chicken and a good, crusty French peasant bread. Although an imported French or Swiss Gruyère adds an interesting winey, nutlike flavor to this salad, any Swiss-style cheese—such as Emmenthaler—could be substituted.

Working time: 20 minutes
Total time: 20 minutes

Two-Bean Salad with Gruyère and Toasted Pecans

6 Servings

1 package (9 ounces) frozen green beans, thawed
½ pound Gruyère, Emmenthaler, Jarlsberg or Swiss cheese
½ pound mushrooms
1 can (15¼ ounces) red kidney beans
1 cup pecan halves
⅓ cup olive or other vegetable oil
¼ cup red wine vinegar or cider vinegar

2 tablespoons grainy or regular Dijon mustard
1 clove garlic, minced or crushed through a press
2 tablespoons chopped parsley (optional)
1 teaspoon tarragon
¼ teaspoon dry mustard
½ teaspoon salt
¼ teaspoon pepper

Step 2

1 Drain the thawed green beans on several layers of paper towel to absorb excess moisture.

2 Grate the cheese. Thinly slice the mushrooms. Drain the kidney beans, rinse under cold running water and drain well.

3 In an ungreased skillet or in a toaster oven, toast the pecan halves. Set aside to cool.

4 In a salad bowl, beat together the olive oil, vinegar, Dijon mustard, garlic, parsley (if using), tarragon, dry mustard, salt and pepper.

5 Add the mushrooms and toss to coat thoroughly.

6 Add the drained green beans and kidney beans and the grated cheese, and toss to combine.

7 Just before serving, add the toasted pecans and toss to distribute.

Step 4

TIME-SAVERS

■ *Microwave tip: To toast the pecans, place them in a shallow microwave-safe bowl or glass pie plate, and drizzle with 1 teaspoon of oil. Cook at 100% for 3 to 4 minutes, stirring once about halfway through.*

■ *Do-ahead: The dressing and the toasted pecans can be prepared ahead. The vegetables and cheese can be prepared ahead and tossed with the dressing and pecans just before serving.*

Values are approximate per serving: Calories: 465 Protein: 18 gm Fat: 37 gm
Carbohydrates: 18 gm Cholesterol: 42 mg Sodium: 552 mg

Step 5

Endive and Avocado Salad with Roquefort Dressing

Its mild flavor and lush, velvety texture make the avocado the perfect counterpoint to the crispness of the Belgian endive and the tang of the blue-cheese dressing in this salad. Piquant French Roquefort, called "the king of cheeses," is one of the most flavorful—and expensive—of the blue cheeses, but a good domestic blue—especially the fine Maytag Blue, which is produced in Iowa—will work well in this recipe.

Working time: 25 minutes
Total time: 25 minutes

Endive and Avocado Salad with Roquefort Dressing

4 Servings

1 egg
⅓ cup sour cream
¼ cup plain yogurt
2 tablespoons white wine vinegar
  or cider vinegar
2 ounces Roquefort or other blue
  cheese, crumbled (about ½ cup)
2 tablespoons chopped parsley
  (optional)

Pinch of salt
1 avocado
16 cherry tomatoes (about half a
  pint)
2 large heads Belgian endive
1 large yellow or red bell pepper

Step 2

1 In a saucepan of boiling water, hard-cook the egg. Rinse under cold running water, peel and set aside to cool.

2 Meanwhile, in a small bowl, combine the sour cream, yogurt, 1 tablespoon of the vinegar, the Roquefort, parsley (if using) and salt.

3 Halve the avocado lengthwise and peel; then cut each half lengthwise into thin slices. Place the avocado in a large serving bowl, sprinkle with the remaining 1 tablespoon vinegar and toss lightly to coat.

4 Halve the cherry tomatoes and add them to the avocado. Cut the endives crosswise into 1-inch lengths and thinly slice the bell pepper; add them to the serving bowl. Gently toss to evenly distribute all of the ingredients.

5 Cut the egg into thin slices. Garnish the salad with the egg slices and serve with the dressing on the side.

Step 3

TIME-SAVERS

■ **Microwave tip:** *To hard-cook the egg: Crack the egg into a custard cup and pierce the yolk and white several times with a toothpick. Cover and cook at 50% for 1½ minutes, or until cooked through.*

■ **Do-ahead:** *The dressing (Step 2) can be made ahead.*

Values are approximate per serving: Calories: 219 Protein: 8 gm Fat: 17 gm
Carbohydrates: 10 gm Cholesterol: 73 mg Sodium: 278 mg

Step 4

Marinated Antipasto Salad

▼

Antipasto, the Italian appetizer course, is typically a platter of olives, cheese, meat and marinated vegetables. Here many of those components are combined in a substantial main-dish salad that includes turkey (or ham) and lots of steamed vegetables, all marinated in an herbed vinaigrette. You can eat the salad immediately, but it's best if left to marinate for at least three hours.

Working time: 15 minutes
Total time: 3 hours

306

6 Servings

½ head of cauliflower
2 large carrots
1 large red bell pepper
1 large yellow bell pepper
1 large green bell pepper
½ pound small mushrooms
1 package (10 ounces) frozen
   artichoke hearts
⅓ cup olive or other vegetable oil
½ cup red wine vinegar

3 tablespoons Dijon mustard
1 garlic clove, minced or crushed
   through a press
1 teaspoon oregano
1 teaspoon salt
½ teaspoon black pepper
1 bunch scallions (6 to 8)
2 cups cubed cooked turkey or ham
   (about ½ pound)

Step 1

1 Separate the cauliflower into bite-size florets. Cut the carrots into matchsticks about 2 inches long. Cut the bell peppers into ½-inch-wide strips. If the mushrooms are small, leave them whole; otherwise, halve them.

2 Place the cauliflower, carrots, bell peppers and mushrooms in a large steamer and steam them until tender, about 6 minutes. Add the artichokes for the last 3 or 4 minutes of steaming to thaw them.

3 Meanwhile, in a small bowl or measuring cup, combine the oil, vinegar, mustard, garlic, oregano, salt and black pepper.

4 Transfer the steamed vegetables to a large bowl and pour the dressing over them.

5 Coarsely chop the scallions. Cube the turkey. Add the scallions and turkey to the vegetables and toss to coat well.

6 Set aside for 3 hours at room temperature or for up to 3 days in the refrigerator, stirring occasionally.

Step 4

Step 5

Values are approximate per serving: Calories: 246 Protein: 15 gm Fat: 15 gm
Carbohydrates: 16 gm Cholesterol: 29 mg Sodium: 660 mg

Sweet Potato Salad

In this out-of-the-ordinary salad, sweet potato chunks are mixed with apples, celery and pecans, and tossed with a light but creamy lime dressing. Choose small potatoes so that they bake in half an hour; larger sweet potatoes may take 45 minutes or more. If you're rushed, you can cut the potatoes into small chunks and boil them instead of baking them whole, but you'll sacrifice some of their flavor and nutrient content.

Working time: 20 minutes
Total time: 45 minutes

Sweet Potato Salad

4 Servings

6 small sweet potatoes (about 1½ pounds total)

⅓ cup plain yogurt

3 tablespoons mayonnaise

1 tablespoon lime juice

¾ teaspoon grated lime zest (optional)

1 teaspoon brown sugar

¼ teaspoon salt

¼ teaspoon pepper, preferably white

1 large Granny Smith apple, unpeeled

2 ribs celery

⅓ cup pecans

Step 2

1 Preheat the oven to 400°. Line a baking sheet with foil.

2 Cut one or two slits in the sweet potatoes to act as steam vents. Place the potatoes on the baking sheet and bake for 30 minutes, or until the potatoes are tender.

3 Meanwhile, in a large serving bowl, combine the yogurt, mayonnaise, lime juice, lime zest (if using), brown sugar, salt and pepper.

4 Coarsely chop the apple, add it to the bowl and toss it with the dressing. Coarsely chop the celery and pecans and add them to the bowl.

Step 4

5 When the potatoes are done and cool enough to handle, peel them and cut them into bite-size pieces. While the potatoes are still warm, add them to the serving bowl and toss to coat with the dressing.

TIME-SAVERS

■ **Microwave tip:** *Pierce the sweet potatoes and place them in the oven on a paper towel. Cook at 100% for 9 minutes, or until just tender, rearranging the potatoes once. If the potatoes are of unequal size, remove them one by one as they test done.*

■ **Do-ahead:** *The dressing (Step 3) can be made ahead. The whole salad can be made ahead but may absorb all of the dressing; if it does, toss with 1 or 2 tablespoons of additional mayonnaise or yogurt just before serving.*

Step 5

Values are approximate per serving: Calories: 308 Protein: 4 gm Fat: 15 gm Carbohydrates: 42 gm Cholesterol: 7 mg Sodium: 241 mg

Greek Green Bean Salad

▼

Olives and olive oil are staples of the Greek kitchen. For authentic flavor in this green bean salad, use a flavorful extra-virgin olive oil and oil-cured Greek black olives. (These deeply flavored olives are soaked in brine before they are packed in oil.) Look for them at supermarket deli counters, where you are also likely to find the feta cheese called for here.

Working time: 15 minutes
Total time: 25 minutes

Greek Green Bean Salad

4 Servings

1 pound fresh green beans or 2 packages (10 ounces each) frozen whole green beans, thawed
3 tablespoons olive or other vegetable oil
3 tablespoons red wine vinegar or cider vinegar
1 clove garlic, minced or crushed through a press
1½ teaspoons oregano
¼ teaspoon pepper
1 small red onion
½ cup oil-cured black olives
½ cup crumbled feta cheese (about 2 ounces)

Step 1

1 Cut the green beans (fresh or frozen) into 2-inch lengths. (If using frozen green beans, drain them on paper towels and skip Step 2.)

2 Place the beans in a vegetable steamer and bring the water to a boil. Steam the beans until they are crisp-tender, about 8 minutes. Cool the beans in a colander under cold running water.

3 Meanwhile, in a small bowl, combine the oil, vinegar, garlic, oregano and pepper.

4 Cut the onion into thin half-rings. Coarsely chop the olives.

5 In a salad bowl, combine the beans, onion, olives and dressing, and toss to coat well. Top the salad with the crumbled feta.

6 Serve the salad at room temperature or chilled.

Step 5

TIME SAVERS

■ *Do-ahead: The green beans can be steamed and the salad dressing (Step 3) made ahead. Or the whole salad can be made ahead.*

Step 5

Values are approximate per serving: Calories: 227 Protein: 4 gm Fat: 20 gm
Carbohydrates: 11 gm Cholesterol: 13 mg Sodium: 756 mg

Cheddar-Scallion Soda Bread

▼

This savory soda bread has a light texture reminiscent of yeast bread, but is made in a fraction of the time. Buttermilk is used here for its tang as well as its acidity (which activates the leavening power of the baking soda). If you don't want to buy a whole carton of buttermilk, you can substitute soured milk: Add 1½ teaspoons of vinegar or lemon juice to ½ cup of milk and let it stand for five minutes.

Working time: 10 minutes
Total time: 50 minutes

Cheddar-Scallion Soda Bread

4 Servings

3 scallions
1⅔ cups flour
½ teaspoon baking powder
½ teaspoon baking soda

¼ teaspoon pepper
2 tablespoons butter, chilled
1 cup grated Cheddar cheese
½ cup buttermilk

1 Preheat the oven to 375°. Lightly grease a baking sheet.

2 Coarsely chop the scallions.

3 In a food processor, combine the flour, baking powder, baking soda and pepper.

4 Add the butter and process for 5 to 10 seconds, or until the mixture is crumbly and resembles coarse cornmeal.

5 Add the scallions and Cheddar and pulse briefly just to combine.

6 Add the buttermilk and pulse briefly, just until the dough forms a cohesive mass.

7 Turn the dough out onto a lightly floured surface and knead for about 30 seconds.

8 Form the dough into a round, domed loaf about 5 inches in diameter. Place the loaf on the prepared baking sheet and bake for 45 to 50 minutes, or until the top is golden and the loaf sounds hollow when rapped on the bottom.

Step 6

Step 7

Step 8

Values are approximate per serving: Calories: 371 Protein: 14 gm Fat: 16 gm
Carbohydrates: 42 gm Cholesterol: 47 mg Sodium: 423 mg

Herb Batter Bread

For the flavor of homemade yeast bread without the work of kneading, try this yeast-raised batter bread. Although it does require some time to rise, it is almost as easy to mix as a quickbread. Serve this hearty, herb-flecked bread with tomato soup, as the base for ham sandwiches or toasted for brunch. Make a double or triple batch and freeze the loaves or give them as gifts.

Working time: 15 minutes
Total time: About 3 hours

Herb Batter Bread

Makes one 8½-inch loaf

½ cup plus 1 tablespoon milk
Pinch of sugar
1 envelope yeast
1 stick (4 ounces) butter, at room temperature
2 whole eggs plus 1 egg yolk
1½ cups flour
¼ cup chopped parsley or scallion greens

1 clove garlic, minced or crushed through a press
¾ teaspoon oregano
¾ teaspoon basil
½ teaspoon salt
¼ teaspoon pepper

1 In a small saucepan, scald ½ cup of the milk and the sugar. Let the mixture cool to lukewarm (105° to 115°).

2 In a large mixing bowl, combine the warm milk with the yeast. Set aside until the yeast begins to bubble, about 5 minutes.

3 Add the butter, 2 whole eggs and ¾ cup of flour and beat until smooth.

4 Coarsely chop the parsley or finely chop the scallion greens.

5 Add the parsley (or scallion greens), garlic, oregano, basil, salt, pepper and remaining ¾ cup flour to the bowl and blend well. Cover the bowl with a towel and set aside in a warm draft-free place until the dough has doubled in bulk, 1 to 1½ hours.

6 Lightly butter an 8½-inch loaf pan or an 8-inch round casserole or cake pan at least 2 inches deep. Transfer the dough to the pan, smooth the surface and set aside, uncovered, for about 40 minutes; the dough will rise but will not double.

7 Preheat the oven to 375°. Meanwhile, in a small bowl, beat together the egg yolk and the remaining 1 tablespoon milk to make an egg glaze.

8 Brush the top of the dough with the egg glaze and bake for 35 minutes, or until the loaf sounds hollow when rapped on the bottom.

9 Let cool in the pan for 5 minutes and then turn out onto a rack to cool completely before slicing.

Values are approximate per ½-inch slice: Calories: 114   Protein: 3 gm   Fat: 7 gm
Carbohydrates: 10 gm   Cholesterol: 57 mg   Sodium: 140 mg

Step 5

Step 6

Step 8

INDEX